2012 AND THE RISE OF THE SECRET SECT

A Revolutionary Spiritual and Physical Survival Guide for 2012–2020

Thousands of years of writing are thought to predict world changing events. *2012 and the Rise of the Secret Sect* unveils the truth behind the prophecies and shows which predictions are true and which are false.

DISCOVERED, COMPILED, AND ANALYZED BY
BOB THIEL, PH.D.
(ALSO KNOWN AS COGWRITER)

Copyright © 2009 by NAZARENE BOOKS
All rights reserved. No part of this publication may be reproduced, stored in a retrieval system, or transmitted in any means, electronic, mechanical, photocopying, recording, or otherwise without the prior written permission of the copyright holder.

NAZARENE BOOKS is wholly owned by Doctors' Research, Inc.

ISBN 978-0-9840871-0-5

Printed in the United States of America

NAZARENE BOOKS

For those seeking knowledge

www.nazarenebooks.com

2012
AND THE RISE OF THE SECRET SECT

A Revolutionary Spiritual and Physical Survival Guide for 2012–2020

Does the year 2012 have any relevance for Christians or Non-Christians?

Might the Mayan calendar, private Catholic prophecies, the I Ching, Hopi traditions, New Age writings, ancient scriptures, interpretations in the Talmud, Islamic plans, a Buddhist prophecy, or even personal Hindu predictions have any bearing on events that may significantly affect you?

Will the "new age to come" be preceded by disaster?

Is Barack Obama apocalyptic or possibly the Antichrist?

What is the documented truth about what will happen in the next decade?

www.thesecretsect.com

DISCOVERED, COMPILED, AND ANALYZED BY
BOB THIEL, PH.D.

CONTENTS

Listing of Photographs 7

Acknowledgments 9

Introduction to the Author and the Book 10

*Author's Preface: Why Bother With
Ancient Predictions?* 12

1. 2012, the Mayans, the Hopis, Scientists,
and the I Ching 15

2. The Sect of the Nazarenes 32

3. Catholic Prophecies (including Nostradamus) that Point to
the 21st Century and an Age of Peace 44

4. Hindu Writings, New Age Hopes, and
Buddhist Goals 62

5. Daniel 9:26-27 and the Rise of the
European King of the North 76

6. The Secret Sect 93

7. The Beginning of Sorrows and the 21st Century 120

8. Barack Obama, Islam, and the End of America 129

9. Does the Bible Point to 2012? When Does
the 6,000 Years End? 150

10. New World Order Prophesied for
the Great Monarch and an Antipope 165

11. Who is 666? 190

12. The Four Verses in the Bible That Use the
Term "Antichrist" 193

13. There Will Be Two Witnesses: Will
You Pay Attention? 199

14. The Great Tribulation is Coming 215

15. The Day of the Lord: Who Wins "the
Battle of Armageddon"? 222

16. Predictions Will Happen in What Sequence? 239

17. 2012 and the Rise of the Secret Sect:
You Will Be Affected 252

Appendix A: Problems with the Pre-tribulation
Rapture Hypothesis 258

Appendix B: Daniel 11: Is the Great Monarch the
King of the North? Will the Great Monarch
Destroy the United States and its Anglo-allies? 285

Appendix C: Endnotes 339

Index 369

LISTING OF PHOTOGRAPHS

Ancient Mayan Temple (a) 16
Mayan Dresden Codex (b) 20
I Ching Coins (c) 26
Solar Particles Interacting with Earth's Magnetosphere (d) 29
Labarum Cross (c) 35
Pope Benedict XVI (c) 56
Nostradamus (c). 58
Gautama Buddha (c) 74
Ruins of Ancient Philadelphia (a) 94
Nun Anne Catherine Emmerich (c). 98
Mary's House in Ephesus (a) 116
U.S.A. National Debt Clock (c). 123
Barack Obama (c) 129
Depiction of Imam Alī ibn Abī Tālib (c) 134
Ecumenical Patriarchate of Constantinople (a) 182
Ancient Babylon Wall (a) 229
Hildegard of Bingen Receiving a Vision (c) 233
Megiddo Junction (c). 234
Canadian and American Warships (e) 296

(a) Photo by Joyce Thiel
(b) Photo courtesy of Foundation for the
    Advancement of Mesoamerican Studies
(c) Photo courtesy of Wikipedia Commons
(d) Photo courtesy of N.A.S.A.
(e) Photo courtesy of the U.S. Navy

Front and back photos under license.

ACKNOWLEDGEMENTS

Putting together a book that attempts to cover so much ground is a difficult project that relies on the works of those who have since died as well as those who are currently alive.

The author would like to thank his wife Joyce for her photographs and technical support, Hugo Schwab for his research support, the Foundation for the Advancement of Mesoamerican Studies, Inc. for the Dresden photograph, Wikipedia for public domain photos, and the ministers and evangelists in Charlotte, North Carolina for their technical support and encouraging comments throughout this project.

Scriptural quotes are taken from the *New King James Version*, sometimes abbreviated as NKJV, throughout this entire text, unless otherwise noted. Copyright © 1979, 1980, 1982 by Thomas Nelson, Inc. Used by permission. All rights reserved.

The *Rheims New Testament*, abbreviated as RNT is sometimes also used, since it is a Roman Catholic accepted standard of the Latin vulgate into the English language. The electronic version used here is by permission of William von Peters.

The author also wishes to acknowledge that although care was taken to minimize problems with references, formatting, and typing, inadvertent errors may still happen. He hopes that the reader will look beyond any that may be found and focus on the bigger picture in order to better understand what lies ahead.

INTRODUCTION TO THE AUTHOR AND THE BOOK

The author was born in Michigan. He has studied philosophy, religion, research, science, and prophecy, both formally and informally for several decades. The author has a Master's degree from the University of Southern California and a Ph.D. from the Union Institute and University. In the past twelve years, he has had scores of articles published on these topics in a variety of print publications such as magazines, newspapers, and journals. He has been a lifelong researcher and has received several research awards. He has also worked for geotechnical and other research companies.

He has been married to his wife Joyce since 1981. Together they have made multiple trips to ancient sites in Central America, Asia Minor, Rome, Greece, and elsewhere. This would include visiting such places as Tikal and Iximche in Guatemala; Ephesus, Smyrna, Pergamos, Thyatira, Sardis, Philadelphia, Laodicea and Patmos in Asia Minor; Vatican City, Rome, and Pompeii in the Italian peninsula; Athens, Corinth, Crete, and Rhodes in Greece; and Constantinople (now Istanbul) and Cappadocia in Turkey. They have also visited ancient ruins in Asia and explored parts of Africa.

The Thiels have three sons and live near the central California coast.

Hundreds of thousands know the author as "COGwriter" and he normally writes one or more articles or online commentaries daily at the popular www.cogwriter.com

INTRODUCTION TO THE AUTHOR AND THE BOOK

website.

Because of his passionate interest in both history and prophecy, the author endeavors to make his discoveries available to the public. His writings strive to explain upcoming world events and the peace that is ultimately coming, despite the fact that extremely difficult times are soon ahead.

Although this book references a variety of terms, including: *saint, blessed, venerable, father, mother, brother, sister, prophet, seer,* to identify writers or sources of predictions, this does not mean that the author agrees that those persons truly held those positions. Those terms mainly are quoted from other sources and/or are included, because they may help in identifying historically who these sources were thought to have been. Also, the term *Roman Catholic* is often used as a distinction from the Eastern Orthodox, the Anglicans, and some others who sometimes use the term *Catholic* to refer to themselves. *Roman* is normally left out when the ties to Rome are obvious by the context, or when something other than the old Roman Catholic Church is mentioned. Seeing "Catholic" in quotation marks is intended to indicate that one clearly was not faithful to certain Catholic traditions or will not be in the future. Also, most dates shown after the name of such "prophets" normally came from the source cited and sometimes are subject to challenge.

It should also be understood that the author often comes to different conclusions or interpretations than did some of the reporters/originators of the ancient writings referenced in this book.

Readers are encouraged to look up the sources and compare them to the end-time conclusions in this book.

AUTHOR'S PREFACE: WHY BOTHER WITH ANCIENT PREDICTIONS?

We're living in exciting and turbulent times. Major national difficulties are eminent in the next few years. Some have already started to occur. How will world economies cope during this time? And, more importantly, will global alliances remain through these difficulties?

Throughout history civilizations have risen to a ruling superpower and then have fallen a short time later because of economic and/or military difficulties.

Some people have predicted major future global events. Many predictions will come to pass, but many will not.

It would be helpful to know which of these predictions are accurate and when the accurate ones should come to pass. You will be affected and you can make decisions based upon them that may actually save your life.

What if you do not believe in predictions of any type? Does not knowing result in safety, or is it preparation that does?

Is there any reason that people in the 21st century should bother themselves with ancient writings, drawings, or other sources of prognostication?

In a word—yes.

Whether or not *you* personally believe that there is any truth in the Bible, Hopi traditions, the *I Ching*, Buddhist writings, scientists' warnings, Shi'ite beliefs, New Age hopes, Catholic private prophecies, Hindu predictions, or the end of the Mayan calendar, billions of people on this planet do. Because billions of people take these predictions seriously, their beliefs and related actions may ultimately affect you. How might that happen, you may wonder?

Here is an example. Are you aware of a report from *Forbes* that there is a centuries-old prophecy by Muhammad's cousin that claims that just before the return of a great Islamic leader, a "tall black man will assume the reins of government in the West" and command "the strongest army on earth"? And whether or not you feel that this can have anything to do with U.S. President Barack Hussein Obama, if enough Muslims do, then they will be more likely to rally behind a religious leader who is (according to some of them) destined to take over the nations of the West and force all to become Muslim or die.

Historically, certain predictions have come to pass, while others have failed. For example, centuries ago writers calling themselves Catholic predicted airplanes, submarines, television, wars, etcetera, while others wrongly claimed the world or the U.S.A. would be gone by the 19th or 20th century. Would you like to know which ones are likely to be correct in the future?

Even if you do believe in the predictions of certain writers or some ancient text, but you do not believe in others, the fact is that those accepting predictions that you may not consider to be of value will ultimately have influence upon you.

For another example, are you aware that people of various faiths around the world are looking for a new age to dawn within the next decade?

There are biblical, Catholic, Hopi, Hindu, Buddhist, New Age, Islamic, Mayan, and various other sources that eagerly anticipate this occurrence.

While those looking forward to this time expect it will be

a golden age of peace, some Catholics, Muslims, and Hindus looking forward to it, believe that it will only come about by the emergence of a militaristic dictator who will insist upon a single religion and who will destroy nearly all of his opposition.

What you might find interesting is that although the Bible, too, predicts that an age of peace will come, it (along with certain non-biblical sources) actually predicts that a horrible militaristic dictator will first come upon the scene and implement a false ecumenical religion while enforcing a militaristic "peace" upon the world.

21st century people need to understand that respected news sources are reporting world events that are converging in ways certain to lead to fulfillment of many prophecies.

We face many challenges ahead. Even respected scientists are verifying that bizarre occurrences are expected in a very few years.

Because the entire world will be involved in coming events, would you not like to know now instead of later, what things must and may shortly come to pass? Billions of people believe in these predictions. They and various world events point to cataclysmic change in the next decade—change that will significantly affect you, even if you don't believe in any prophecies. This book will help you learn what to expect and the survival choices that you will face.

Bob Thiel, Ph.D.

CHAPTER 1
2012, THE MAYANS, THE HOPIS, SCIENTISTS, AND THE I CHING

For several years we have heard a variety of claims concerning the year 2012. Most of them are focused upon a possible "end of the world" or "dawn of a new age" based upon ancient Mayan documents and/or other sources. Some claims are said to be based upon the Bible, other ancient texts, scientific insights, and/or personal "revelations."

While most people do not seem to expect anything unusual, some believe that doom and destruction awaits humanity beginning December 22, 2012. Some others believe that a new golden age will dawn for humanity.

Instead, however, it may be a time of temporary peace leading to turmoil.

Why December 22, 2012?
Why would anyone be concerned about the date of December 22, 2012?

That date is of interest, because a rare astronomical event takes place the day before. *USA Today* reported:

> Part of the 2012 mystique stems from the stars. On the winter solstice in 2012, the sun will be aligned with the center of the Milky Way for the first time in about 26,000 years. This means that "whatever energy

typically streams to Earth from the center of the Milky Way will indeed be disrupted on 12/21/12 at 11:11 p.m. Universal Time"...[1]

So there is an astronomical event that occurs on December 21, 2012 (some astronomers contend it is not the actual center of the Milky Way, nor of any real significance). That alone might not have been considered to be of any consequence, except for the fact that the ancient Mayans also produced some materials that point to that date as well.

And why would anyone care about the ancient Mayans?

Partially because the ancient Mayans were obsessed with keeping an accurate calendar.

They were so obsessed with the accuracy of their calendar that they produced a calendar that is actually more accurate than the one most of the world uses in the 21st century.

Mayan Temple, Tikal Guatemala, 2006

Thus, the accuracy of the Mayan calendar is one reason that some people do not dismiss other Mayan documents as mere superstition.

After reviewing information about 2012 predictions, Lawrence E. Joseph, author of *Apocalypse 2012* concluded:

2012 is destined to be a year of unprecedented turmoil and upheaval...[2]

Why Do Some See Doom and Destruction?

If the celestial events of December 21, 2012 are just the results of normal astronomical cycles, why do some predict doom and destruction?

Basically the reason has to do with some Mayan calendar interpretations, certain writings, and how they seem to coincide with many other ancient traditions.

First, a little more background might be helpful. The ancient Mayan calendar consists of days, months, years, and a variety of other cycles such as *katuns* (7,200 days) and *baktuns* (144,000 days). Thirteen was an important number for the Mayans, and thirteen *baktuns* creates a cycle commonly referred to as the Mayan long-count calendar.

This current cycle is believed to have begun August 13, 3113 B.C. and is to come to an end on December 21, 2012.

Steve Alten, author of *Domain*, claimed on *The History Channel*:

> The four prior cycles all ended in destruction. So when we talk about the Mayan doomsday prophecy, we're talking about the end of the fifth cycle, the very last day, which equates to December 21, 2012.[3]

Thus we are now in the current fifth cycle, which many believe will also end in destruction. Some believe it means total destruction. Some interpret it to be a time of chaos or transition.

A pre-Columbian relic commonly called the "Aztec Calendar Stone" (some claim it is technically not Aztec) or the "Mexica Sun Stone" is believed by some to point to destruction between December 21st and December 24, 2012.

Certain beliefs of the Hopi Indians also indicate at least some destruction soon. Notice the following from the popular book *2012 The Return of Quetzalcoatl*:

> According to the Hopi, we are currently completing the cycle of the Fourth World Tuwaqachi, "World Complete"—on the verge of the transitioning, or emerging, into the Fifth World, with several more worlds to follow. In each of the three previous conditions, humanity eventually went berserk, bringing ruin upon themselves through destructive practices, wars, misused technologies, and the loss of the connection to the sacred.[4]

Hence, the Hopi prophecies tend toward doom, though *not* the destruction of all life.

Another view (which is consistent with that Hopi one and an ancient Chinese one[5]) holds that because of the cosmic alignment event, there may be a change in the polarity of the earth (something quite remote, but seemingly not impossible as it apparently has happened before) and/or that the passing of this alignment will result in more catastrophic weather patterns in the future.[6] Some believe that this could represent some type of tipping point from which the planet will not be able to recover without supernatural support.

Considering the chaotic weather patterns in the past several years, it is certainly possible that some shift in planetary alignment might have some impact on the weather.

Did the Mayans Predict Massive Flooding in 2012?

There are two Mayan documents that indicate some type of destruction by flood.

The most famous, perhaps, is commonly referred to as the Dresden Codex (named after the town in Germany whose library housed it).

The Dresden Codex is one of only four remaining "books" (called codices) from the ancient Mayan (pre-Columbian) civilization. In the 16th century the Spaniards destroyed many ancient Mayan records; they believed those records involved too many pagan practices. But before all could be destroyed, a Catholic priest prevented some of them from being burned. And one of those is now known as the Dresden Codex. It is the final page of it that has generated much attention in the past several years.

There are also nine writings called *Chilam Balam* (meaning "oracular priest" "jaguar") that seem to combine Mayan and Spanish beliefs that were written in the early 16th century after some Mayans learned a character writing system from the Spaniards. Notice what it says about a flood coming at the end of Mayan time ("when the law of the katun has run its course"):

> But when the law of the katun has run its course, the God will bring about a great deluge again which will be the end of the world. When this is over, then our Lord Jesus Christ will descend over the valley of Jehoshaphat besides the town of Jerusalem where he redeemed us with his holy blood.[7]

However, since the *Chilam Balam* shows Spanish and biblical influence, many prefer to focus on the Mayan documents that pre-date the Spaniards (like the Dresden Codex).

Final Page of Mayan Dresden Codex

The last page of the Dresden Codex depicts large quantities of water coming out of the mouth of some type of possibly demonic serpent entity (snakes have been considered a symbol of the devil since Genesis 3:1).

Because it is the final page, many feel that the picture is

trying to tell us that at the end of the Mayan calendar the world comes to an end, as it will be destroyed by a massive flood. While according to Quetzil Castañeda, some Mayans in Mexico have claimed that 2012 is a "gringo invention",[8] the fact is that centuries ago (in the *Chilam Balam*) some Mayans did predict a flood to occur at the end of their calendar.

Some people are so frightened about this that thousands of Dutch and Flemish people (much of the Netherlands is below sea level) believe that the world will end then, and many of them are taking steps to try to survive the aftermath of December 21, 2012.[9]

The World Will Not Be Completely Destroyed By Flooding

Even though some believe that the Mayans were accurately forecasting a worldwide flood, this is not the case.

According to ancient Hebrew prophecies (that Jews, Christians, and Muslims also recognize), it is not possible that the entire world will be destroyed again by flood:

> [11] Never again shall all flesh be cut off by the waters of the flood; never again shall there be a flood to destroy the earth…[15] the waters shall never again become a flood to destroy all flesh (Genesis 9:11,15, NKJV throughout unless otherwise specified).

Thus, from a biblical perspective, the entire world is *not* prophesied to end by flood. Therefore, those relying on the Bible do not believe the Mayan predictions related to December 21, 2012 will be fulfilled by a massive flood that will destroy humanity.

But two other floods seem to be prophesied in the Greek scriptures (which Christians and Muslims somewhat recognize, but Jews do not).

The New Testament refers to Satan the Dragon (also known as the devil) as a serpent (Revelation 12:9). The Book of Revelation refers to a time when the "the serpent" will cause a flood (Revelation 12:15). Both the Mayan picture and the Bible show water coming out of the mouth of a serpent, which is certainly a similarity. This "biblical flood" is near the beginning of the Great Tribulation and is an attempt to destroy the highly faithful church while it is fleeing (signified by the woman in Revelation 12:15). The Bible also shows that the church will be helped and not destroyed by that flood (Revelation 12:16). Because the Bible mentions that "the woman" (the church) is fleeing then and those in the Mayan Dresden picture are not fleeing, it would seem that these are not the same two floods.

However, a flooding of islands and apparently rising sea levels are shown in the Bible (and are expected by many scientists). Yet, contrary to certain interpretations of the Mayan Dresden picture and the *Chilam Balam*, this appears to be predicted to occur after 2012 according to biblical prophecies (for more information, please see Chapter 16, Appendix A, and Appendix B).

"Blood-Vomit" in The *Chilam Balam*

There are also some 16th century writings within the *Chilam Balam* which state:

> You shall not call the katun which is to come a hostile one, when Jesus, the guardian of our souls shall come...
>
> The katun is established at Chichen Itzá. The settlement of the Itzá shall take place <there>. The quetzal shall come, the green bird shall come. Ah Kantenal shall come. Blood-vomit shall come. Kukulcan shall come with them for the second time. <It is> the word of God.[10]

The *katuns* in these writings do not seem to be the same precise time periods, yet some feel that they are related to 2012.

These writings do document that there was a belief that some type of disaster ("blood-vomit") would come. Blood-vomit may signify liquid (like a flood), chaotic times, or perhaps disaster. And, perhaps because they were influenced by the Spanish missionaries, the Mayan writing suggest that Jesus would return (the Bible calls Jesus the "Word" and God, cf. John 1:1,14).

However (as will be discussed later in this text), it would not seem possible for Jesus to return by December 21, 2012, so if the above are referring to a future event, it would seem that they would need to be referring to a time after December 21, 2012.

It should be noted that *Kulkulcan* can mean "serpent"[11] or "feathered serpent"[12] and hence instead of Jesus returning, that section of the *Chilam Balam* may be referring to a Satanic power rising up at a time of turmoil who claims his word is that of God. And that could happen shortly after 2012.

Some Old Predictions Look for a New Age to Dawn

Some who look into the Mayan prophecies, however, simply feel that the water on the last page of the Dresden Codex signifies a new birth, and that a new age of peace will come. The water that comes out of the mouth of the serpent seems to possibly be directed at covering two darkened figures that might possibly be considered to represent all evil.

Because water is universally used for cleansing, the Mayan Dresden picture might be suggesting that evil may be cleansed from the world, or that there will be two evil rulers.

Interestingly, the Bible teaches that two evil rulers (a male military leader and the false prophet who represents a church) will be purged from the earth before the real age of peace comes (though they are killed via fire per Revelation 19:20). As no one really knows what the ancient Mayans intended by their drawings, this may be how that last page could be fulfilled. Although the Mayan picture shows a male and a female, a female can symbolize a false church according to Revelation 17:1-6, meaning this interpretation might be feasible.

This interpretation seems to be consistent with other sources (not part of the Mayan prophecies) that also suggest a change and elimination of evil is due soon.

A couple of thousand years ago the so-called Sibylline prophecies (or Sybilline oracles) predicted what seems to be the end of human existence. Some believe that the last generation is supposed to have started around the year 2000[13]:

> Cumaean Sibyl lived in ancient Rome around the 6th century BC. She was highly regarded by Roman authorities... She predicts the world will last for 9 periods of 800 years, and that the 10th generation will begin around 2000 AD, and that it will be the last generation.[14]

There were, though, various Sibyls. Here is a quote from what seems to be one of the later Sibylline oracles:

> But when the tenth generation shall go down
> To Hades, then shall come the mighty power
> Of one of female sex; and God himself...
> With a strong tempest, he will waste the earth.
> And there shall be a rising of the dead;
> The lame shall swiftly run, the deaf shall hear,
> The blind shall see, those who spoke not shall speak,
> And life and wealth shall be alike to all.[15]

Thus, if the Sybil was correct, then the end of humanity as we know it would be expected to happen sometime in the 21st century and God will return also in the 21st century.

Additionally, there are Hindu, Tibetan, and other prophecies that seem to suggest that sometime in the next decade a type of new age will dawn and humanity will benefit because of it (see Chapter 4).

Furthermore, a website called the *2012Wiki* reported that instead of destruction, there may be some positive predictions in the Hopi prophecies:

> The Hopi prophecy is an oral tradition of stories that Hopis say predicted the coming of the white man, the world wars and nuclear weapons. And it predicts that time will end when humanity emerges into the "fifth world." The Mayan calendar predicts a similar end in 2012; some Hopis have said their prophecy roughly coincides with that time. The tradition says the years after 2012 could be a golden age with humans at peace. It also says the world will go through a time of trial, suffering and purification before a time of "one-heartedness.[16]

And while 2012 is just a little bit too early for a truly peaceful new age to dawn, there are various predictions that seem to point to that timeframe for some type of major change.

The *I Ching*

Perhaps one of the more fascinating 2012 predictions is related to the *I Ching*.

The *I Ching*, or Book of Changes, is a common source for both Confucianist and Taoist philosophy. It is believed to have been put together between four thousand and five thousand years ago. The book contains a symbol system used to identify order in chance events, rules for manipulating these symbols, poems, and commentary.

Three Coins Used for I Ching Divination

The *I Ching* originated in China and is used by some as a relatively quick way of performing divination or making a prediction for the future. It is still commonly used today.

Using the *I Ching* for predictions is sort of like throwing three dice (though they are not dice, they are small coin-like discs) and coming up with a prediction based upon several outcomes. Each time the discs are thrown, a series of lines (either full, called *Yang*, or broken, called *Yin*) is written out based upon the discs. Sixty-four possible outcomes/hexagrams can be obtained by throwing the three discs. The alleged meaning of the series of full or broken lines obtained from the tossing is essentially explained in the *I Ching*.

While the *I Ching* does not seem to have been intended to make massive long-term predictions using it the normal way, there have been some calculations made based upon looking at all sixty-four possible combinations and plotting the associated full and broken lines that seem to point to something happening around 2012. Although those predictions related to the *I Ching* slightly remind me of the so-called "Bible Code," some believe that it may be indicating a change in the early 21st century.

Robert Blast has reported:

> **Fractal time and the I Ching**—Ethnobotanists and fractal time experts Terrence and Dennis McKenna... Their studies began with the *I Ching*, which is composed of 64 hexagrams, or six-line figures. It struck them that 6 x 64 = 384, which is exceptionally close to the number of days in 13 lunar months (29.5306 x 13 = 383.8978), and that maybe the *I Ching* was originally an ancient Chinese calendar...
>
> The McKenna brothers arrived at the 2012 end date by using fractals. Starting from a table of differences between one hexagram and the next, they developed a Mandelbrot fractal in which each level is 64 times greater then the one below it. They then laid this fractal pattern on top of a time scale. The peaks and troughs of the pattern relate to the level of connectedness or novelty in any span of time, whether it covers a day, millennia or even since the beginning of time. By matching the levels of the pattern with key periods in history, they determined it would fit best if the end of the time scale was December 22, 2012...and everything that happens is new.[17]

So, some believe that December 22, 2012 has long been considered to have been the date for the world as we know it to change (note: others believe that the McKenna brother's "*I Ching*" date was originally November 17, 2012[18]).

Scientists, Mayans, and the Sun

While various scientists have differing opinions on many

subjects, there is one related to warnings about 2012 that perhaps should be mentioned here.

Some scientists believe that there will be an increase in sunspot activity that will affect the earth in 2012.[19] Notice the following from N.A.S.A.:

> **Solar Storm Warning**: Researchers announced that a storm is coming—the most intense solar maximum in fifty years. The prediction comes from a team led by Mausumi Dikpati of the National Center for Atmospheric Research (NCAR)...
>
> Solar physicist David Hathaway of the National Space Science & Technology Center (NSSTC)...has confidence in the conveyor belt model and agrees with Dikpati that the next solar maximum should be a doozy. But he disagrees with one point. Dikpati's forecast puts Solar Max at 2012. Hathaway believes it will arrive sooner, in 2010 or 2011...Either way, a storm is coming.[20]

Solar outbursts have been proposed that could essentially wipe out modern civilization.

Depiction of solar particles interact with Earth's magnetosphere

Notice a scenario that is based on a report from the U.S. National Academy of Scientists (although the precise date seems to be speculative):

> IT IS midnight on 22 September 2012 and the skies above Manhattan are filled with a flickering curtain of colourful light...Within 90 seconds, the entire eastern half of the US is without power.
>
> A year later and millions of Americans are dead and the nation's infrastructure lies in tatters. The World Bank declares America a developing nation. Europe, Scandinavia, China and Japan are also struggling to recover from the same fateful event - a violent storm, 150 million kilometres away on the surface of the sun...
>
> According to the NAS report, a severe space weather event in the US could induce ground currents that would knock out 300 key transformers within about 90 seconds, cutting off the power for more than 130 million people...

First to go - immediately for some people - is drinkable water...With no electricity to pump water from reservoirs, there is no more...

There is simply no electrically powered transport: no trains, underground or overground...For hospitals, that would mean about 72 hours of running a bare-bones, essential care only, service. After that, no more modern healthcare.

The truly shocking finding is that this whole situation would not improve for months, maybe years...[21]

Another N.A.S.A./N.O.A.A. report has indicated that the next solar cycle peak may be later, like May 2013.[22]

While biblical sources indicate that the world cannot actually be destroyed that early, it is certainly possible that major electrical outages can occur from solar activity. This could cause various blackouts and could greatly damage civilization as we know it.

And this is consistent with the views of some other scientists. "Russian geophysicists believe that the Solar System has entered an interstellar energy cloud...Their predictions for catastrophe resulting from the Earth's encounter with this energy cloud range from 2010 to 2020."[23]

There also seems to be a couple of Mayan predictions recorded in the 16th century that suggest some type of solar flare-up will affect the earth:

Chilam Balam (Mayan priest): Heaven and earth shall burn...It is the holy judgment, the holy judgment.[24]

Napuctun (Mayan priest): It shall burn on earth; there shall be a circle in the sky.[25]

The Bible itself warns of a time of scorching solar heat (Revelation 16: 8-9; see also Chapter 15).

So What?

Are these predictions coincidences? Or may they be related to something else?

Are all the converging predictions purely coincidental? But by now you may be asking yourself, so what?

You may have concluded:

> If there is not going to be a catastrophic flood, I will be fine.

> If there will be solar flares, there is nothing I can do about that.

> If there is not going to be an "age of peace", I am no worse off than I am now.

> If there is going to be an "age of peace", I will be even better off than I am now.

> Therefore, it is logical to conclude that I will be fine and none of this matters.

And while on the surface these positions may seem logical, adopting them would be ignoring other ancient texts and beliefs (as well as modern happenings) that will affect you.

The reality is that more than one false time of peace will be declared relatively soon. Worldwide devastation is predicted in many sources.

You will be affected, and you may not survive.

CHAPTER 2
THE SECT OF THE NAZARENES

Before getting into more predictions, perhaps this would be a good time to briefly overview the sect sometimes called the Nazarenes.

Unlike the rest of this book, this chapter mainly delves (briefly) into matters of history that help set the foundation for events that must come to pass.

You may or may not know this, but Christians were often called and/or considered to be Nazarenes in the 1st century or so after Jesus was crucified.

The Bible itself teaches that "Jesus" would "be called a Nazarene" (Matthew 2:1,23). Seventeen times the Bible (NKJV) uses the expression "Jesus of Nazareth," probably because Jesus used to live there (Matthew 2:23). The New Testament uses the expression Nazareth, Nazarene, or Nazarenes thirty-one times.

In the Book of Acts, the Apostle Paul was considered to be a leader of the Nazarenes by his enemies. Here are two translations:

> [2] Paul...[5] For we have found this man a plague, a creator of dissension among all the Jews throughout the world, and a ringleader of the sect of the Nazarenes (Acts 24:2,5, NKJV).

> [2] Paul...[5] We have found this man pestiferous, and

raising seditions to all the Jews in the whole world, and author of the sedition of the sect of the Nazarenes (Acts 24:2,5, RNT).

So, from the beginning of the Christian church, we find that Jesus was to be called a Nazarene, and His followers were considered to be members of a small sect called the Nazarenes.

Prior to the destruction of Jerusalem in 70 A.D. by the Romans, there is an old tradition that the Nazarenes were warned to flee from it. Many fled to Pella in Paraea, east of the Jordan (southeast of Jenin), before the beginning of the siege of Jerusalem.[26] Some Nazarenes ended up in Asia Minor (such as the Apostles Philip and John).

After the destruction in 70 A.D., some Nazarenes returned. However, because of the Bar Kokhba revolt of 132–135 A.D. of the Jews against Rome, those Nazarenes who had certain original Christian practices were prohibited by Emperor Hadrian to live in Jerusalem[27] (which he renamed Ælia Capitolina), and ultimately many ended up in Asia Minor (and some later went back to Jerusalem).

Nazarenes a Type of Secret Sect

Apparently some ancient Jews felt that the early Christians, whom they called Nazarenes, were a type of secret sect according to some late 19th/early 20th century writers:

> The dispersed Nazarenes were a secret sect that had no affiliation with the Jews...[28]

> The title Nazarene was given by the Jews to those strange people outside their own religion that seemed to belong to some type of secret sect...[29]

They were probably considered to be a "secret sect" by the Jews because many tended to distance themselves from the Jews in the first few centuries A.D.

But the Nazarenes were not just of Jewish heritage, though they had many practices some have considered to be Judeo-Christian.

Christian leaders, often of Greek lineage, were appointed by the apostles (i.e. Timothy, Acts 16:1; also Polycarp of Smyrna[30]) and led churches in Asia Minor in the first and second centuries. Their spiritual descendants apparently appointed other leaders (cf. Acts 8:18) there in the third and fourth centuries. Some of these leaders, such as Polycarp and Theophilus (of Antioch) have been called or considered to be Nazarenes [31] and are also considered to be saints by the Greco-Roman churches.

It is likely that the Christians from Pella/Jerusalem, and Asia Minor later got together, as there is some evidence that they communicated with each other in the 2nd century.[32] Some who apparently fled Antioch in the 3rd century (after an Imperial persecution by Emperor Septimius Severus that lasted until 211 A.D.) probably also joined them.

Partially because of Imperial persecutions and partially because of differences in theological interpretations, there was a major separation of the two main "proto-orthodox" groups claiming Christianity in the second and third centuries (there were also varieties of minor groups). [33]

Early (2nd/3rd century) theological writers such as Clement of Alexandria[34], Irenaeus of Lyon[35], Tertullian[36], and Origen[37] noted that there were two major groups: one with ties to Asia Minor and one with ties to Rome (and those writers mainly supported the Roman version). But they specifically tied leaders with Judeo-Christian practices like Polycarp to the early apostles in Asia Minor such as Philip and John.

Those who were most heavily-based in Italy and Northern

Africa tended to accept a more allegorical and mystical approach to understanding the Bible, while most of those in Antioch and Asia Minor (until at least the early 3rd century) took a more literal approach and retained more of what are commonly-called Judaeo-Christian beliefs. But of course, there were people of both persuasions (as well as mixtures of both) in both areas.

Those that took the more literal approach and followed the practices of the original Jewish converts to Christianity are further referred to in this book as original Nazarenes Christians, as they were labeled that way by others in the 4th century.

Edicts of Emperors

The 4th century saw both good and bad to come from Imperial authorities. On the positive side, the empire-wide persecution of all who professed Christ, began by Emperor Diocletian, was stopped.

Just prior to a major battle in 312 A.D. (Battle of the Milvian Bridge), Emperor Constantine claimed to see a Chi-Rho (Labarum) cross and had his soldiers start to wear one.[38]

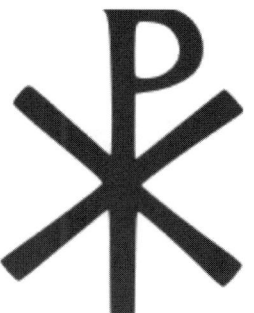

Labarum Cross

Emperor Constantine's cross-bearing army won that battle.

Then in 313 A.D., Constantine issued an edict (the *Edict of Milan*[39]) that essentially legalized all religions claiming a Christian tradition.

Sadly, this Imperial favor did not last.

Because of various controversies, Emperor Constantine decided that a council of bishops would be held in Nicea in 325 A.D., with himself as a self-appointed "bishop"[40] (he had not then even been baptized into any form of Christianity) to oversee the council. He proposed and supported various measures that were passed by the attending bishops. Some of the items discussed resulted in orthodox conclusions. Two items related to dates that differed from the biblical Passover and weekly worship practices that the apostles (including John and Philip), the original Jerusalem Christians, and the 2nd century Asia Minor Christians had observed. The bishops/leaders of "Nazarene" churches with those practices did not attend the Emperor's Council of Nicea.[41]

After this council, Emperor Constantine later decided he would not tolerate people who did not accept his version of religion, and issued his *Edict Against the Heretics*.[42]

Death Penalty Issued Against Those with Original Nazarene Practices

While there were many actual heretics that Constantine's edict covered, his edict represented a change in the empire. No longer were all types of "Christianity" tolerated, but instead those that did not accept the religion endorsed by Constantine were subject to persecution. In one odd edict for the Jerusalem area, Emperor Constantine decreed the death penalty to Christians who would not eat pork.[43]

In the 4th century, Emperor Constantine endorsed and/or encouraged a number of changes, including changes in the appearance of the clergy. Much of the Constantinian-accepting clergy then began to wear unusual vestments that none of the Christian clergy had worn in periods prior.[44] The Nazarene clergy, however, did not follow the example of the Constantinians.[45]

Thus, there was a further separation between those Constantinians and the original Nazarene Christians (they are often called "original Nazarenes" in this text to distinguish them from the group dating to the 19th century that refers to itself as "the Church of the Nazarene" but does not have the same "Judeo-Christian" practices). With the support of Imperial Rome, the Constantinian supporters greatly increased in numbers and in influence.

Many later Roman Emperors also issued decrees and edicts against the Nazarenes and others who claimed Christ. E. Gibbon records that a later Roman Emperor decreed the death penalty for continuing one original Christian practice related to Christ's last Passover. He then oddly noted:

> The theory of persecution was established by Theodosius, whose justice and piety have been applauded by the saints.[46]

How any one who was truly a "saint" could applaud the killing of people for keeping the same practices that Jesus, the Apostles, and their faithful followers (like Polycarp[47]) did is absurd. Yet, *The Catholic Encyclopedia* of the early 20th century called Theodosius I "Great" and one who "reigned as a just and mighty Catholic emperor."[48]

Thus, in the 4th century there were still at least two "proto-orthodox" groups professing Christ in the old Greco-Roman empire. There was the major one who sometimes persecuted under the authority of the Roman authorities, and the other smaller one that was the persecuted (there were also other persecuted groups).

Some have viewed this Constantinian intervention as

a good thing. Notice a bizarre title of a book chapter and comment from a clergyman named Jesse Hurlbut:

> FROM THE EDICT OF CONSTANTINE, 313 A.D., TO...476 A.D. – THE VICTORY OF CHRISTIANITY...
>
> Christianity as the official religion of the Roman empire, and a Christian emperor held supreme authority...
>
> But while the triumph of Christianity resulted in much that was good, inevitably the alliance with the state and the church also brought in its train many evils.[49]

It is bizarre how Jesse Hurlbut can declare the murderous as the victors of Christianity, and then admit that this brought evils. It perhaps should be noted that prior to the time of Constantine (for about three centuries), nearly all who professed Christ would not participate in carnal warfare.[50]

Of course, the truly faithful Church of Jesus Christ never brought evils among those that truly practiced it (cf. 3 John 11). Christians were always pacifists. And the truly faithful never became murderous persecutors, but became their victims (cf. John 16:2-4).

People of all faiths should strive to follow the Apostle Paul's admonition to "live at peace with everyone" (Romans 12:18, NIV).

Nazarenes Were Not Originally Considered to be Heretics

Although all Christians were called Nazarenes originally, by the end of the 4th century, only those with practices like those of Apostle John[51] and Polycarp were called Nazarenes by writers such as Jerome[52] and Epiphanius[53]. Catholic writers such as Jerome considered many second and 3rd century leaders who held Nazarene views as part of the original church,[54] yet Jerome more strongly supported the church with ties to Rome himself.

The Nazarenes had long existed, but until the time of Constantine, they simply were not considered to be heretics by those in Rome nor Alexandria.

The 19th century Protestant historian Philip Schaff noted:

> A portion of the Jewish Christians … propagated themselves in some churches of Syria down to the end of the fourth century, under the name of Nazarenes… They…deeply mourned the unbelief of their brethren, and hoped for their future conversion in a body and for a millennial reign of Christ on the earth. But they indulged no antipathy to the apostle Paul. **They were, therefore, not heretics**, but stunted separatist Christians. They stopped at the obsolete position of a narrow and anxious Jewish Christianity, and shrank to an insignificant sect.[55]

While calling the Nazarenes "stunted" and "insignificant" does not seem nice, the reality is that those with Nazarene beliefs have tended to have been considered as a separatist sect throughout history.

Dr. Ray Pritz noted:

> …the earliest heresiologists did not include the Nazarenes for the simple reason that they did not consider them to be heretics…we arrive at this important conclusion: the lack of polemic against the Nazarenes until the fourth century does not show that they were a late phenomenon; rather it shows that no one until Epiphanius considered them heretical enough to add them to older catalogues…no one until

Epiphanius felt it necessary to include the Nazarenes, even though they existed from the earliest times...[56]

Notice an interesting, but highly important, related observation by the Catholic priest and scholar Bellarmino Bagatti:

> In conclusion, **regarding the Nazarenes, both St. Epiphanius and St. Jerome have nothing to condemn them for except the observance of customs forbidden by the Councils.**[57]

Thus, both Catholic and non-Catholic sources admit that those with Nazarene views were not originally considered to have been heretics.

Now, Priest Bagatti pointed out an interesting and major difference between the Nazarenes and many who profess Christ today. Many non-Nazarenes seem to accept some of the Imperial/Church Councils as authoritative (there are still differences between the Greco-Romans about which Councils they mutually accept), but are selective, as some contradict others (for example the 359 Council of Rimini endorsed a semi-arian/binitarian view of the Godhead,[58] whereas the 381 Council of Constantinople endorsed a particular trinitarian view[59]).

Yet, those who claim descent through these 4th century Nazarenes (while not in disagreement with some parts of some Councils) never have accepted any of the Councils as divinely authoritative.

By the end of the 4th century, even though they still existed, various writers decided that they no longer existed,[60] or that they had become an insignificant hidden separatist[61] or even heretical secret sect.[62]

The Woman Fled to the Wilderness

Because of Imperial edicts against non-conforming religions, those continuing to hold differing beliefs often had to flee and hide.

It seems that this was foretold in the Book of Revelation:

> [6] Then the woman fled into the wilderness, where she has a place prepared by God, that they should feed her there one thousand two hundred and sixty days (Revelation 12:6).

The above passage indicates that many of the faithful may have had to flee and become hard to find for 1260 years (some passages in the Bible use a day to represent a year, cf. Isaiah 34:8; Ezekiel 4:4-6; Numbers 14:34). Others have reported that the Nazarenes had a "rapid disappearance from the historical scene" and were "clandestine" and "hiding" for centuries in order to avoid persecution.[63]

Perhaps it should be noted that the Bible sometimes indicates that a woman represents the faithful church (cf. Ephesians 5:31-32; 2 John 1) and that traditional Catholic theologians also teach that the above passage in Revelation 12:6 is referring to the woman as the church.[64]

Interestingly, the Third Lateran Council of 1179, which took place under Pope Alexander III, referred to some of those that the Greco-Romans had persecuted as "secret."[65]

One Catholic writer, speaking of groups that appeared to be Nazarenes (they professed Christ, yet retained certain "Jewish practices") during this general period, referred to them as "Secret Jews."[66] (Some in the Middle East seemed to be called *nasrdm*, Nazarenes, around that time,[67] but whether they were truly faithful Christians is difficult to determine.)

Of course, the Crusades also occurred during these times and those that resisted the "cross bearers" (which is where the term "Crusaders" came from) in various lands were subject to severe punishments.

Despite persecutions, the Inquisition, and other hardships, those with original Nazarene practices did not die out.

In the 16th century, there were some with Roman Catholic backgrounds that rose up to condemn practices such as indulgences and the use of statues in worship. Yet, some of the "Reformers" condemned those who held to original Nazarene Christian beliefs such as an earthly millennium[68] —and even called for the deaths of some who taught against infant baptism with such expressions as "drown the dippers."[69]

On a more positive note, partially because of these reformers, political situations also changed, which ultimately led to the more public emergence of the Nazarene Christians. They became much more "public," but still were also sometimes considered secretive.

(For a much more comprehensive history of the faithful "Nazarene Christians," please read *The Beginning and the End of the Christian Church Era: An Alternative View of Church History by One Who Actually Believes the Bible*.[70])

Hidden Groups Start to Emerge

Around the beginning of the 17th century, groups with Nazarene-like practices began to emerge more publicly as persecution for religion became less acceptable in various parts of the world. Some of them found refuge in Europe, while others came to Rhode Island, the only colony in the Americas at that time that truly offered freedom of religion.

During the 17th to 21st centuries, some groups with names that included the expressions "Church of God" or "Church of Christ" held many of the practices of the original Nazarene Christians (though all groups who used those names did not have certain "Nazarene" practices). And, of course, some groups were more faithful to those original practices than were others.

Though overt persecutions basically stopped, the groups with these practices have often been distanced from those who hold to the beliefs of the mainstream churches.

In the 21st century, there are many small groups that hold to a lot of the practices and beliefs of the original Nazarene Christians. Some of them have primary characteristics of at least one of the four churches mentioned in Revelation 2 & 3 (Thyatira, Sardis, Philadelphia, and Laodicea).

In the twentieth and twenty-first centuries, some with Nazarene practices became more publicly effective, and they boldly proclaimed the religion of peace and the good news of the coming kingdom of God. They had more reach than they had achieved since perhaps the 1st century.[71]

That part of Nazarene history is consistent with biblical prophecy, as the Bible shows that at the time of the end, there will be a small church that will go through doors that Christ opens to proclaim the Gospel (Revelation 3:7-8; cf. 2 Corinthians 2:12; Luke 12:32).

The Bible shows that they will somehow fulfill Matthew 24:14 more than it has ever been fulfilled before, and **then the end will come,** as that verse states. Those who are associated with this church that has "Judeo-Christian" practices (cf. Revelation 3:9) will rise up as the "secret sect" that certain religious writers (as well as certain scriptures) have predicted throughout the centuries. And its major rise may occur next decade.

CHAPTER 3
CATHOLIC PROPHECIES (INCLUDING NOSTRADAMUS) THAT POINT TO THE 21ST CENTURY AND AN AGE OF PEACE

Mayan and biblical prophecies, of course, are not the only source of predictions for the end-time that seem to point to the 21st century.

There are several "Catholic" "private prophecies" (some of which have an official imprimatur or similar approval) that suggest a major change in the world is likely to occur in the 21st century. Perhaps it should be mentioned that the official position of the Church of Rome is that believing these "private revelations" can be helpful, but is not required for followers of the Vatican.[72]

Certain Roman Catholic writings clearly indicate that the end of civilization could not occur before the 20th century and some seem to point to the 21st century as the end.

Notice two of them:

> *Sister Bertina Bouquillion* (died 1850): The beginning of the end will not come in the nineteenth century but certainly in the twentieth century.[73]

> *E. Culligan* (20th century): …there is convincing evidence…that the Antichrist was born on February 5, 1962…The Antichrist will be a Jew by race and religion.[74]

Hence, because certain Catholic predictions indicate that

the beginning of the end starts in the 20th century, they are consistent with the view that the end is likely to happen in the 21st century.

But there are more. Here is another from two sources about the same French predictor (the first has his name translated into English also):

> *St. John of the Cleft Rock* (14th century). It is said that 20 centuries after the incarnation of the Word, the Beast in its turn will become man. About the year 2000 A.D., Antichrist will reveal himself to the world.[75]
>
> *Jean de Roquetaillade* (died 1365): Because it is said that twenty centuries after the incarnation of the *Verb,* the Beast would also be embodied and she would threaten the earth with evils as impressive as the graces brought by the divine incarnation.[76]

These sources indicate that the Beast (likely a reference to the ten-horned beast of Revelation 13:1-8; who also is the one known as the final King of the North) would be born prior to the 21st century. If they have any accuracy, this would indicate that the end will be in the 21st century as human biology would suggest that the Beast would have to act in the twenty-first century in order to have much power.

An archbishop seemed to have a similar view that the last days of this current era began in the 20th century:

> *Archbishop Fulton Sheen* (1950): We are living in the days of the Apocalypse--the last days of our era.... The two great forces of the Mystical Body of Christ and the Mystical Body of Antichrist are beginning to draw up the battle lines for the catastrophic contest.[77]

Notice that the Archbishop also was concerned that two great forces were then rising up. Could this be between the "secret sect" and an ecumenically-oriented religion?

Furthermore, notice two accounts about a pontiff who had a vision in 1884:

> Pope Leo XIII had a vision of a confrontation between God and Satan. Pope Leo was made to understand that Satan would be allowed one hundred years to tempt and try to destroy the Church. In the vision, Satan chose for his one hundred years the Twentieth Century.[78]

> Pope Leo XIII had a remarkable vision…When asked what had happened, he explained that, as he was about to leave the foot of the altar, he suddenly heard voices - two voices, one kind and gentle, the other guttural and harsh. They seemed to come from near the tabernacle. As he listened, he heard the following conversation:

> The guttural voice, the voice of Satan in his pride, boasting to Our Lord: "I can destroy your Church."

> The gentle voice of Our Lord: "You can? Then go ahead and do so."

> Satan: "To do so, I need more time and more power."

> Our Lord: "How much time? How much power?"

> Satan: "75 to 100 years, and a greater power over those who will give themselves over to my service."

Our Lord: "You have the time, you will have the power. Do with them what you will."[79]

If the 20th century alone was meant, then the Pope's vision was completely false (as opposed to being a reverse mirror image of God's plan as some private prophecies seem to be). In order for the above to fit in with other Catholic private prophecies, it would probably need to be interpreted that the seventy-five to one hundred years started at about the same time as the timeframe that Nun Emmerich indicated (in a few upcoming paragraphs). If so, then the seventy-five years ended in 2008, and the outside date for the one hundred would be about 2033. Hence, unless this Pope had it completely wrong, some part of the end would need to occur fairly soon.

A Greek Eastern Orthodox scholar named H. Tzima Otto has claimed that the "Great Monarch", Antichrist, and the antipope are alive now, hence the end, according to her, must be in the 21st century.[80]

Notice what one mystic nun wrote:

> *St. Hildegard* (died 1179): After the birth of Anti-Christ **heretics will preach** their false doctrines undisturbed, **resulting in 'Christians having doubts about their Catholic faith'**.[81]

Thus, it would seem that the first half of the 21st century may see the rise of those who are preaching a message that some Greco-Roman Catholics might embrace.

Furthermore there are other private prophecies that mention that the rise of the secret sect starts in the 20th century:

> *Ven. Sor Marianne de Jesus Torres* (17th century): During this epoch the Church will find herself attacked by waves of the secret sect...Know, beloved daughter, that

when your name is made known in the 20th Century, there will be many who do not believe, claiming this devotion is not pleasing to God...[82]

Nun Anne Catherine Emmerich (about 1820): I heard that Lucifer (if I don't mistake) will be freed again for awhile fifty or sixty years before the year 2000 A.D. I have forgotten many of the other dates were told.[83]

These mystics seemed to believe that while events to get ready for the end would not begin until the 20th century, that the end would apparently come shortly thereafter. And it should be noted that a "secret sect" with Nazarene characteristics did disturb the changing Greco-Roman churches utilizing a variety of media for 50–60 years before the year 2000.[84]

As far as when the great tribulation can begin, notice the following:

Mother Shipton (16th century). The great chastisement will come when carriages go without horses...[85]

Automobiles, of course, used to be called horse-less carriages, and they were not used to any extent before the 20th century. Some say that "Mother Shipton" was a myth, and that the predictions were composed by others, but a book including these predictions came out before the 20th century. And according to Yves Dupont, she was a Catholic prophetess. Some might call her predictions coincidences, but as there is a spirit world, you readers are challenged to consider whether "coincidence" makes more sense than a spirit-based explanation.

"Mother Shipton" was born Ursula Sontheil in 1488 in a cave beside the river Nidd in North Yorkshire, England and reportedly taught:

> When pictures seem alive with movements free when boats like fishes swim beneath the sea, when men like birds shall scour the sky then half the world, deep drenched in blood shall die.
>
> For those who live the century through in fear and trembling this shall do. Flee to the mountains and the dens to bog and forest and wild fens.
>
> For storms will rage and oceans roar when Gabriel stands on sea and shore And as he blows his wondrous horn old worlds die and new be born...
>
> The tides will rise beyond their ken to bite away the shores and then the mountains will begin to roar and earthquakes split the plain to shore.
>
> And flooding waters, rushing in will flood the lands with such a din that mankind cowers in muddy fen and snarls about his fellow men.
>
> He bares his teeth and fights and kills and secrets food in secret hills And ugly in his fear, he lies to kill marauders, thieves and spies.
>
> Man flees in terror from the floods and kills, and rapes and lies in blood And spilling blood by mankinds hands will stain and bitter many lands.[86]

So, it appears that she predicted automobiles, submarines, airplanes, and television. Now if by century, the 20th century itself is indicated, then the above prophecy was partially false (also, it is likely that some prophesies ascribed to her were not actually penned until the 19th century[87]).

However, if the century that "Mother Shipton" was referring to began once television became available ("When pictures seem alive with movements free"), then the century would not have begun until sometime in the 1920s, hence, this may indicate that flood and other prophecies are expected before 2030 (but after 2012).

An Ecumenical Forced Age of Peace is Expected Soon

The Bible tells of a time when people all over the world will be forced to worship the Beast's religion, and that this is not a good thing. The Bible essentially shows that intimidation, economic blackmail, and even the threat of death will be used to cause people to comply (Revelation 13:15-17).

Some Catholic prophets/writers, have themselves warned about a coming false peace that many will believe in:

> *The Ecstatic of Tours*: When everyone believes that peace is assured, when everyone least expects it, the great happenings will begin…[88]
>
> *LaSalette Prophecy* (1846): There will be a kind of false peace before the advent of Antichrist.[89]
>
> *Priest R. Gerald Culleton* (1943): We have also been warned against various prophets…Thus they say, "Peace, Peace": yet there is no peace.[90]
>
> *Robert Conte, Jr.* (21st century): They will obtain a kind of false peace, which is an exterior-only peace brought about by severities in law enforcement, by excessively harsh punishments…There will also be little or no war, except between the kingdom of the North (Europe)

and the kingdom of the South (Israel, Middle East, northern Africa)...The Antichrist then decides to try to destroy the Church from within, by making it legal for these apostates and heretics to openly practice their perverse version of Catholicism. He give {sic} them control of church buildings and he alters laws, customs, and culture in order to support their ideas.[91]

Interestingly, there is a Chinese prophecy from astrologers in the Tang Dynasty (618-907 A.D.) that warns of a "false peace" at the same time that a "dragon" (leader) is rising up.[92]

Yet, contrary to the fact that the Bible does not teach a true age of peace before Antichrist (it instead discusses four times of false pronouncement), astoundingly some supposedly "Catholic" writers have taught that prior to the return of Christ an "age of peace" will come from one sometimes called the Great Monarch.

> *D. Birch* (20th century): This would be a Minor Chastisement preceding an Age of Peace. It is not the Tribulation...The Great King will establish Peace and justice in civil matters on a worldwide basis, and protect the primacy of the Church in spiritual matters. [93]

> *H. Kramer* (20th century): Verses 20 and 21 presage a time of peace between the first reign of terror in the second woe and the reign of Antichrist.[94]

> *Y. Dupont* (20th century): a period of peace...In short, virtually the whole world will be Catholic.[95]

> *Telesphorus of Cozensa* (16th century): A powerful French Monarch and French Pope will regain the Holy

Land after terrible wars in Europe. They will convert the world and bring universal peace.[96]

Mother Alphonse Eppinger (1867): After God has purified the world faith and peace will return. Whole nations will adhere to the teachings of the Catholic Church.[97]

Werdin d' Otrante (13th century): The Great Monarch and the Great Pope will precede Antichrist...All the sects will vanish. The capital of the world will fall... The Great Monarch will come and restore peace and the Pope will share in the victory.[98]

John of the Cleft Rock (1340): The White Eagle (Great Monarch), by order of the Archangel Michael, will drive crescent from Europe where none but Christians will remain--he himself will rule from Constantinople. An era of peace and prosperity will begin for the world. There will no longer be Protestants or Schismatics...[99]

St. Methodius (4th century). But a Great King will arise to fight the enemies of God. He will defeat them, and peace will be given to the world, and the Church will be freed from her anxieties.[100]

Venerable Bartholomew Holzhauser (died 1658): He will root out false doctrines and destroy the rule of the Moslemism. His dominion will extend from the East to the West. All nations will adore God their Lord according to Catholic teaching... The reign of the Great Ruler may be compared with that of Caesar Augustus, who became Emperor after his victory over his enemies, thereby giving peace to the world... The Fifth Epoch of time dates from the reign of Charles V until the reign of the Great Monarch [101]

Hence some type of forced age of peace supposedly precedes the Great Tribulation according to some private prophets/writers. It supposed to occur fairly soon. This prediction seems in contrast to the biblical order. The Bible itself warns that before Christ returns some will falsely proclaim peace:

> [6] They have envisioned futility and false divination, saying, 'Thus says the LORD!' But the LORD has not sent them; yet they hope that the word may be confirmed. [7] Have you not seen a futile vision, and have you not spoken false divination? You say, 'The LORD says,' but I have not spoken." [8] Therefore thus says the Lord GOD: "Because you have spoken nonsense and envisioned lies, therefore I am indeed against you," says the Lord GOD. [9] My hand will be against the prophets who envision futility and who divine lies; they shall not be in the assembly of My people, nor be written in the record of the house of Israel, nor shall they enter into the land of Israel. Then you shall know that I am the Lord GOD. [10] Because, indeed, because they have seduced My people, saying, 'Peace!' when there is no peace …(Ezekiel 13:6-10).

> [3] For when they say, "Peace and safety!" then sudden destruction comes upon them, as labor pains upon a pregnant woman (1 Thessalonians 5:2-3).

So, the Bible warns that before some great time of sudden destruction, many will rely on false prophecies. It also warns that many people love false prophecies (Jeremiah 5:31).

Now this is not saying that all private prophecies (Catholic or otherwise) are false. However, they need to be consistent with the testimony of the Bible, or Christians (and hopefully others) should decide that they are somehow unreliable:

> [19] And when they say to you, "Seek those who are mediums and wizards, who whisper and mutter," should not a people seek their God? Should they seek the dead on behalf of the living? [20] To the law and to the testimony! If they do not speak according to this word, it is because there is no light in them (Isaiah 8:19-20).

Hence, any "private prophecies" (from any sources) that are in conflict with scripture are either false or are not being understood correctly.

Even the current Pope teaches that private prophecies should not be accepted if they are in conflict with the historical teachings of his church[102]—and many (even some in books with imprimaturs) are. Perhaps it should be added that no Catholic that I have thus far spoken to is personally looking forward to a militaristic leader to rise up and kill the amounts of people that the "Great Monarch" seems prophesied to kill. No Catholic (or anyone else) should later change and support such a leader when he rises up, even if at first he professes peace.

The Malachy Prophecies

While some may scoff at some of the Catholic writings thus far cited, there is an old and extremely interesting one that perhaps most clearly points to the 21st century. It was given by an Irish Catholic Archbishop of Armagh Malachy.

Near the middle of the 12th century, Malachy claimed to have a vision where he listed some comments about every future pope from then to the last one. A complete list of each of the popes (including *several* of the antipopes) through John Paul II (number 110 on that list) is included in a Catholic approved (contains an imprimatur from a bishop) prophecy book from the 20th century.[103]

Here are come Catholic comments about *Malachy's* list:

> *Y. Dupont*: St. Malachy...has given fitting descriptions of every pope since the 16th century, when it was discovered.[104]

> *E Connor*: [W]hen Malachy visited Pope Innocent II in Rome in 1139, he was given a vision of all the Holy Fathers of the future...Of the 112 popes described on the list 74 had already reigned when the list was discovered... Proponents of the prophecy...stand on the fact that the prophetic utterances did fit all the popes *after* 1590 with uncanny aptness...**A study of the entire prophecy shows that fulfillment is made possible only by including anti-popes**...[105]

> *P. Bander*:....the vast majority of Malachy's predictions about successive Popes is amazingly accurate...[106]

> *A. Devine*: In 1139...St. Malachy gave his manuscript to Innocent II to console him in the midst of his tribulations, and that the document remained unknown in the Roman Archives until its discovery in 1590...These short prophetical announcements, in number 112, indicate some noticeable trait of **all future popes from Celestine II, who was elected in the year 1143, until the end of the world**. They are enunciated under mystical titles. Those who have undertaken to interpret and explain these symbolical prophecies have succeeded in discovering some trait,

allusion, point, or similitude in their application to the individual popes, either as to their country, their name, their coat of arms or insignia, their birth-place, their talent or learning, the title of their cardinalate, the dignities which they held etc.[107]

It should emphasized that Malachy's list includes several leaders that the Roman Catholics identify as antipopes (e.g. Clement VII, Benedict XIII, etc.[108]) and that, thus, many are inserted sometimes together as opposed to always being in strict chronological order. Hence, since "God is not the author of confusion" (1 Corinthian 14:33) while the list has a certain accuracy, it would not appear that its origins are truly divine. God would not allow His true prophet to make that type of error. But the list is still of interest.

The second to the last pope on the Malachy list is the current Pope Benedict XVI (number 111 on the Malachy list).

Pope Benedictus XVI is Number 111 on the Malachy List

This means that *if* all the future popes are supposedly forecast here (which is what the list suggests, although some have questioned that[109]), there is only one left. And if only one is left, this would point to the last one being alive in 2012 and almost assuredly dying in the 21st century. That one may be the final antipope[110] (see also Chapter 10).

Nostradamus and Barack Obama?

Michel de Nostredame ("Michael of Our Lady," usually Latinized to Nostradamus), was a French apothecary and reputed Catholic seer who published collections of prophecies that have since become famous worldwide.

And while some Catholics distance themselves from his writings, Nostradamus was a Roman Catholic. One Catholic writer wrote:

> Nostradamus...A member of the third order of St. Francis, he enjoyed the friendship of Pope Pius IV. He was a devout Catholic all his life...Nostradamus was an authentic seer.[111]

Nostradamus probably is best known for his book, *Les Propheties* (The Prophecies), which was first distributed in 1555. It contained a series of 100 sets (called Centuries) of four verse prophetic passages (called Quatrains) that many believe were often written cryptically to help preserve his life from government/church authorities. Others believe that they were written cryptically to make them subject to almost any interpretation, thus of no real predictive value.

Whether they do or do not have real predictive value, the fact is that a lot of people around the world believe that they may. Thus, some might be influenced by them. For purposes of this book, there are a couple of them that we should look at.

Nostradamus: Original portrait by his son Cesar

The first is Century 4 Quatrain 50 from Nostradamus, with the *Comment* below it from a Catholic writer:

> Under the sign of Libra, America shall reign, Shall hold power in the sky and on land, Shall never perish under Asian forces, Until seven Pontificates have passed.[112]

> *Comment on the above from Yves Dupont*: "As a great world power, the U.S.A. began its "reign" during the first World War—but it was not the *greatest* world power...In 1945, however, the U.S.A. was, by and large, the greatest world power. I think it is from the reign of Pius XII that the seven Pontificates must be counted, and this brings us to the last Pope according to St. Malachy's list—when the world will end."[113]

It appears that the above writings suggest that the end of the U.S.A. will thus be in the 21st century. And as far as Asian forces go, this could be interpreted to include terrorists from places like Afghanistan and others parts of Asia. The U.S.

has had troops battling "Asian forces" for some time, and its current president Barack Obama has increased the presence of American troops in Afghanistan.

Here is another translation of Quatrain 50 that perhaps should be shown, as it implies something a little bit different:

> Libra will see the western lands (America) to govern, Holding the rule over the skies and the earth No one will see the forces of Asia destroyed Until seven hold the hierarchy in succession.

Here is a comment about that Quatrain by a writer in India (R. Chopra) who then cites Quatrain 74:

> The "seven" are the seven millennia in Nostradamus' calculations which end in A.D. 2000, which also links this quatrain to the quatrain below:

> The year the great seventh number is accomplished Appearing at the time of the games of slaughter, Not far from the age of the great millennium (2000) When the dead will come out of their graves.[114]

Now the above suggests that the forces of Asia will not be destroyed until the "seven hold the hierarchy in succession," which apparently is in the 21st century. The Bible does warn that the "kings of the east" will come together at Armageddon (Revelation 16:12-16) and that a 200,000,000 man army will be destroyed (Revelation 9:13-20; 16:16). If you are Asian, you might want to warn your people now to help prevent some of them from supporting that army.

Now, regardless of which of the translations of Quatrain 50 is more accurate, the fact is that if Y. Dupont is correct about the seven being popes until the last one on the Malachy prophecy list, then it is possible that Barack Obama may be the last leader of the America to govern before the end. And if the Indian writer is correct that the seven times refers to the end coming in this millennium, the end is coming soon.

If Barack Obama is re-elected and survives in office, then he would remain U.S. president until January 19, 2017. Because the current Pope Benedict XVI was born on 16 April 1927, he would be 89 3/4 then if he remains alive—and while he may, it seems more likely that the next pope (the final one on the Malachy list) could be in place before a re-elected Barack Obama would leave his office.

There is only one pope left on the Malachy list. Some Catholics suspect that this could be an antipope (one not true to Roman Catholicism) who could be the Antichrist (see Chapter 9).

And *if* that pope is the antipope and the final Antichrist, then the following one of Nostradamus' other Quatrains (Century 10 Quatrain 66) may possibly apply to Barack Obama (perhaps the one identified as "Reb" below):

> The chief of London through the realm of America, The Isle of Scotland will be tried by frost: King and "Reb" will face an Antichrist so false, That he will place them in the conflict all together.[115]

Quatrain 66 suggests that the leader of the United Kingdom (chief of London and involving Scotland) will be influenced by the western realm of America, with the leader called "Reb" (America rebelled against England in 1776) and will encounter an Antichrist that will ultimately place them into conflict.

Hence Quatrain 66 could be an end-time reference that might take place soon.

So there appears to be at least two quatrains from

Nostradamus that *might* point to Barack Obama and something terribly important happening in the 21st century.

Lost Writings of Nostradamus?

There are certain drawings (actually more like small paintings) that some have indicated that Nostradamus produced. These drawings are said to predict the end of the world in 2012. While it is not certain that Nostradamus himself made those colored drawings (his *Les Propheties* book does not have any), they came out in his era, and he may have produced some that others copied.

Basically, if one interprets certain of those paintings to indicate that the cosmic alignment that many believe will occur on December 21, 2012, then Nostradamus could have indicated that something bad would occur then. Some believe that Nostradamus was pointing to the same flooding as the Mayan Dresden Codex.[116] And while that might be, we know the Bible is clear that the entire world will not be destroyed by a flood (Genesis 9:11), hence even *if* the drawings are from Nostradamus (which is questionable) and he did intend them to be fulfilled in 2012, they should not be interpreted to mean that the world will end around December 22, 2012, as it will not.

However, regardless of any drawings, paintings, or writings by Nostradamus, there is still only one pope left on the Malachy list.

Thus, translation and interpretation issues not withstanding, there seem to be several writings from Catholic sources suggesting that the end should occur sometime in the early part of the 21st century.

CHAPTER 4
HINDU WRITINGS, NEW AGE HOPES, AND BUDDHIST GOALS

In addition to the Mayans, Hopi, and *I Ching*, there are many writings that do not come from a Judeo-Christian perspective that look forward to a new age to come—a time most often considered by their believers, to be an "age of peace."

Some of these writings point to an unspecified time in the distant future, while others are more specific.

This chapter will look at some related to Hindu, New Age, and Buddhist traditions.

Hindu Writings and 2012

There are a variety of claims that Hindu writings point to the next decade. Many Hindus seem to be looking toward a time of a rebirth of the planet.

The following Hindu prediction is intriguing, and is a good place to begin. A Hindu from India named Vijay Kumar (he refers to himself as "The Man who Realized God In 1993") makes the following claims about 2012:

> 2012 shall be remembered in history of mankind forever. Why?
>
> From the position of planetary movements and

astrological calculations...A significant upheaval on the whole shall be the order of the day.

Adharma (lawlessness) would be rooted out for ever. 2012 and beyond is the period of spiritual elevation. 2012 rings start of golden era. Beyond 2012 it shall be harmony and peace all over...

The spiritual wisdom would become the order of the day. 2012 is the year of sacrifice. Both... the sinner (committer of crime) and the innocent will be sacrificed. One who has committed crime shall face the gallows. Those who uphold and cherish values in the society would sacrifice their lives for the sake of humanity...

The sacrifice by the eminent would be by will. To cleanse the society of its ills in 2012...many would come forward and sacrifice self on the altar of God. Unless that happens...the upheaval in the society is not possible. **The blood of the innocent would be spilled. There is no other remedy**...

For the society to climb back to its pristine glory of the golden era... **even the meek would handle metal (pick arms).** Whatever the poor and the downtrodden lay their hands upon would become their weapon. In the last phase of the Kali Yuga we are passing through... the complete society has been taken to ransom by about 6% corrupt population comprising of politicians, bureaucrats, judiciary and police force...

2012 is the year of the Avatar of the era (god almighty manifest in human form)... people await with abated breath the coming of Bhagwan Kalki...one who delivers the mankind from the existing ills of today. **Bhagwan Kalki would be a spiritual master of the highest order with the deadly combination of a wise dictator** (Chanakya of the modern era)...[117]

Notice that Vijay Kumar's writings support a warring power—something the Bible warns against in Revelation 13:3-10. This type of warring power will not bring in a true age of peace, even though many may proclaim that it will (cf. Ezekiel 13:10-16; 1 Thessalonians 5:3).

Also notice the following about the Avatar/Bhagwan Kalki:

> **Whenever there is a withering of the law
> and an uprising of lawlessness on all sides,
> then I manifest Myself.
> For the salvation of the righteous
> and the destruction of such as do evil,
> for the firm establishing of the Law,
> I come to birth, age after age.**
> —*Bhagavad Gita, Book IV, Sutra 5, 7, 8...*

In all, the Hindu text of Kalki Purana is comprised of 6100 verses describing ... Kalki, who is considered the last Avtar or incarnation of Vishnu or the Supreme Being, who will establish the Age of Truth or Age of Purity on Earth.... As agreed by all the religious prophecies, the Awaited One will not be a man of peace like Jesus Christ or Buddha, but a man of war who will destroy evil and establish righteousness on the earth.[118]

If views like these become predominant in the future, it may be that they will help lead to Hindus at least temporarily accepting a new religion of the coming False Prophet and the authority of the coming militaristic dictator known as Beast that the Bible warns will rise up at the end.

It also probably should be mentioned that many Hindu "prophecies" tend to point to dates later than 2012. Here is an astrological one related to a Hindu deity:

The Coming Age of Transition...

> Thereafter Saturn will govern for **19 years** when it will spread Sahaja Yoga in the Whole world. Saturn means the masses, the Virata and Shri Mataji will witness Kalki (Mercury) Power manifesting over the whole World. **21 – 02 - 2013**.[119]

So, apparently a time of change is being predicted that may be clearer by February 21, 2013 (a frequent Hindu festival called "Ekadashi" is also to take place then). Hence this may point to the rise of a great leader or power in 2013.

Certain Hindus, however, seem to be looking a little later, while recognizing certain astronomical aspects of 2012:

> As far as Hindus are concerned the important date is {sic} 2014 & 2013.
>
> In 2012 the plane of our Solar System will line up exactly with the plane of our Galaxy,
>
> On the winter solstice in 2012, the sun will be aligned with the center of the Milky Way for the first time in about 26,000 years.
>
> According to Srimad Bhagavatam - Kalki is destined to appear when the Sun, Moon and Jupiter together enters

> Pushya nakshatra ...it then goes to give the description of his birth etc. This astrological phenomenon happens on 26/27th. July 2014 A.D. at 3:10 P. M. on a Sunday. [120]

Thus, it is clear that not all Hindus are looking toward 2012, but some do seem to be looking to the next decade with some changes taking place then. And although we in the "secret sect" do not believe in practicing astrology (cf. Jeremiah 10:2), astrology is part of the Hindu faith. Therefore, those who do believe in astrology can be highly influenced by movements in the sky—so much so, that perhaps they will temporarily accept some of what the European Beast power teaches.

This is especially true because many Hindus are looking forward to the time of the coming "Kalki" (also known as Maha Avatara, an incarnation of Vishnu, who will come to end the present age of darkness and destruction).

Hindus look forward to an age of peace, but as the following also suggests, many feel that a strong human leader is needed for it to come to pass:

> Kalki Incarnation...shall herald the Golden Age of peace and plenty—the Satyayuga. Since Kalki will be an age making Avatar, he has to be powerful and potent.[121]

New Age Movement is Correct that Peace is Coming, but ...

There are various groups around the world who consider that the world as we know it must change or humankind faces disaster. Some operate under the broad category known as the "New Age Movement." Some use that term, while others do not. Some associated with it have alluded to 2012.

Similarly, notice what the Ontario Consultants on *Religious*

Tolerance have reported about the New Age Movement:

> The New Age Movement is in a class by itself. Unlike most formal religions, it has no holy text, central organization, membership, formal clergy, geographic center, dogma, creed, etc. They often use mutually exclusive definitions for some of their terms. The New Age is in fact a free-flowing spiritual movement; a network of believers and practitioners who share somewhat similar beliefs and practices, which they add on to whichever formal religion that they follow...
>
> **New Age beliefs**:
>
> A number of fundamental beliefs are held by many New Age followers...
>
> ■ **Universal Religion:** Since all is God, then only one reality exists, and all religions are simply different paths to that ultimate reality. The universal religion can be visualized as a mountain, with many **sadhanas** (spiritual paths) to the summit. Some are hard; others easy. There is no one correct path. All paths eventually reach the top. They anticipate that a new universal religion which contains elements of all current faiths will evolve and become generally accepted worldwide.
>
> ■ **New World Order** As the **Age of Aquarius** unfolds, a **New Age** will develop. This will be a utopia in which there is world government, and end to wars, disease, hunger, pollution, and poverty. Gender, racial, religious and other forms of discrimination will cease. People's allegiance to their tribe or nation will be replaced by a concern for the entire world and its people.[122]

Notice that many of those within the New Age movement look forward to a new age with a universal ecumenical religion.

In his book, *Peace is the Way*, Deepak Chopra wrote that we are on the verge of a global shift in consciousness that will lead the world toward an age of peace, because many in the West are becoming more accepting of New Age values. Deepak Chopra stated that those values included a shift away from what he calls "religious fundamentalism," [123] and apparently toward a more ecumenical humanistic religion.

The idea that some type of change would occur at the end of the Mayan calendar in 2012 was originally popularized by José Argüelles. Dr. Argüelles was one of the original founders of "Earth Day" in 1970 and is considered a leader with New Age beliefs. Here is some of what he has written:

> When we look at the calendar…the thirteenth subcycle of this beam, began in 1618 and runs to 2012…
>
> There are actually many points of convergence among the Mayan galactic code, I Ching, the Book of Revelations, and many other systems…
>
> [Y]ou have the mathematical code of the Book of Revelations, which is based on 7 and 13, and 144 and 144,000; it's the same number of the Mayan Code. The Mayan Code is the master code. It's the galactic code. It's the master program.[124]

Now, those of us who accept a literalistic interpretation of the Bible would not consider that the Mayan Code is the "master code." But we often find predictions interesting when they align with scripture.

In his book on 2012, Gregg Braden includes the following

HINDU WRITINGS, NEW AGE HOPES, AND BUDDHIST GOALS

from James O'Dea:

> Our collective emergence will be defined by feelings of oneness and communion with "all our relations." It will be accompanied by feelings of great expansiveness and generosity.[125]

Thus, some feel that a collective emergence will become more pronounced. This seems to lean toward the acceptance of some type of universal ecumenical faith.

Because of its limited structure and apparent beliefs, it seems likely that the New Age Movement will be influenced by one who proclaims peace, accompanied by signs and wonders (2 Thessalonians 2:9; Revelation 16:14).

Like some of the Hindus, when a leader rises up proclaiming a new ecumenical religion that he will likely claim will lead to an "age of peace," (on more than one occasion) many within this movement may decide that this leader is the one that their movement needs in order for the world to have peace.

Thus from various (Catholic/Hindu/New Age) sources, it is clear that many look for a new religious leader to rise up and establish a new age. This book challenges them to remain true to the idea that peace will not be implemented by a militaristic human being.

While a new age will temporarily come (and will make many people wealthy for a time per Revelation 18:11-16, this is not the age of the Kingdom of God. The Bible shows that prior to the real age of peace, a warring ecumenical religion will take over much of the world through force and economic blackmail (Revelation 13:2-17). And this warring age will come to an abrupt end when God orchestrates it (Revelation 18:17-20).

The Bible is also clear that while God wants people to pray

for peace (Psalm 122:6), that it is God, and not humankind, who will bring peace to earth.

Those in the New Age Movement are correct that a new peaceful age is needed. And they are correct that peace is coming. Hopefully this book will help those in the New Age Movement better understand how and when a real age of peace will actually come about.

Buddhism Looks Forward to Peace

Tibetan Buddhists reportedly also look toward 2012 and the dawning of an age of peace:

> The Tibetans Kalachakra contains a prophecy that 860 years after its introduction into Tibet, which happened in 1127, the conditions would be fulfilled for a twenty-five year period that would culminate in the appearance of the Tibetan version of New Jerusalem, the hidden city of Shamballa. Eight hundred and sixty years after 1127 is 1987, and 25 years after that is 2012.[126]

(Perhaps it should be pointed out that a "New Jerusalem" is prophesied to come, but according to the Bible, it is to come after the millennial reign of Christ (Revelation 21:1–2.)

When a flood does NOT destroy the planet in 2012, some who are Hindu, Buddhist, New Age, and even ecumenically-inclined Catholic will likely claim that their hoped for "age of peace" is dawning, because if anything, that is what some will claim the Mayan 2012 calendar really represented. Hence, many are likely to accept the coming ecumenical religion.

Interestingly, certain Roman Catholic writers consider that the "pagans" (which is a term that many have historically used for Buddhists and Hindus) will become part of the final militaristic ecumenical religion that will likely call itself the "Catholic Church":

Jerome Savonarola (15th century): My Lord wants to reformulate the Church And convert each barbaric people…There shall be one shepherd and one sheepfold… And so much blood shall flow…[127]

St. Bridget (14th century): Before Antichrist comes, the portals of Faith will be opened to great numbers of pagans.[128]

Cardinal La Roque (c. 18th century): **A regeneration of Faith will appear in Asia**…the Great Monarch will be in Europe.[129]

Jane Le Royer (died 1798): The Church in Council will strike down anathemas…religions shall be abolished {other than the one calling itself "Catholic"}…the altars shall be reestablished…Then will a universal peace be proclaimed.[130]

Gonçalves Annes Bandarra (16th century): I see a great King coming…He will defeat the fantasies…All will have one love Heathens and pagans, The Jews will be Christians, With no mistake anymore.[131]

Although Gonçalves Annes Bandarra mentioned "one love," this is not the "one love" that the Jamaica-based Rastifaris (who are not Buddhists) talk about. No real universal love is going to come to pass because of a "great King" forcing everyone to become a new type of ecumenical "Catholic."

But this is what some who have held to some version of "Catholicism" have claimed, despite the fact that their views appear to conflict with scripture. While they are correct that a "regeneration of faith will appear in Asia," those who suggest that it will take a militaristic human king for this to come to pass are not true to either original Catholicism (as practiced in the 2nd century) nor the Bible.

God Will Bring Peace

Perhaps it should be mentioned that the Buddhists are correct that humans are not to be militaristic and should to try to be peaceful; real Buddhists hope for peace:

> *Ron Epstein* (20th century): Buddhism teaches that whether we have global peace or global war is up to us at every moment. The situation is not hopeless and out of our hands. If we don't do anything, who will? Peace or war is our decision. The fundamental goal of Buddhism is peace...The doctrine of karma teaches that force and violence, even to the level of killing, never solves anything... The most fundamental moral precept in Buddhist teaching is respect for life and the prohibition against taking life... Unlike almost all other religions, Buddhism teaches that there are no exceptions to this prohibition and no expedient arguments are admitted. [132]

It should be understood that despite this position, Buddhists do sometime engage in warfare—although based upon the above, those that do would not appear to be faithful Buddhists.

Also notice the following "Shamballa" prophecy:

> *Lama*: A great epoch approaches. The Ruler of the World is ready to fight. Many things are manifested. The cosmic fire is again approaching the earth. The planets are manifesting the new era. But many cataclysms will occur before the new era of prosperity.[133]

HINDU WRITINGS, NEW AGE HOPES, AND BUDDHIST GOALS

The above is actually fairly correct. A great epoch is approaching. Of course, Buddhists should be wary of a coming "Ruler of the World" who will fight. After he does, the Day of the Lord (See Chapter 15) will produce cataclysms. Then when Jesus returns, the REAL age of prosperity will come.

Also notice the following:

> *Anagata-vamsa*: The Maitreya (Pali: Metteya) is predicted to be the future Buddha in the scriptures of both Theravada and Mahayana Buddhism. In both traditions some consider him as the future Messiah who will usher in the new age of bliss and consummation.[134]

A blissful age, that the Buddhists and others look forward to, will ultimately come. But hopefully the Buddhists will not accept a militaristic leader as the Buddha to come.

Notice the following from the *Encyclopedia Britannica*:

> Buddhist literature contains predictions of a certain Buddha Maitreya, who will come as a kind of saviour-messiah to inaugurate a paradisaical age on earth. Gautama the Buddha himself, the 6th-century-bc founder of Buddhism, mentioned this prediction.[135]

And while a savoir will come for the Buddhists and all others, the Bible shows that this will be Jesus. So, Buddhists should not believe any "savior" claim prior to His return. It should be added, however, that certain Buddhist sects do not look towards the coming of any single being as Messiah—but the real Messiah will still come.

Gautama Buddha, 1st century
The "Great Monarch" is not the Buddha

This peaceful age is shown in the Bible to come from God intervening and stopping the world from destroying itself after that vain and false leader has risen up.

Notice the following:

> [15] "Therefore when you see the 'abomination of desolation,' spoken of by Daniel the prophet, standing in the holy place" (whoever reads, let him understand), [16] then let those who are in Judea flee to the mountains. [17] Let him who is on the housetop not go down to take anything out of his house. [18] And let him who is in the field not go back to get his clothes. [19] But woe to those who are pregnant and to those who are nursing babies in those days! [20] And pray that your flight may not be in winter or on the Sabbath.

> ²¹ For then there will be great tribulation, such as has not been since the beginning of the world until this time, no, nor ever shall be. ²²And **unless those days were shortened, no flesh would be saved**; but for the elect's sake those days will be shortened (Matthew 24:15-22).

After God stops humanity from destroying the planet, Jesus will return and God will establish the new age that many cultures have looked forward too:

> ²⁹ "Immediately after the tribulation of those days the sun will be darkened, and the moon will not give its light; the stars will fall from heaven, and the powers of the heavens will be shaken. ³⁰ Then the sign of the Son of Man will appear in heaven, and then all the tribes of the earth will mourn, and they will see the Son of Man coming on the clouds of heaven with power and great glory (Matthew 24:29-30).

This will usher in the true "age of peace" that people all over the world have longed for.

There will be major problems and a falsely claimed, terrifying, "age of peace" first, though.

CHAPTER 5
DANIEL 9:26–27 AND THE RISE OF THE EUROPEAN KING OF THE NORTH

The Bible (an ancient text that around three billion or so people have a religious connection with) and other sources have foretold of a time when a powerful, but diabolical, militaristic leader rises up. This leader is predicted to be so fierce that he will attempt to put an end to religious views different than those he will impose.

Interestingly, this prophesied leader is described in a way similar to a leader that certain Hindus, Muslims, and some others have predicted. Hence, much of the world is, in a very real sense, waiting for someone like this to rise up.

Not only I, but many biblically-oriented Protestant and Catholic theologians believe this leader is still prophesied to rise up, based upon the writings in Daniel and elsewhere.

Note what Daniel was led to write:

> [24] The ten horns are ten kings
> Who shall arise from this kingdom. And another shall rise after them;
> He shall be different from the first ones, And shall subdue three kings.
> [25] He shall speak pompous words against the Most High,

> Shall persecute the saints of the Most High,
> And shall intend to change times and law.
> Then the saints shall be given into his hand
> For a time and times and half a time (Daniel 7:24-25).

So, Daniel wrote that someone will rise up from a prior kingdom, but that he will be different than those who were before him. And this leader will persecute the saints of the Most High. Both Protestant and Catholic commentators[136] agree that the last of the four kingdoms in Daniel 7:7-8 is the Roman Empire. Thus the idea that the final Beast leader comes from some revised version of that empire appears consistent with the historical views that many religious writers have put forth.

Now, in the book of Daniel there is another prophecy related to the end times that states: [26] And the people of the prince who is to come Shall destroy the city and the sanctuary. The end of it shall be with a flood, And till the end of the war desolations are determined. [27] Then he shall confirm a covenant with many for one week; But in the middle of the week He shall bring an end to sacrifice and offering.

And on the wing of abominations shall be one who makes desolate, Even until the consummation, which is determined, Is poured out on the desolate (Daniel 9:26-27).

Notice that there is a "prince to come" from the people who destroy "the city" (probably Jerusalem; cf. Revelation 11:2) and that he will stop sacrifices and be related to an abomination that brings desolation. This leader will apparently change from a peaceful one to a militaristic one (cf. Isaiah 10:5-11).

There are several reasons for referring to a future top leader from a developing superpower rising in Europe. (cf. Isaiah 10:5-11). The Roman Empire, however, offers the most compelling reason to suspect that this leader will arise in

Europe. Much of the current European Union (EU) covers areas once controlled by the old Roman Empire. The people of the Roman Empire fulfilled the portion of Daniel 9:26 in the 1st century as they destroyed the city (Jerusalem) in 70 A.D. And verse 27 refers to the "prince" coming from the people who had destroyed that city. Hence, this prophecy tells us that a leader will start to rise up about 3 1/2 years before the great tribulation.

There is another reason to suspect that the area involves the territories of Europe. Millennia ago, Daniel wrote a prophecy that discussed a little horn that would mainly expand to the south and east:

> [8] And out of one of them came a little horn which grew exceedingly great toward the south, toward the east, and toward the Glorious Land. [10] And it grew up to the host of heaven; and it cast down some of the host and some of the stars to the ground, and trampled them. [11] He even exalted himself as high as the Prince of the host; and by him the daily sacrifices were taken away, and the place of His sanctuary was cast down. [12] Because of transgression, an army was given over to the horn to oppose the daily sacrifices; and he cast truth down to the ground. He did all this and prospered (Daniel 8:9-12).

And while the above has had a past fulfillment, this prophecy seems to be dual (compare with Daniel 11:27--39)- and seems to be for our time.

What is now the EU began as a small organization involving three small countries located in the northern and western regions of Europe (Netherlands, Belgium, and Luxembourg, called the Benelux nations)—they then helped form the European Economic Community. This

European Economic Community expanded mainly south and east of the Benelux nations, into what had become the expanded European Union. Now, about 500 million people are under a new (though not completely united) government headquartered in Brussels, Belgium.

Some Related Catholic Writings

There have been writings from various Catholics suggesting that prior to the rise of a "Great Monarch," Catholics will become lax in their religion and something will happen in Europe.

Some believe that God will punish the nominal Catholics with civil unrest and war in Europe. As there already has been civil unrest in Europe (and according to secular sources, more is expected[137]), it is possible that the following (to some degree) also may come to pass:

> *Jean Paul Richter* (died 1809): Through a terrible purgatory Europe will return to the faith.[138]
>
> *Monk Hilarion* (15th century): The people of the peninsula of Europe will suffer by needless wars until the Holy Man comes. The Lion will come from a high mountain in the enlightened nation.[139]
>
> *Dionysius of Luxemburg* (died 1682): Pastors in many places will neglect the service of God...Even the religious will crave for worldly things. The churches will be dreary and empty like deserted barns...From the midst of His Church He will raise up a Christian ruler who will perform most remarkable deeds. With divine assistance this ruler will not only lead erring souls back to the true Faith but also deal a heavy blow to the foes of the empire; the Turks, to take away their

empire and restore it to Christianity.¹⁴⁰

Brother Louis Rocco (19th century): All over Europe there will rage terrible civil wars...The German sections of Austria will join Germany, so will also the commercial cities of Belgium and Switzerland. A Catholic descendant of a German imperial house will rule a united Germany with peace, prosperity and great power, for God will be with this sovereign (the Great Monarch?)...A Great Monarch will arise after a period of terrible wars and persecutions in Europe. He will be a Catholic...¹⁴¹

D. Birch (20th century): At some time in the future, the corrupt faithless age we live in now will come to an end either through repentance (immediately followed by an age of peace)--or there will be a chastisement. This would be a Minor Chastisement preceding an Age of Peace. It is not the Tribulation of the Antichrist... A man who will subsequently be known as a great saint will ultimately be elected pope near the end of the Chastisement. He will be heavily responsible for the French acceptance of a king to be their military and civil leader...¹⁴²

The Ecstatic of Tours...The revolution will spread to every French town. Wholesale slaughter will take place. This revolution will last only a few months but it will be frightful; blood will flow everywhere because the malice of the wicked will reach its highest pitch. Victims will be innumerable. Paris will look like a slaughter-house...The French people will ask for the good King, he who was chosen by God. He will come, this saviour whom God has spared for France,

> this King who is not wanted now because he is dear to God's Heart. He will ascend to the throne; he will free the church and reassert the Pope's rights...[143]

Despite the destructive nature, this unrest has been called "the minor chastisement" by some Catholics.[144]

Some believe this civil unrest will result in the rise of a militaristic leader who will quell that particular violence, establish a new religious order, and reign with a pope who will perform miracles (see also Chapter 10).

One interesting 15th century Catholic prophecy foretells a time when a "great prince" will rise up. "All Germany" will apparently convert to the ecumenical religion, and then massive conversions in "all countries" "will happen quickly".[145]

A 4th century Byzantine prophecy states that one of the divisions of the army of the coming monarch will have 18 languages.[146] As there are 23 official languages currently in the European Union, it appears that a European monarch is what the Orthodox expect.

The descriptions of the Great Monarch/Prince in many ways parallel the description of one the Bible refers to as the "prince" in Daniel 9:26-27, final "King of the North" in Daniel 11:27-45 (see also Appendix B, as well as the Beast of Revelation 13).

Protestants on Daniel 9

While there have been various understandings of the Daniel 9:26-27, notice what three Protestant commentators basically correctly state (**bolding**/*italics* in source):

> *Matthew Henrys Commentary:* It is here foretold that *the people of the prince that shall come* shall be the instruments of this destruction, that is, the Roman

armies, belonging to a monarchy yet to come...That the desolation shall be total and final: *He shall make it desolate, even until the consummation*, that is, he shall make it completely desolate...And when it is made desolate, it should seem, there is something more determined that is to be *poured upon the desolate* (v. 27), and what should that be but the *spirit of slumber*...[147]

Wycliffe Bible Commentary: C. F. Keil (*Comm., in loco*) is correct in asserting that the **prince** is said to be *coming* (***habba'***), because he has already been introduced and discussed in the prophecy of chapter 7...The Romans who destroyed Jerusalem (A.D. 70) were his **people** because they and he belong to the fourth stage (the Roman) of world empire (chs. 2; 7)...

> **And he shall confirm the covenant with many for one week** (make a *firm covenant*, ASV). The language ***higbir*** from ***gabar***, "be strong" does not signify confirmation of a covenant but causation of a firm covenant. *And he shall cause to prevail* is an excellent translation. The most natural antecedent for **he**, the subject of the clause, is the wicked "prince" of verse 26... Evidently the covenant is to be made...when the Jews are back in their homeland in the last days. The exact nature of the covenant is unknown.

The evil and destructive events described in the remainder of this verse should be interpreted as summary information concerning the final "time of Jacob's trouble" (Jer 30:7 and context) set forth rather more fully in Dan 12:1 ff; 2 Thess 2:1 ff; Rev 13; 14; and other passages.[148]

> *Dr. J.F. Walvoord:*...the covenant of Daniel 9:27 is not the covenant of grace...this refers to the coming world ruler at the beginning of the last seven years...He will make a covenant with Israel for a seven-year period.[149]

The two commentaries correctly identified this leader as one who will be part of a "Roman Empire," and is also the leader warned about in Daniel 7:23–26. Dr. Walvoord correctly indicated that a prophetic week is generally understood to refer to seven years. And half a week is 3 1/2 years.

The leader mentioned in Daniel 9:26–27 is only referred to as a "prince" when he confirms the one week covenant. He may not be known as the "king" (or some other title indicating the top ruler) until shortly before he breaks the covenant at the mid-week point. Most likely he will be considered simply one of several leaders negotiating a treaty when this deal in Daniel 9:27 is initially made.

And lest some feel that the idea of a European deal with Israel is far-fetched, even within Israel, many suggested such a deal.[150] So, while there is still some time left, it may not be very much time.

Islam Seems to Be Expecting this Deal

Interestingly, within Islam, there is a belief that someone who sounds like the biblical "King of the South" of Daniel 11 (see Chapter 8), who they tend to call the Mahdi or 12th Imam will participate in a deal like the one in Daniel 9:27.

Notice the following which is attributed to Mohammed (there are several accepted spellings):

> Rasaullah [Muhammed] said: "There will be four peace agreements between you and the Romans [Christians].

> The fourth agreement will be mediated through a person who will be the progeny of Hadrat Haroon [Honorable Aaron -- Moses' brother] *and will be upheld for seven years.*[151]

Thus, a deal between someone from Europe (Romans above) and Israel (descendant of Aaron) and an Islamic leader is expected.

An Islamic prophetic writer wrote the following:

> ...a life of peace as a result of a peace agreement between you and the Banil Asfaar (Romans) which they will break and attack you.[152]

Hence, some within Islam seem to understand that a temporary, but false peace, will happen with it broken by an attack from the Europeans.

Thus, it seems clear that Muslims should approach that deal with extreme skepticism—but biblically it appears that it will still be made.

There is Still Some Time, but It May Not be Much Past 2013

Because the deal of Daniel 9:27 has not been made (at least not publicly), even if it were made today, the end (meaning the beginning of the great tribulation and the last 3 ½ years before the second coming) cannot happen prior to 2013. (If you add 3 ½ years from this book's publication date, you end up in the year 2013.)

Hence, this appears to be additional biblical evidence that the end will *not* come in 2012 as many have publicly indicated. However, if the deal is made soon, the end may come shortly after the Mayan 2012 date.

And while many do not consider that the European Union

is much of a military power that perception is likely to change in or after 2013.

Why 2013 or after?

In 2013, the Europeans are planning on having their own global positioning system (GPS), called Galileo, available for military applications.[153] This will allow the Europeans to track the world and attack others without relying on the U.S.A.'s GPS. This will be the first time in the 21st century that Europeans will be able to have that type of independent military capability.

Furthermore, according to a 2009 report from the U.S. government, the U.S. Air Force *may* have to start relying on the European Galileo system (at least to a degree) beginning in 2013, as the U.S. GPS capabilities are expected to deteriorate by then [154] (other problems are also appearing in the newer U.S. satellites[155]). Because the Europeans will be able to control Galileo, they will also likely be capable of derailing certain sophisticated U.S. military applications. This will give the Europeans a unique defensive (as well as offensive) capability that no others on the planet will have.

But there is more. The Europeans now also have the world's leading-edge physics project called the Large Hadron Collider (the world's largest and highest-energy particle accelerator).[156] It was built by the European Organization for Nuclear Research (also referred to as CERN), and is apt to provide the Europeans with unique military capabilities in several years. No other nation or group of nations will have complete access to what will develop from the Large Hadron Collider.

The Bible is clear that the final "Beast power" (which will be primarily European) will have such unique military capabilities that the entire world will marvel (cf. Revelation 13:3–4). It appears that these capabilities are being developed now.

The Deal Will Be Made, the Secret Sect Will Claim It, and the Secret Sect Will Rise Up

Those of us who take the Bible literally do believe that the deal in Daniel 9:27 will be made and/or confirmed.

It is also possible that a nation such as the United States may broker such a deal initially, and that it will simply be confirmed by some, including the "prince to come"—but it is at least as likely that the "prince" will propose the deal himself. As the United States continues to face various problems, some in Israel are now calling for a deal similar to the one in Daniel 9:27 to take place soon.[157]

It is my belief that after this deal has been made and/or confirmed by "the prince to come," that the group that best represents the "sect of the Nazarenes" (the remnant of the Philadelphia era of the church per Revelation 3:7–11) in the 21st century will begin to publicly identify the person who confirmed the deal ("the prince") as the one who fulfilled Daniel 9:27. If this deal is made public, others, without the same Nazarene ties, may also claim it.

(If the details of this deal are not made public, the "secret sect" may be able to partially identify it, if some type of a deal is completed involving the nation of Israel and the EU in the Fall of some year. For just like the children of Israel fled Egypt in the Spring at the time of the Exodus, the sect would likely flee around the same time of year. And because one would need to flee about 3 ½ years after this deal is made, a Fall date for the deal seems quite likely.)

The "secret sect" is basically unknown to most around the world. Once the various media begin to report on the group's information about this deal, the "secret sect" will get a lot of publicity. In that sense, the "secret sect" will rise up.

A year or two after this Daniel 9:27 deal is made, women may wish to be careful about becoming pregnant, as Jesus warned that the time right at the beginning of the Great

Tribulation would be hard on those who are pregnant or nursing (Matthew 24:19).

In addition to claiming that the individual is the "prince to come" in Daniel 9:27, this "Nazarene sect" will also teach more about him and what he is prophesied to do. This will upset him enough to begin horrible persecutions (see also Appendix B).

The "Prince" Will Become the King of the North

In the Book of Daniel, a leader called "the King of the North" is mentioned.

And the Bible seems to show similarities between him and the "prince to come." Notice the following:

> [31] And forces shall be mustered by him, and they shall defile the sanctuary fortress; then they shall take away the daily sacrifices, and place there the abomination of desolation...[33] And those of the people who understand shall instruct many; yet for many days they shall fall by sword and flame, by captivity and plundering...[40] the king of the North…(Daniel 11:31,33,40).

This seems to be the same individual as the one mentioned in Daniel 9:27 and Daniel 7:24-25.

Furthermore, because a "prince" is one who can become a king, it *may* be that the Bible is teaching that there will be a way to identify the future King of the North while he is simply an up and coming leader on the world scene—he will be the "prince" who confirms a seven-year peace treaty that he will break in the middle of that seven year period (Daniel 9:26-27).

This King of the North seems to be identified in various "Catholic" (including some which would be considered Eastern Orthodox) writings as the head of a resurrected

Roman Empire; hence he apparently is a European:

> *Bl. Rabanus Maurus* (died 856): Our principal doctors agree in announcing to us, that towards the end of time one of the descendants of France shall reign over all the Roman Empire; that he shall be the greatest of the Empire; and that he shall be the greatest of the French monarch, and the last of his race. After happily governed his kingdom, he will go to Jerusalem, and depose on Mount of Olives his sceptre and crown. This shall be the end and conclusion of the Roman… Empire.[158]

> *Monk Adso* (died 992): Some of our Teachers say that a King of the Franks will possess the entire Roman Empire. This King will be the greatest and the last of all Monarchs, and after having prosperously governed his kingdom, he will come in the end to Jerusalem and he will lay down his sceptre and his crown upon the Mount of Olives and immediately afterwards, Anti-Christ will come.[159]

> *Desmond A. Birch* (20th century): Several private prophecies of canonized Saints specifically state that there will be a latter restoration of the Holy Roman Empire and that there will be at least one last Holy Roman Emperor.[160]

> *Aystinger the German* (12th century?): There shall arise in the last times a Prince sprung from the Emperor Charles who shall…reform the Church. He will be Emperor of Europe. [161]

> *St. Methodius* (385): A day will come when the enemies

of Christ will boast...Then a Roman emperor will rise in great fury against them....In the last period Christians will not appreciate the great grace of God who provided a Great Monarch, a long duration of peace, a splendid fertility of the earth...Many men will wonder if the Catholic faith is the true and only saving one and whether the Jews are perhaps correct when they still expect the Messias.[162]

We need to understand that the secret sect is not against Christ (it is truly Christian, so it could not be considered as Christ's enemy), but that it will be warning about the ecumenical church that will be in the process of rising up under the influence of a European leader that will pretend to be "Catholic." This European leader will try to persuade people throughout the world that he is the one to bring the "age of peace" that many have longed for.

And publicly identifying him will be a major factor leading to the rise of what some will consider "the secret sect," as they may be the ones that fulfill the predictive claim about "the enemies" boasting. It should also be noted that an Byzantine Orthodox prophet (Hieronymus Agathaghelos, 1279) suggested that those with Nazarene practices will be publicly involved when the Great Monarch rises up and that he will take steps to silence them.[163]

Has Daniel 11 Been Completely Fulfilled?

It may come as a shock, but in the 21st century, some accepted (but in my view apostate) scholars seem to teach that Daniel 11 has been fulfilled and hence that no one needs to be concerned about it being fulfilled.

Note this Roman Catholic bishop-approved writing:

The First six chapters of the Book of Daniel contain

older stories about a wise man, Daniel, from an earlier era. The stories are set during the Babylonian exile in the sixth century B.C. (see Ezekiel 14:14; 28:3), whereas Daniel 7 through 12 present visions received during the later Hellenistic period of writing (second century B.C.). As most apocalypses did, the visions in Daniel are presented as if namely, the hero of Daniel 1–6. This follows the Jewish practice of writing under the names of ancient authors. Internal historical references in the visions prompt scholars to ascribe their visions quite narrowly to a Jewish seer suffering under the persecution of the later Greek emperor, Antiochus IV Epiphanes, in 167–164 B.C., the same persecution that 1 and 2 Maccabees describe.[164]

But, of course, this is also a modern change, as the idea that Daniel 11 still has future fulfillment has been the Catholic position for many centuries.

Notice the following:

> *Archbishop Jacob Voragine* (13th century): Daniel xi... Antichrist and his complices shall give abomination and desolation to the temple of God in this time...he shall destroy the law of God.[165]

Furthermore, Jerome ran into the same 21st century heresy in the 4th century, as he wrote:

> *St. Jerome* (4th/5th century): Porphyry wrote his twelfth book against the prophecy of Daniel, denying that it was composed by the person to whom it is ascribed in its title, but rather by some individual living in Judaea at the time of the Antiochus who was surnamed Epiphanes. He furthermore alleged that "Daniel" did

> not foretell the future so much as he related the past, and lastly that whatever he spoke of up till the time of Antiochus contained authentic history, whereas anything he may have conjectured beyond that point was false, inasmuch as he would not have foreknown the future...
>
> But inasmuch as it is not our purpose to make answer to the false accusations of an adversary, a task requiring lengthy discussion, but rather to treat of the actual content of the prophet's message for the benefit of us who are Christians, I wish to stress in my preface this fact, that none of the prophets has so clearly spoken concerning Christ as has this prophet Daniel. For not only did he assert that He would come, a prediction common to the other prophets as well, but also he set forth the very time at which He would come...
>
> Verse 24...those of our persuasion believe all these things are spoken prophetically of the Antichrist who is to arise in the end time...Verses 40, 41...the king of the North.[166]

Hence, Jerome had to deal with some who preferred to deny the highly prophetic nature of Daniel. And, on the specific point that there was future fulfillment in Daniel 11 involving a King of the North, Jerome was correct. Those affiliated with Rome who teach (or who will teach) that Daniel 11 has been completely fulfilled are teaching heresy.

Therefore, this has been a problem before, and it looks as if it will be a problem again. It should probably be mentioned that within Protestantism, a minority of scholars also seems to believe that Daniel 11 has been completely fulfilled by Antiochus Epiphanes[167], but any such "scholars" are also in error.

These relatively modern changes among some within Catholicism/Protestantism will make it easier for many weak ones to not understand end-time prophetic events, including the coming even more ecumenical religion that will take the name "Catholic." (More on the King of the North can be found in Appendix B.)

CHAPTER 6
THE SECRET SECT

If the "secret sect" (the Philadelphian remnant of the true Church) exists today, is it a large church? And if there is a small secret sect today that will rise up, why would any one care? And if it matters, what would it look like?

As far as size is concerned, according to the Bible, the true end-time church would be small. Notice what Jesus taught:

> [32] Do not fear, little flock, for it is your Father's good pleasure to give you the kingdom (Luke 12:32).

But before going further, let me state that I do not believe that the only real Christians are those that are part of the Nazarene Philadelphia remnant. The true church is not limited to any corporation, nor are all who attend any church necessarily faithful themselves. The Bible teaches that Christians are those who have "the Spirit of Christ" dwelling within them (Romans 8:9).

This may be a good time to add that the Bible is clear that salvation is open to "Jews" and "Gentiles" (Acts 10:39 45; 13:42), and that the faithful "contend earnestly for the faith which was once for all delivered to the saints" (Jude 3).

Jesus Himself stated that His Church would be subject to persecutions. He also suggested that His followers, when feasible, should try to avoid those persecutions:

Ruins of Ancient Philadelphia, 2008. My wife Joyce and I have visited all the ruins of the seven churches of Revelation 2 &3, and Philadelphia is now the least physically impressive.

> [11] Blessed are you when they revile and persecute you, and say all kinds of evil against you falsely for My sake. [12] Rejoice and be exceedingly glad, for great is your reward in heaven, for so they persecuted the prophets who were before you (Matthew 5:11-12).
>
> [23] When they persecute you in this city, flee to another. For assuredly, I say to you, you will not have gone through the cities of Israel before the Son of Man comes (Matthew 10:23).
>
> [9] Then they will deliver you up to tribulation and kill you (Matthew 24:9).

Jesus seems to be warning that the truly faithful Christians would sometimes hide, flee, and/or be secretive to avoid persecution. He also taught that they would be a little flock, and that sometimes, while under persecution, their secrecy would be betrayed.

The Bible (Acts 8:1) and secular history records that this was in fact true, as Christians were for centuries considered to be a secret cult or a secret sect by various ones.

Note one account of the early persecutions by Graeme Snooks:

> Christianity was a more exclusive, secret, and potentially more subversive, cult than all the others. The followers of Christ rejected the old gods completely, they refused to sacrifice to the emperor and his gods, and they established an empire-wide network of secret cells practising strange rites. Not surprisingly, this cult attracted suspicion and hostility from the Roman state, particularly when its members refused to worship publicly the emperors and gods of war. Christians attracted, therefore, sporadic imperial persecution in the second century AD which became more systematic and determined in the third and fourth centuries...[168]

Notice that early Christians (who would not participate in military warfare nor engage in emperor worship) were considered a secret cult, but that despite that, they existed throughout the empire. Many today do not realize that the Christians were originally considered to be a secret cult, a secret sect.

The same type of situation is expected at the end. There will be small groups of Christians who will refuse to accept the new ecumenical emperor worship that the militaristic Beast and False Prophet will encourage; they will resist this religion even though it will likely adopt the name "Catholic." They may be branded as a cult or secret sect.

The Non-Compromisers Were and Will Be Denounced

As mentioned in Chapter 2, there have been groups or sects that have not been willing to change their doctrines to those Council decisions that many ultimately adopted.

Some "Catholic" writers denounced them as Christians who were secretly Jews or who were part of secretive sects. Sometimes they were just called heretics or apostates.

Interestingly, as mentioned in chapter 3, in the 20th century, at least one mystic claimed that the secret sect would start to rise up:

> *Ven. Sor Marianne de Jesus Torres* (17th century): But this knowledge will only become known to the general public in the 20th Century…. During this epoch the Church will find herself attacked by waves of the secret sect … Know, beloved daughter, that when your name is made known in the 20th Century, there will be many who do not believe, claiming this devotion is not pleasing to God….[169]

The above indicates that "the secret sect" would rise up and attack the main changing ecumenical church in waves. And it will likely be part of the many who claim that "this devotion" (private prophecy based upon an apparition or locution) is not of God. While it could be argued that several groups might fit the above, there were "Nazarene" Christians that did this in the 20th century.

And there are still Nazarenes in the 21st century that fit other prophecies involving "the secret sect."

More on the Secret Sect

There are additional private prophecies that discuss "the secret sect." Studying them should give some clues to the group that certain writers have felt will rise up in the latter times.

Notice:

Jeanne le Royer (died 1798): My Father, God has manifested to me the malice of Lucifer, and the perverse and diabolical intentions of his emissaries (secret societies) and the Holy Church of Jesus Christ. At the command of their master **these wicked men have traversed the earth like furies, with the intention to prepare the way and place for Anti-Christ whose reign is approaching**...They have succeeded in confounding all sound principles, and spreading everywhere such darkness as to obscure the light both of faith and of reason...[170]

Anna-Katarina Emmerick (19th century): I saw a great renewal, and the Church rose high in the sky...I saw **the secret sect relentlessly undermining the great Church**...Very bad times will come when non-Catholics will lead many people astray.[171]

Anne Catherine Emmerich (19th century): I saw again the present Pope and the dark church of his time in Rome. It seemed to be a large, old house like a town-hall with columns in front. I saw no altar in it, but only benches, and in the middle of it something like a pulpit. They had preaching and singing, but nothing else, and only very few attended it...The whole church was draped in black, and all that took place in it was shrouded in gloom...I saw the fatal consequences of this counterfeit church ; I saw it increase ; I saw heretics of all kinds flocking to the city. I saw the ever-increasing trepidity of the clergy , the circle of darkness ever widening... **Again I saw in vision St. Peter's undermined according to a plan devised by the secret sect whilst,** at the same time, it was damaged by storms; but it was delivered at the moment of greatest distress....Then I saw the church speedily rebuilt and more magnificent than before, for its defenders brought stones from all parts of the earth.[172]

Anne Catherine Emmerich Spoke of a Secret Sect

This document that you are now reading could be considered part of a plan evolved by one who hopes he is a part of the "secret sect"—that is the Philadelphia remnant of the true church to undermine the coming changing ecumenical Church.

The faithful "Nazarenes" are not actually "secret," though apparently sometime soon in the 21st century they will go into hiding per Revelation 12:14-16. The faithful sect will ultimately be perceived as relentless in attacking the rising ecumenical Church since at least the early/mid-20th century, and that its effectiveness came in waves.

Notice that according to the many private prophecies, this secret sect causes problems for the Catholic church near the time of the end, but these problems lead into a time of religious renewal and a new form of imperial dominance—a dominance of an empire that will not tolerate variations from the official religion of that State.

Instead of getting even further from original Christianity, those not part of the "secret sect" need to embrace the original practices (cf. Jude 3) of the original Christians (Acts 24:5).

Gospel of the Millennial Kingdom Condemned

It may be interesting to note that mystics believed that there would be a group of whom *Jeanne le Royer* called "wicked men" who "prepare the way and a place for Anti-Christ, whose reign is approaching" by attacking "the great Church." The reason that this is interesting is that in the 20th century, the Nazarene Christians began to clearly focus on the message of proclaiming the gospel of the coming millennial kingdom of God, and again began to send men all over the world to do this.

It is a known fact that many in the Greco-Roman churches who have been considered early saints (Papius, Irenaeus, Melito, Justin, etc.) held to a literal millennial reign of Christ on the earth. Even some Roman Catholic leaders held to it in the 19th century, but this position changed.[173]

It may be partially because of the millennial teachings of the secret sect that the Vatican made a clarifying change in its position in the 1940s:

> Millenium {sic}: Since the Holy Office decreed (July 21, 1944) that it cannot safely be taught that Christ at His Second Coming will reign visibly with only some of His saints (risen from the dead) for a period of time

before the final and universal judgment, a spiritual millennium is seen in Apoc. 20:4-6. St. John gives a spiritual recapitulation of the activity of Satan, and the spiritual reign of the saints with Christ in heaven and in His Church on earth.[174]

This strong anti-millennial stance from the Vatican suggests that Satan has been gone a thousand years (as the Bible teaches he is bound away for that same thousand years)—something that world history would suggest has not yet happened. This is a change from the Bible and the early church), and sadly seems to point to additional changes from those that will occupy Vatican City.

It may be of critical importance to understand that an important relatively recent writing now warns that the message of the millennial kingdom is a significant doctrine of Antichrist. Notice what the revised *Catechism of the Catholic Church* teaches:

> **676** The Antichrist's deception already begins to take shape in the world every time the claim is made to realize within history that messianic hope which can only be realized beyond history through the eschatological judgment. The Church has rejected even modified forms of this falsification of the kingdom to come under the name of millenarianism…[175]

The above is the only teaching associated with the Antichrist in the current *Catechism of the Catholic Church*.

Notice what Joseph Ratzinger wrote in a paper titled *The Theology of History in St. Bonaventure* prior to becoming the current pope:

> …both Chiliasm [the teaching of the Millennium] and

Montanism were declared heretical and were excluded from the universal church; for they both denied this vision [the "Christ is the end of the ages" vision] and awaited still another period of more definitive salvation to follow after the age of Christ...[176]

So although most scholars (Catholic and otherwise) are aware that the early true Church did teach the millennial reign of Christ on the earth, it is now sadly being warned against as doctrine of Antichrist.

The millennial teaching (also known as chiliasm) was first formally condemned at Emperor Theodosius' Council of Constantinople in 381 A.D., even though people considered as saints by the Roman and Orthodox Catholics taught it prior to that.[177] But, despite that condemnation, many Catholics, Orthodox, and Protestants have believed it throughout history.

Now it may be helpful to understand that the "secret sect" has long also believed in the idea that there is an age to come (Matthew 12:32; Mark 10:30). Many early professors of Christ believed in it. The fact is that this doctrine of "apocatastasis" (an age to come where all who had not been offered salvation would be resurrected and offered it, and nearly all would be saved) was abandoned and condemned by some in the 4th century[178]. Yet, there are hundreds of verses in the Bible that support this teaching.[179]

Certain theologies, like some Eastern Orthodox beliefs, still hold to this idea that salvation is available up until the time of final judgment[180]. So, surely the current pontiff in the 21st century does not mean that it was not an early Christian belief, as it, just like millennialism, clearly was. The existence of this doctrine by a small sect was even documented in the Middle Ages by an Inquisitor.[181]

The fact is that the Nazarenes have (from no later than

when the Apostle John taught them what Jesus showed in the Book of Revelation) always held to a belief in the literal millennial reign of Christ on earth and still do so until this day (as do many Protestant and some Orthodox groups).

Furthermore, the Nazarene sect has always believed that after the millennium God will resurrect all who were not resurrected prior (Revelation 20:4-5). People will be physically resurrected (some might prefer the term reincarnated) in their own reconstructed human bodies (Ezekiel 37:4-10; 11:16-20; Job 19:26), salvation will be offered (Isaiah 55:1-5; Jeremiah 25:31; Ezekiel 20:33-38; Luke 3:6), and nearly all that ever lived will be saved (Isaiah 62:1-5; Romans 11:26-27; Romans 9:6-8,22-24).

The Nazarene Christians actually believe that a God of love (1 John 4:8, 16), who is all wise, is smart enough to have a plan of salvation that will result in everyone who ever lived being offered salvation. Certainly the God of the universe will do right (cf. Genesis 18:25) and at least properly make that offer. The Bible shows that nearly everyone (regardless of their present religious orientation or lack thereof, Psalm 66:3-4) will ultimately be saved. Hundreds of Bible verses support this teaching[182], and throughout history, many writers without a biblical background have advocated similar notions). And this is God's will (2 Peter 3:9; John 3:16-17).

The Nazarenes, however, especially the Philadelphia remnant, will be condemned for teaching it.

Secret Sect: Christians with "Jewish" Practices

Lest it seem that this book has been overly presumptuous about the Philadelphia remnant of the Church being portrayed as a "secret sect" or referred to as "Jews," various writings show that some have considered Christians who hold to early Nazarene/Jewish Christian practices to be Jews or Nazarenes. This goes back until at least 326 A.D. (and later in the fourth century) according to the Catholic scholar Bagatti:

> From 326...The authors speak of "inhabitants" and of "Jews", and these can only be the Judaeo-Christians...
>
> Epiphanius...these Christians of Jewish race {are} not to be called Christians or Jews but Nazarenes. A late confirmation that the community of Jerusalem was not considered "Christian" but Nazarene is found in the relation of Severus ibn al Moqaffa (10th century) inserted into the *History of the Councils*... [183]

An anonymous Catholic clergyman writing under the name Maurice Pinay in the nineteenth century provides additional documentation on this subject. He indicated that in the Middle Ages, the Popes and the Councils successfully destroyed what some call Jewish revolutionary movements appearing within Christianity. He considered some were Christians in appearance, but he felt that they were Jews in secret, spread false teachings. Pinay stated:

> In the Middle Ages, the Popes and the Councils were successful in destroying the Jewish revolutionary movements which appeared within Christianity in the form of false teaching and which were introduced by those who were Christians in appearance but Jews in secret. The latter then recruited upright and good Christians for the arising heretical movement by persuading the latter in a crafty way.
>
> The secret Jews organised and controlled in secret manner the movements, which were the creative and driving force of wicked false teachings, such as those of **the Iconoclasts, the Cathars**, the Patarines,

the Albigensians, the Hussites, the Alumbrados and others.[184]

Pinay's book is still recommended by and for many "Catholics" (though others wisely distance themselves from it). Hence, sometimes those who were historically faithful Nazarene Christians (such as a few of the Cathars and Albigenses) were improperly considered to be a secret Jewish group that only professed Christ.

The fact is that all in the early church were also "iconoclasts" (against the use of idols or icons as part of Christian worship)—as the use of idols is something that the Bible, up until its very last chapter (Revelation 22:15) condemns—hence those who still have that view should not be condemned for that belief.

Orthodox seers and writers have also taken positions against those with Nazarene practices. One example would be a 1249 A.D. vision of "Blessed Hieronymus Agathaghelos" which claimed that their "blasphemies...have stained and soiled for many centuries."[185]

Does the Secret Sect Harm the True Church?

Certain mystics have taught that a secret sect will harm the final "Catholic" Church, and many believe this is bad.

The Bible suggests that success of the "secret sect" proclaiming the gospel message is prophesied to precede and/or lead to the end (Matthew 24:14).

This successful preaching may lead to the persecuting events foretold in Daniel 11:28-35 and Matthew 24:9-10, including the persecution of the Philadelphians mentioned previously. It will also lead to reprisals by the future ecumenical church that will eventually affect others, including the non-Philadelphian Christians.

The following private prophecies support the idea of reprisals from the future ecumenical church and that their enemies and a sect, are rendered inconsequential by their leaders:

> *Blessed Anna Maria Taigi* (died 1837): On this terrible occasion so many of these wicked men--enemies of His Church and of their God--shall be killed by this divine scourge that their corpses round Rome will be as numerous as the fish which a recent inundation of the Tiber had carried into the city. **All the enemies of the church, secret as well as known, will perish over the whole earth during that universal darkness, with the exception of the some few**, whom God will soon after convert. The air shall be infected with demons, who will appear under all sorts of hideous forms.[186]

> *Palma Maria d'Oria* (died 1863): There shall be three days darkness during which the atmosphere will be infected with **innumerable devils, who will cause the death of large multitudes of unbelievers and wicked men**...Blessed candles alone shall preserve... Catholics...the enemies of religion and mankind shall be universally destroyed. **A general pacification** of the world and universal triumph of the Church are to follow.[187]

> *Saint Bridget of Sweden* (died 1373): ...an emperor of Spanish origin will be elected, who will, in a wonderful manner, be victorious through the sign of the Cross. He shall destroy the Jewish and Mahometan sects: he shall restore the Santa Sophia (in Constantinople), and all the earth shall enjoy peace and prosperity; new cities will be erected in many places.[188]

> *Anne Catherine Emmerich* (Purification day 1822): I saw

during the last few days marvelous things connected with the Church. St. Peter's was **almost entirely destroyed by the sect**, but their labors were, in turn, rendered fruitless and all that belonged to them, their aprons and tools, burned by the executioners on the public place of infamy. They were made of horse-leather, and the stench from them was so offensive that it made me quite sick...[189]

Notice that a false time of peace ("pacification") is expected after this persecution of all those who will not support the ecumenical church.

It would seem to be that the "sect" being described is the Philadelphia church or its offspring (cf. Revelation 12:17) as they would not use the cross as a mark. The comments about being burned by executions, and the stench of horse leather may refer to some true Christian literature and/or true Christian people being burnt up, as Daniel 11:33 refers to persecution involving death "by sword and flame" (see also Appendix B).

As with other persecutions throughout history, though, it is unlikely that the ecumenical confederation will only limit the persecutions to those actually in the Philadelphian Church.

The following prophecy that mentions secret societies and a particular false religion may specifically apply to the remaining sect of the Philadelphians in our time:

> *Sister Jane Le Royer* (died 1798): **When the time of the reign of Antichrist is near, a false religion will appear** which be opposed to the unity of God and His Church. This will cause the greatest schism the world has ever known. The nearer the time of the end, the more darkness of Satan will spread on Earth, the greater

will be the number of children of corruption, and the number of Just will correspondingly diminish.[190]

The above suggests that secret societies will impugn the most sacred dogmas and doctrines of the end-time "Catholic" religion. Before Jesus (who some mystics seem to identify as the Antichrist as noted in Chapter 15), comes, a "false" religion will arise.

This may be used to describe the rise of the Philadelphia era of the Church in the 20th century and its remnant in the 21st century. Alternatively, it might possibly be applied to the final ecumenical religion that will call itself "Catholic."

While the Christian church has existed since Pentecost in Acts 2, as far as many are concerned, the Philadelphia portion recently simply appeared out of nowhere.

Many people are not willing to accept that there is a small Nazarene group church that can trace its spiritual roots throughout history—a group that also claims strong ties to the faithfulness of the earliest apostolic successors, such as Polycarp of Smyrna and Polycrates of Ephesus.

Because of the number of times the New Testament uses the expression "Church of God" (Acts 20:28; 1 Corinthians 1:2; 10:32; 11:16,22; ;15:9; 2 Corinthians 1:1; Galatians 1:13; 1 Thessalonians 2:14; 2 Thessalonians 1:4; 1 Timothy 3:5,15), it is fairly certain that the last organized form of the secret sect will somehow include that expression in its name.

While the Philadelphians are not the only ones who can write books that Roman Catholics disapprove of as a false religion, as it gets closer to the end, it appears that Nazarene Philadelphian writings will become a serious threat to the future ecumenical church. Notice what is pointed out in the following private prophesies:

Nursing Nun of Bellay (19th century): At the same time, the

Great Monarch ascends the throne of his ancestors... All these things shall come to pass once the wicked have succeeded in circulating large numbers of bad books.[191]

Trappistine Nun of Notre Dame des Gardes: Chastisement will come when a very large number of bad books have been spread.[192]

Abbe Voclin: People will speak only of money. Horrible books will be freely available. Intellectuals will argue fiercely among themselves. Then war will break out that will see the rise of the Great Monarch.[193]

The Philadelphian remnant, and others, currently write books and booklets that some may feel partially fulfill the above. As it gets closer to final times, it appears that some future materials (and also apparently including this book) will be considered to fulfill those prophecies more fully relatively soon, especially within the next several years. That is when the ecumenical Great Monarch is expected to rise up.

Furthermore, private prophecy suggests that someone will attempt to attack the future ecumenical church at its very foundations during a time that seems to parallel the "minor chastisement."[194] Some suggest this will happen before the future ecumenical church gains its major end-time prominence.

Notice one account:

Elizabeth Canori-Mora (died 1825): All men shall rise one against the other, and they shall kill one another without pity. During this sanguinary conflict the avenging arm of God will strike the wicked, and in His mighty power He will punish their pride and presumption. God will employ the powers... for the extermination of these **impious and heretical persons who desire to overthrow the Church and destroy it to its very foundation...God will allow the demons to strike with death those impious men** because they gave themselves up to the infernal powers and had formed with them a compact against the Catholic Church...[195]

Notice that some of the mystics claim that *demons* will kill those working to expose the changing "Catholic" church at its very foundations.

An Orthodox mystic seem to teach the Great Monarch, who may be demonically influenced (cf. Revelation 16:13), will kill his enemies:

Saint Andrew Fool-for-Christ (c. 4th century): {Through the reign of} this King...for their blasphemous religion...the remaining ones will be annihilated, they will be burned to death and they will die a cruel death...The entire world will fear this King. He will instigate through fear...[196]

The Bible itself shows that demons have influenced prophetic events (I Kings 22:20-23), will do so in the future (2 Corinthians 11:13-15), and that cruel demons will clearly be supportive of the Beast and the False Prophet (Revelation 16:14). These private prophecies suggest that some *mystics have confused those on the side of Jesus and those on the side of demons.* Accepting the ecumenical form of religion in the future will mean choosing the side of demons—not truly the side of God.

Jesus was clear that the persecutors, while not always understanding what they were doing, were not the faithful ones, but that His faithful would be persecuted:

> **... they will lay their hands on you and persecute you**, delivering you up to the synagogues and prisons. You will be brought before kings and rulers for My name's sake (Luke 21:12).
>
> **If they persecuted Me, they will also persecute you** (John 15:20).
>
> ... yes, the time is coming that whoever kills you will think that he offers God service. And **these things they will do to you because they have not known the Father nor Me**. But these things I have told you, that when the time comes, you may remember that I told you of them (John 16:2-4).

Despite the persecutions (that they expect), the secret sect understands that "God is love" (1 John 4:16), and they "know that all things work together for good to those who love God, to those who are the called according to His purpose" (Romans 8:28), thus they will endure persecution.

Enduring persecution seems to be related to the faith and "patience of the saints." (Revelation 14:8-12) This is a challenge that many readers of this book might face.

A Falling Away

Christians and others should all understand that the Bible tells of a time after a falling away, that a lawless leader will rise up.

He will have signs and lying wonders (influenced by demons per Revelation 16:13–14), and people all around the world who are not expecting this will fall for it:

> ³ Let no one deceive you by any means; for that Day will not come unless **the falling away comes first**,

and the man of sin is revealed, the son of perdition, [4] who opposes and exalts himself above all that is called God or that is worshiped, so that he sits as God in the temple of God, showing himself that he is God... [7] For the mystery of lawlessness is already at work; only He who now restrains will do so until He is taken out of the way. [8] And **then the lawless one will be revealed**, whom the Lord will consume with the breath of His mouth and destroy with the brightness of His coming. [9] **The coming of the lawless one is according to the working of Satan, with all power, signs, and lying wonders,** [10] **and with all unrighteous deception** among those who perish, because they did not receive the love of the truth, that they might be saved. 1[11] And for this reason God will send them strong delusion, that they should believe the lie, [12] that they all may be condemned who did not believe the truth but had pleasure in unrighteousness (2 Thessalonians 2:3–4,7–12).

This is after a falling away of apparently true believers. (1 Timothy 4:1.). And while there have been times throughout history where the faithful have fallen away, perhaps there will be one more major falling away.

But also notice, that in a sense, this biblical passage is teaching that people all over (including non-Christians) will be influenced by seeing power, signs, and lying wonders. Hence they will also "fall away," in a sense, from their traditional beliefs and support this lawless power.

That is precisely what this book is meant to warn about.

People often believe what they see through their own eyes. And different signs and wonders may affect various people. For example, while many of those in Islam are apparently going to be misled for a shorter time than almost any one else (as they are to be the first major power to turn on the Beast per Daniel 11:40-43), they too will, at least slightly, accept some agreement with the ecumenical movement (for a very short while).

It should also be noted that many Orthodox and Roman Catholics expect signs and wonders will announce the Great Monarch, as he will be a lesser known leader before coming into power. Here is one from an Orthodox source:

> *Anonymou Paraphrasis* (10th century): The one true King..will hear the voice and instructions by an Angel appearing to him...he has foresight and is cognizant of the text of the prophecies...the name of the King is hidden [concealed] among the nations...And the particular manner of the king's manifestation to the public [to the world] will take place as follows: A star will appear for three days...And a herald speaking with a very loud voice in the course of the three days will summon and unveil the hoped for one...There will become visible in the sky a 'nebulous firmament of the sun'...under that image will be suspended a cross...And the invisible herald from Heaven with his thunderous voice will say to the people: Is this man agreeable to you? At that moment everybody will be taken by fear and terror.[197]

Orthodox scholar H. Tzima Otto believes that the cross referred to will be red, because other signs in the sky, like a comet, will also be present.[198]

Notice the following two from Roman sources:

> *Josefa von Bourg* (died 1807): God will choose a descendant of Constantine...who has been tried by a long period of disappointment...to rule over Europe.

He will have the sign of the cross on his breast...

Abbe Soufrand (died 1828): The Great Ruler will perform such great and noble deeds that the infidels will be forced to admit the working of God's providence.[199]

So, from both the Roman and Orthodox Catholics we learn that someone who seemed not significant is expected to appear on the scene with signs and wonders.

What About Mary and Other Wonders?

Apparitions claiming to be Mary may have an end-time role. Some believe that Mary will have power during the time of the Great Monarch, and this will lead to many conversions:

R. Gerald Culleton (20th century): During the reign of the Great Monarch and the Angelic Pastor the Catholic Church will spread throughout the world, conversions will be innumerable...The Blessed Virgin will be the chief one in gaining victory over all heresy and schism because of her power over the demons in the last ages of the world will be especially great.[200]

Saint Louis de Montfort (18th century): These great souls, full of grace and zeal, shall be chosen ... and they shall be singularly devouted to our Blessed Lady, illuminated by her nourishment, led by her spirit, supported by her arm, and sheltered under her protection, so that they shall fight in one hand and build with the other. With the one hand they shall fight, overthrow and crush the heretics with their heresies, the schismatics with their schisms....[201]

> *Pope Pius IX* (died 1878): We expect that the Immaculate Virgin and Mother of God, Mary…will bring it about that our Holy Mother the Catholic Church, after the removal of obstacles and overcoming all errors, will gain in influence from day to day among all nations and in all places, prosper and rule from ocean to ocean…to the ends of the earth…there will be one fold and one shepherd.[202]

Thus, there seems to be an end-time tie between the Great Monarch, an ecumenical religion, and apparitions claiming to be Mary.

In an apparition in Pfaffenhofen, Germany (which is not one of "the nine major approved Marian apparitions of modern times" by the Vatican[203]), one claiming to be Mary, the mother of Jesus, made the following assertions, on June 25, 1946, according to two related accounts:

> In secret I will work marvels…till the number of victims is filled…shorten the days of darkness… **Then, I can manifest myself to the world**…Pray and offer sacrifices through me…[204]

> The Father wants the world to recognize His handmaid…My sign is about to appear. God wills it…**I cannot reveal my power to the world as yet…Then I will be able to reveal myself**…Pray and sacrifice through me!…I will impose crosses on my children that will be as heavy and as deep as the sea.[205]

Notice that this apparition is claiming that in a future time, she will become known to the world. This may mean that some apparitions claiming to be Mary may publicly appear in many places next decade. And many people will tend to accept these appearances as valid.

This is also confirmed by another non-Vatican approved apparition to one calling herself Mariamante in 1987:

> The wickedness of man would destroy my plan if possible...You will know by the sign in the heavens which is I myself that the time is at hand for the instant conversion of the multitude.[206]

Thus, there are apparitions that seem to warn that someone will oppose these false apparitions, and that apparitions claiming to be Mary will be instrumental in converting multitudes of peoples.

It should be mentioned that there have been many claimed statements from "Mary" that have been proven to have been false. This has happened so many times, that the Vatican took steps in 2009 to prevent its followers from mentioning them until they have been researched in depth.[207] For what it is worth, there is a book titled *Thunders of Justice;* its authors believe in the Marion apparitions and locutions. The book contains dozens of accounts of predictions that turned out to be false, after the book was published.

Other false apparitions are highly likely. Even some Eastern Orthodox writers have been concerned that apparitions of "Mary" will be used as an ecumenical symbol for a false unity for Catholics, Muslims, and others that will lead people to follow the final Antichrist:

> *Peter Jackson* (20th century): To which Mary are Muslims and Protestants being drawn?... Rome began to see her more and more as a "goddess," a fourth Hypostasis of the Trinity...Today, as heterodox Christians become more and more ecumenist and

work toward creating a "One World Church," the search has begun for a Mary of universal recognition, one who will appeal not only to those who bear the name Christian, but apparently to Muslims and others as well, just as attempts are likewise being made to identify the "new Christ" with the Muslim concept of their coming Mahdi and with the Messiah still awaited by the Jews. This, of course, will be no Christ at all but the antichrist.[208]

It may be a surprise to some to learn that Jesus' mother Mary has long been important to Muslims. Mary (called *Miriam* in Arabic) is actually mentioned more times in the Qur'an than in the New Testament.

"Mary's House" near Ephesus — Lighter, Upper, Portion Added

In Turkey there is even a festival related to Mary each year.

The house where Mary may have lived out her last days is in the primarily Islamic nation of Turkey. My wife Joyce and I have visited it.

Thus, it is possible that an apparition claiming to be Mary might appear in Turkey and/or elsewhere, that may persuade some Muslims to temporarily consider that somehow God might be working through a Western religious leader. This will not last (see also Appendix B), but it seems to have been predicted:

> *Blessed Maria of Agreda* (died 1665): The power of Mary in the latter days will be very conspicuous. Mary will extend the reign of Christ over the heathens and the Mohammedans...[209]

Perhaps it should be mentioned that there are certain Catholic prophecies that suggest many Muslims in Turkey will somewhat accept the Catholic faith:

> *Brother Louis Rocco* (19th century): Terrible wars will rage all over Europe. God has long been patient with the corruption of morals; half of mankind He will destroy. Russia will witness many outrages. Great cities and small towns alike will be destroyed in a bloody revolution that will cause the death of half the population. In Istanbul (Constantinople) the Cross will replace the half-moon of Islamism, and Jerusalem will be the seat of a King. The southern Slavs will form a great Catholic Empire and drive out of Europe the Turks (Mohammedans), who will withdraw to North Africa and subsequently embrace the Catholic faith.[210]

Many people of all persuasions, including apparently atheists are going to fall away from their current beliefs in vast numbers (even according to many Catholic leaders) to embrace one who will promote a powerful ecumenical religion that is to be accompanied by what will appear to be real miracles.

But, a small group will not be deceived, even by such

wonders:

> ²⁴ For there shall arise false Christs, and false prophets, and shall shew great signs and wonders; insomuch that, if it were possible, they shall deceive the very elect (Matthew 24:24, KJV).

The "very elect" that Jesus spoke of will apparently be the "secret sect," as well as those who decide to fully support them as they point out the identity of the King of the North (and will suffer persecutions from his wrath for doing so; see also Appendix B).

Jesus Promises a Specific Protection to the Secret Sect

Jesus indicated that near the time of the end, the "secret sect" would be persecuted, would flee, and during the time of the Great Tribulation and Day of the Lord be protected (cf. Revelation 12:14-16).

The Orthodox have recognized that the faithful will have to flee:

> *Saint Caesar of Arles* (542): ...the church of God...will be forced to flee...[211]

It was specifically to the Philadelphians that Jesus promised:

> ¹⁰ Because you have kept My command to persevere, I also will keep you from the hour of trial which shall come upon the whole world, to test those who dwell on the earth. ¹¹ Behold, I am coming quickly! Hold fast what you have, that no one may take your crown (Revelation 3:10-11).

So, though there will be troubles for the secret sect, Jesus will protect them. But others will not receive this same protection. Because the secret sect is not now closed off to the world, many who are not now part of it may decide to support it.

(More on this protection is shown in Appendix A and Appendix B.)

CHAPTER 7
THE BEGINNING OF SORROWS AND THE 21ST CENTURY

Considering all of the natural disasters such as earthquakes, floods, food shortages, and economic problems in the past few years, perhaps this would be a good time to explain that the Bible shows that these problems were expected to occur prior to the great tribulation. Those outside the Bible have sometimes referred to a time such as this as a time of transition or chaos.

The Apostle Paul warned:

> [1] But know this, that in the last days perilous times will come: [2] For men will be lovers of themselves, lovers of money, boasters, proud, blasphemers, disobedient to parents, unthankful, unholy, [3] unloving, unforgiving, slanderers, without self-control, brutal, despisers of good, [4] traitors, headstrong, haughty, lovers of pleasure rather than lovers of God, [5] having a form of godliness but denying its power. And from such people turn away! (2 Timothy 3:1–5)

And we certainly do appear to be in a period of perilous times. There will be a generation that will experience end-time events, beginning with "sorrows," including the Great Tribulation, heavenly signs, and finally the return of Jesus

THE BEGINNING OF SORROWS AND THE 21ST CENTURY

Christ (Matthew 24:5-34).

Notice what Jesus taught would happen just prior to the end:

> ⁴ And Jesus answered and said to them: "Take heed that no one deceives you. ⁵ For many will come in My name, saying, 'I am the Christ,' and will deceive many. ⁶ And you will hear of wars and rumors of wars. See that you are not troubled; for all these things must come to pass, but **the end is not yet**. ⁷ For nation will rise against nation, and kingdom against kingdom. And there will be famines, pestilences, and earthquakes in various places. ⁸ **All these are the beginning of sorrows**. ⁹ Then they will deliver you up to tribulation and kill you, and you will be hated by all nations for My name's sake. ¹⁰ And then many will be offended, will betray one another, and will hate one another. ¹¹ Then many false prophets will rise up and deceive many. ¹² And because lawlessness will abound, the love of many will grow cold. ¹³ But he who endures to the end shall be saved. ¹⁴ And this gospel of the kingdom will be preached in all the world as a witness to all the nations, and then the end will come.
>
> ¹⁵ "Therefore when you see the 'abomination of desolation,' spoken of by Daniel the prophet, standing in the holy place" (whoever reads, let him understand), ¹⁶ then let those who are in Judea flee to the mountains. ¹⁷ Let him who is on the housetop not go down to take anything out of his house. ¹⁸ And let him who is in the field not go back to get his clothes. ¹⁹ But woe to those who are pregnant and to those who are nursing babies in those days! ²⁰ And pray that your flight may not be in winter or on the Sabbath. ²¹ For then there

will be great tribulation, such as has not been since the beginning of the world until this time, no, nor ever shall be…" (Matthew 24:4-21).

Recent ordeals such as earthquakes and food shortages should, at most, be considered as related to "the beginning of sorrows," and not the "great tribulation" itself. Pestilences (insect outbreaks and/or infectious disease outbreaks) are also expected.

The "great tribulation" does *not* begin until verse 21. And while "tribulation" is involved in verse 9, this seems to be referring the persecuting tribulation that true Philadelphia Christians will face just prior to the great tribulation (see also Appendix B).

Mark recorded the same account of this time from his perspective:

> [3] Now as He sat on the Mount of Olives opposite the temple, Peter, James, John, and Andrew asked Him privately, [4] "Tell us, when will these things be? And what will be the sign when all these things will be fulfilled?" [5] And Jesus, answering them, began to say: "Take heed that no one deceives you. [6] For many will come in My name, saying, 'I am He,' and will deceive many. [7] But when you hear of wars and rumors of wars, do not be troubled; for such things must happen, but the end is not yet. [8] For nation will rise against nation, and kingdom against kingdom. And there will be earthquakes in various places, and **there will be famines and troubles. These are the beginnings of sorrows**. [9] But watch out for yourselves, for they will deliver you up to councils, and you will be beaten in the synagogues. You will be brought before rulers and kings for My sake, for a testimony to them. [10] And the

gospel must first be preached to all the nations. [11] But when they arrest you and deliver you up, do not worry beforehand, or premeditate what you will speak. But whatever is given you in that hour, speak that; for it is not you who speak, but the Holy Spirit..." (Mark 13:3-11).

Thus, in both Matthew and Mark it is clear that a time called "the beginning of sorrows" precedes the Great Tribulation.

Notice that in Mark's account he uses the term troubles. Troubles would seem to include economic and political problems, in addition to those specifically mentioned, such as wars, famines, natural disasters, and pestilences.

The accumulation of debt prior to the end time was also warned against (Habakkuk 2:3, 6-8), and this will cause disaster for those most highly indebted nations (for more detail, see Chapter 8).

U.S.A. National Debt Clock as of April 19, 2008. The Debt Clock Displayed $11,397,711,606,020 on July 3, 2009.[212]

Because the Bible foretells the rising up of a great economic power (Revelation 13:17; 18:3) near this time, it also makes sense that troubled events in the world today will likely fall into place for these end-time prophecies to be fulfilled.

That is what we are now seeing in the news on a regular

basis.

Sometime during the beginning of sorrows, a prince will start to rise up who will be the biblical King of the North. The Orthodox seem to realize that he may be identified around then. Near the end of the 4th century, there was an exchange between two important Orthodox leaders pertaining to their future King and the beginning of sorrows:

> *Epiphanius*: When will come the end of the world? What are the 'beginning of sorrows' and when shall they take place? From what signs and events shall humanity be able to know that the end of the world is near and what signs will be manifest?...
>
> *Andrew the Fool-for-Christ*: Now son, how can I relate to you without tears the events of the beginning of sorrows and the end of the world? During the End Times, God will reveal as King a certain poor man... This king will rule...Happiness will reign in the world as it did in the days of Noah. People will become very rich...The entire world will fear this king...he will pursue all persons of the Jewish religion out of Constantinople...and the people will rejoice like in the time of Noah until the deluge came.[213]

So, some ancient Orthodox writings indicate that the Great Monarch will rise up during the time of the beginning of sorrows—and that is correct. The comment about "persons of Jewish religion" may refer to persecution of the Nazarene sect as Orthodox and Roman Catholics have often indicated that the those with Nazarene practices are actually Jews pretending to be Christian. However, it also needs to be understood, that while the above Orthodox discussion indicates that having things as they were in the days of Noah is a positive thing, the Bible warns that this occurrence comes after the tribulation has begun and is a sign that Jesus is about to return (Matthew 24:37-44).

In these latter days, Christians generally realize that they are to pay attention to many world and national events that line up with the Bible. Notice what Jesus taught:

> [31] So you also, when you see these things happening, know that the kingdom of God is near. [32] Assuredly, I say to you, this generation will by no means pass away till all things take place. [33] Heaven and earth will pass away, but My words will by no means pass away.
>
> [34] "But take heed to yourselves, lest your hearts be weighed down with carousing, drunkenness, and cares of this life, and that Day come on you unexpectedly. [35] For it will come as a snare on all those who dwell on the face of the whole earth. [36] Watch therefore, and pray always that you may be counted worthy to escape all these things that will come to pass, and to stand before the Son of Man" (Luke 21:31-36).

Hence, Jesus clearly taught that His followers were to pay attention to end time events, and that those who heeded His words could escape. (See also Appendix A and Appendix B.)

Christians wishing to comply with Jesus' admonition to "watch" might find that having some understanding of end-time beliefs of non-Christians (cf. 1 Corinthians 9:19-23) can be helpful. This is one reason why they are in this book. Paul also made it clear that Christians should not be in darkness about prophetic matters (see 1 Thessalonians 5:4).

Those who do not consider themselves to be Christian would do well to heed the signs of the times as well. We are near the time (if not actually in it) that Jesus called "the beginning of sorrows." Considering the chaotic weather patterns in the past several years, it is certainly possible that some shift in planetary alignment might happen in December 2012, and that this may have some impact on the weather and/or earthquakes.

While the "day and hour" of some events were known in Jesus' time (Matthew 24:36), that was nearly 2000 years ago. Even secular sources warn that things are lining up for famines and major disruptions in the first half of the 21st century. Notice one such scientist from March 19, 2009:

> The demand for resources will create a crisis with dire consequences, Prof. Beddington predicts...
>
> Demand for food and energy will jump 50 per cent by 2030 and for fresh water by 30 per cent, as the global population tops 8.3 billion, he is due to tell a conference in London.
>
> Climate change will exacerbate matters in unpredictable ways, he will add.
>
> "It's a perfect storm," Prof. Beddington will tell the Sustainable Development UK 09 conference...
>
> Prof Beddington said the "storm" would create war, unrest and mass migration...
>
> He said food reserves are at a 50-year low but the world requires 50 per cent more energy, food and water by 2030.
>
> Prof. Beddington said climate change would mean Northern Europe would become new key centres for

food production and other areas would need to use more advanced pesticides.

The United Nations Environment Programme predicts widespread water shortages across Africa, Europe and Asia by 2025. The amount of fresh water available per head of the population is expected to decline sharply in that time. [214]

The beginning of sorrows can begin any time (if it has not started already). The world's reserve food supply is already at a fifty-year low.

Also notice the following from late 2008:

> Gerald Celente, the CEO of Trends Research Institute, is renowned for his accuracy in predicting future world and economic events...
>
> Celente says that by 2012 America will become an undeveloped nation, that there will be a revolution marked by food riots, squatter rebellions, tax revolts and job marches, and that holidays will be more about obtaining food, not gifts... adding that the situation would be "worse than the great depression".
>
> "America's going to go through a transition the likes of which no one is prepared for," said Celente...
>
> Celente, who successfully predicted the 1997 Asian Currency Crisis, the subprime mortgage collapse and the massive devaluation of the U.S. dollar, told UPI in November last year that the following year would be known as "The Panic of 2008," adding that "giants (would) tumble to their deaths," which is exactly

> what we have witnessed with the collapse of Lehman Brothers, Bear Stearns and others. He also said that the dollar would eventually be devalued by as much as 90 per cent.
>
> The consequence of what we have seen unfold this year would lead to a lowering in living standards, Celente predicted a year ago.[215]

Hence, many more sorrows may happen relatively near the Mayan 2012 date, whether or not one believes what Jesus taught. Severe problems of many types may well occur before the start of the Great Tribulation.

Although some have actually claimed that the Great Tribulation has begun (or is even over[216]), at most we are at or near the times that Jesus referred to as "the beginning of sorrows."

CHAPTER 8
BARACK OBAMA, ISLAM, AND THE END OF AMERICA

On January 20, 2009, Barack Hussein Obama became the 44th President of the United States. His first presidential term is to include the year 2012.

Official Photograph of Barack Obama, President of the United States

By virtue of his timing, Barack Obama will likely implement policies for many prophecies to be fulfilled. Others have stated that he is personally mentioned or alluded to by Kenyan, Shi'ite, Nostradamus, and other sources.

Regardless of possible outside prophecies, the Bible itself warns that if His people sinned and did not repent, the following would happen:

> ⁴³ The alien who is among you shall rise higher and higher above you, and you shall come down lower and lower (Deuteronomy 28:43).

> ¹² As for My people, children are their oppressors, And women rule over them. O My people! Those who lead you cause you to err, And destroy the way of your paths (Isaiah 3:12).

> ¹⁶ For the leaders of this people cause them to err, And those who are led by them are destroyed (Isaiah 9:16).

Since multiple millions of the physical descendants of Israel reside in the United States, and we are getting close to the end, the above prophecies are likely to be fulfilled, to a degree, during Barack Obama's presidency.

While Barack Obama was born an American citizen (birth certificate controversies notwithstanding), because Barack Obama's father is Luo Kenyan AND because he was partially raised in Indonesia (a Muslim nation), he could be perceived as an alien. Hence, part of the biblical prophecy in Deuteronomy 28:43 MIGHT apply to Barack Obama, and it does also have multiple applications. Because of his timing, however, it seems that he will partially fulfill the previously mentioned two prophecies from Isaiah, as will other end-time leaders in the Anglo-American nations.

The end of the 6,000 years God has granted humanity to rule itself will likely be over in the next decade (see next chapter). Thus, simply by the virtue of his timing, Barack

Obama is destined to aid in the fulfillment of end-time biblical prophecies.

Additionally, one of the first things that Barack Obama has done as U.S.A. president is to sign into to a law a bill that will greatly increase the debt of the U.S.A. He has also indicated that he will need to pursue policies that will increase that debt during at least his first administration, although he ultimately hopes to change that, as even he claims that the U.S. debt is "unsustainable."[217]

However, he and others may not realize that the Bible strongly warns about what will happen to a huge debtor in the end time. Notice what the seer Habakkuk wrote over 2,600 years ago:

> [3] For the vision is yet for an **appointed time; But at the end** it will speak, and it will not lie. Though it tarries, wait for it; Because **it will surely come**, It will not tarry...
> [6] "Will not all these take up a proverb against him,
> And a taunting riddle against him, and say,
> 'Woe to him who increases
> What is not his—how long?
> And to him who loads himself with many pledges'?
> [7] **Will not your creditors rise up suddenly?** Will they not awaken who oppress you? **And you will become their booty.** [8] Because you have plundered many nations, **All the remnant of the people shall plunder you..."** (Habakkuk 2:3,6–8).

Hence, Barack Obama seems to currently be fulfilling the part of that prophecy of increasing pledges/debt. And, of course, it is possible that the rest of the above prophecy might be fulfilled while he is U.S.A. president. This prophecy, if it is applicable to the U.S.A, also suggests that American dollars will ultimately be of no value to creditors by then (or to probably anyone else).

Furthermore, as discussed in previous chapters, the Bible predicts that at the appointed time, a King of the North and a King of the South with rise. Various statements that Barack Obama has made suggest that he will implement policies that will likely help lead to the multi-national formations that will ultimately have these kings.

Islamic Prophecy: Barack Obama to Aid the Rise of the King of the South?

According to a commentary by Amir Taheri in *Forbes*, there is an amazing old Shi'ite prophecy that some in Iran believe seems to fit Barack Hussein Obama personally:

> Is Barack Obama the "promised warrior" coming to help the Hidden Imam of Shiite Muslims conquer the world?
>
> …a pro-government Web site published a Hadith (or tradition) from a Shiite text of the 17th century. The tradition comes from ***Bahar al-Anvar*** (meaning Oceans of Light) by Mullah Majlisi, a magnum opus in 132 volumes and the basis of modern Shiite Islam.
>
> According to the tradition, **Imam Ali Ibn Abi-Talib** (the prophet's cousin and son-in-law) **prophesied** that at the **End of Times** and just before the return of the Mahdi, the Ultimate Saviour, a "tall black man will assume the reins of government in the West." Commanding "the strongest army on earth," the new ruler in the West will carry "a clear sign" from the third imam, whose name was Hussein Ibn Ali. The tradition concludes: "Shiites should have no doubt that

he is with us."

> In a curious coincidence Obama's first and second names–Barack Hussein–mean "the blessing of Hussein" in Arabic and Persian. His family name, Obama, written in the Persian alphabet, reads O Ba Ma, which means "he is with us," the magic formula in Majlisi's tradition.[218]

Because we are near the end of times *and* Barack Hussein Obama is considered to be black *and* he is now the new "ruler in the West" *and* he does lead the" strongest army on earth", it makes sense that a lot of Shi'ite Muslims apparently believe that he may fit that Islamic prophecy. Apparently this prediction shows that some type of deal is made between the Mahdi (Arabic for "the guided one") and the West.

Is any of that specific to Barack Obama?

It is difficult to know for certain, other than to say that some Shi'ites seem to believe their writings have alluded to Barack Hussein Obama in prophecy. Irrespective of that writing, some have long believed that an Islamic military leader would rise up and successfully fight the "crusaders"—this is even now advocated by groups like Al Qaeda, which is extremist Sunni. [219]

The fact that his name also seems to closely fit that prophecy suggests that he may. And while Barack Hussein Obama himself probably does not believe that "he is with us" (as "o bama" apparently means in Persian) refers to him in that prophecy, the fact is that no other U.S.A. president has ever been as close to Muslims as President Obama. His historic June 2009 speech in Cairo laid out the fact that the U.S.A. is now taking a different, more cooperative, stance with the Islamic world.[220]

Now, it needs to be made clear that the Bible predicts

the rise in the end time of a Future King of the South (see Appendix B)—and this person may be the one that Muslims will consider to be their prophesied "Mahdi." But the Bible is clear that Jesus will return (even the Muslims believe this), and that it is He and not some "Mahdi" that will bring God's kingdom to the earth.

The Shi'ites claim descent though Muhammad's cousin Ali, whom they consider to have been an Imam (a great Islamic leader). It should be mentioned that one of the differences between the Sunni and Shi'ite Muslims is that most Shi'ites strongly believe that a great leader will rise up, help destroy the West, and ultimately force everyone to become Muslim or die.

A Depiction of Imam Alī ibn Abī Tālib

On the other hand, certain Muslims believe that Jesus returns after the Mahdi and that the arrival of a Mahdi is a necessary step. Notice the following from the *New Encyclopedia of Islam*:

> The last days, as described in Islam, are marked by the figures of Gog and Magog (Juj wa Jajuj), the Mahdi, the Antichrist (Dajjal), and Jesus...Gog and Magog, representing the forces of chaos, have been kept at bay...At the end of time, chaos will break through the wall of Divinely imposed order, and the world

will succumb to "outer darkness". At the same time, it is believed, there will be a countercurrent, or a brief return to the state of spiritual lucidity and primordial integrity that obtained at the dawn of time. This is the reign of the Mahdi, the "rightly guided one"...

The reign of the Mahdi will be followed by that of the Antichrist... once the Antichrist has led away his followers, Jesus will then come to destroy the Antichrist in the closing moments of the cosmic drama.

Belief in the Mahdi has been rejected by noted Sunni authorities...[221]

Some in Islam seem to believe that the reign of the Beast and Antichrist will happen after the Mahdi's death. Now this is true, to a degree, for the Arab lands. However, the Beast (King of the North) and the final Antichrist (False Prophet) will rule in Europe and in some of the American land, prior to the European reign over Arab lands (hence the final Antichrist will have power prior to the death of the biblical King of the South, who seems to be the Islamic Mahdi).

The belief in a Mahdi is apparently a minority Sunni view, even though "the Muslim World League issued a *fatwa* in October of 1976 commanding Sunni Muslims to believe in the concept of an Islamic Savior called the Mahdi."[222]

Sunnis (who vastly outnumber the Shi'ites) should not change their anti-Mahdi views, however (various Sunni scholars also agree[223]). Shi'ites also would do well to recognize that just because someone may claim to be the final Imam (or Mahdi), does not mean that God will agree that he should be followed. Neither Sunnis nor Shi'ites should support one who will appear to possibly be the final Imam in the next decade; whoever claims to be will be defeated soundly (Daniel 11:40-

43; see also Appendix B).

Jesus and the Koran

All Muslims, whether they are Shi'ite or Sunni, however, expect Jesus to return at the time of judgment. Notice what the Koran (Qur'an) teaches:

> *043.057*
> **YUSUFALI:** When (Jesus) the son of Mary is held up as an example, behold, thy people raise a clamour thereat (in ridicule)!
> **PICKTHAL:** And when the son of Mary is quoted as an example, behold! the folk laugh out,
>
> **SHAKIR:** And when a description of the son of Marium is given, lo! your people raise a clamor thereat
>
> *043.061*
> **YUSUFALI:** And (Jesus) shall be a Sign (for the coming of) the Hour (of Judgment): therefore have no doubt about the (Hour), but follow ye Me: this is a Straight Way.[224]

So, when Muslims see Jesus return, they should hopefully accept the truth of His coming.

Now without seeing the actual Shi'ite prophecy that *Forbes* reported about (which would have been written in either Persian or Arabic), it is not certain that Barack Obama will meet all of the criteria of that prophecy (or if reports on it are entirely accurate). However, if Barack Hussein Obama is the President of the United States until 2013-2017, his administration will help (most likely inadvertently) lead to the rise of the future King of the South who is mentioned in end time Bible prophecy.

Is Barack Obama Muslim?

Many have wondered, "Is Barack Obama Muslim?"

No, not if one needs to proclaim Islam to be one. Barack Obama's personal religion is not Islam.

Here is what his "Fight the Smears" website claims:

The Truth About Barack's Faith

> Barack Obama is a committed Christian. He was sworn into the Senate on his family Bible. He has regularly attended church with his wife and daughters for years.
>
> But shameful, shadowy attackers have been lying about Barack's religion, claiming he is a Muslim instead of a committed Christian.[225]

Barack Obama says he is not a secret Muslim. In that sense, he will not fit prophecies that indicate that a committed Muslim will do anything.

Yet, some have argued that because his father (or at least grandfather) was considered a Muslim, that Barack Obama is considered to be one also by birth, even if he has never embraced Islam. Thus, in that sense, some may consider him to be a Muslim.

Barack Obama, himself, claims Christ, although he does not seem to be highly involved with religion. For example, in the first few weeks after the election, he did not attend any church service, according to new reports.[226]

However, because he does not seem to have much focus on end-time biblical prophecies (though that could change), Barack Obama will likely not understand many end-time events. This will lead him to be more accommodating to the rise of the Beast power than one who understands end-time prophecy would likely be.

He and all others should open their Bibles and practice genuine Christianity, before they are subject to being misled by the modified, ecumenical religion that will come upon the whole world (cf. Revelation 13:3-4).

Is Barack Obama a Muslim Sympathizer?

Many have wondered if Barack Obama is a Muslim sympathizer. The answer to that question is unclear. He did grow up in Muslim Indonesia, however, and has had more early Muslim contacts than has anyone else ever elected as President of the United States. Therefore, he would probably have more reasons than most U.S. presidents to have sympathy for certain Muslim perspectives.

Here is some of what Barack Obama's "Fight the Smears" website quotes about this:

> *Newsweek*: Obama's only personal contact with Islam came as a boy when he moved to Jakarta, Indonesia, with a stepfather who mixed his Islam with Hindu and Animist traditions...
>
> *Boston Globe*: His Kenyan paternal grandfather and Indonesian stepfather were Muslim...

Thus, while the selected quotes seem to have been intended by the Obama campaign to minimize his ties to Islam, Barack Obama has more early ties to Islam than has any President of the United States in history. He also repeated his full name, Barack Hussein Obama, twice at his inauguration as U.S.A. president (and some believed that he seemed to emphasize his middle name, Hussein).

But irrespective of any tie to Islam, it seems that his

policies may lead to greater cooperation between the Arabic and non-Arabic Muslim nations, which at some point, must end up with a leader (whom the Shi'ites tend to call a Mahdi) whom the Bible warns will be the Future King of the South.

Is Barack Obama the Antichrist?

No, Barack Obama is *not* the prophesied Antichrist. The Bible shows that the final Antichrist is a religious leader as opposed to a primarily political one. This would indicate that Barack Obama is not the final Antichrist (for the scriptures, please see Chapter 12).

However, many on the Internet have given a variety of reasons why they believe that he is actually the Antichrist.

Here are seven claims that supposedly indicate that Barack Obama is the Antichrist, along with brief explanations as to why each of them is in error.

> CLAIM 1. The Beast is 666. 6+6+6=18, the number of letters in Barack Hussein Obama, whose Chicago power base includes the 60606 zip code. On November 5 —the day after the election —in Obama's home state of Illinois—the evening "Pick 3" lottery number was 6-6-6.

The Bible says that the number is *six hundred*, and sixty-six (Revelation 13:18), rather than three sixes (see also Chapter 10). Thus, nothing in that claim ties Barack Obama to 666.

> CLAIM 2. False Prophets Will Precede. Antichrist will be heralded by false prophets. Jeremiah Wright and Father Pfleger, who claim to be in the prophetic tradition, compared Barack to Jesus. Louis Farrakhan called Barack "the Messiah.

Actually, the Bible teaches that one called the false prophet will do miracles and cause people to worship the image of the Beast (Revelation 16:13-14; 13:12-15). Neither Jeremiah Wright nor the other two mentioned above have thus far qualified according to the Bible.

> CLAIM 3. Satanic Palindrome. Sasha is only the nickname of Obama's oldest daughter. Her legal name is NATASHA—the reverse of AH SATAN.

Natasha is the Russian version of the name Natalie. It is a female given name: from a Latin word meaning "birthday." Those who claim that putting his daughter's name backwards has something to do with him being Antichrist is a low blow. She has enough concerns as a president's daughter. She does not need to be picked on because of her name. His daughter's name is simply not relevant.

> CLAIM 4. Antichrist is a Charismatic Speaker Worshipped By The Masses. The Book of Daniel says the Beast will arise in a country made up of "diverse" people from "all kingdoms" [which could describe the USA] …
>
> The charismatic Barack is conceited and is worshipped throughout the world, including in the European Union—the successor to the Roman Empire.

The Beast is *not* the final Antichrist (see Chapter 12). The Beast will be the King of the North, and a European. The United States is *not* the heir to the ancient Roman Empire—Europe is.

> CLAIM 5. New Nostradamus Quatrains Scholars

for the Smithsonian Institute have uncovered new interpretations that may relate to Barack Obama ...

Professor Eugene Randell, Deputy Director of the Smithsonian Institution Archives has released information pertaining to the up and coming US elections. The Institute which holds some very rare Nostradamus manuscripts, believes that some of the quatrains written by the 16th century soothsayer are very close to describing the fight for the White House that is happening now...

243 *The great empire will be torn from limb, The all-powerful one for more than four hundred years: Great power given to the dark one from slaves come, The Aryana will not be satisfied thereby.*[227]

The above story (though popular on the internet) is an apparent a satirical hoax. There does not appear to have ever been a Professor Eugene Randell who was Deputy Director of the Smithsonian Institution Archives; nor is this new Quatrain 243 legitimate. The publisher of the above (*The Daily Squib*) also would not verify, nor respond at all, concerning its story, even after two requests were made.

> CLAIM 6. Mayan 2012 Calendar. The Beast/Antichrist will rule for 42 months of relative peace and prosperity...in the middle of the fourth year of his reign...{is the} the Battle of Armageddon. The fourth year of Barack's presidency will be 2012, the year the Mayan calendar comes to an end, the year of a rare planetary alignment...

While Barack Obama's first term as president includes the

year 2012, the end will not come then as some believe that the Mayan 2012 prophecies indicate.

As the seven-year deal in Daniel 9:27 has not happened yet, it is not possible that the so-called "Battle of Armageddon" could begin in Barack Obama's first term (plus the Great Tribulation needs to start about 3 ½ years before the Armageddon related battle, see Chapter 14). And it is almost impossible for this battle to occur in his second term (presuming his reelection to a consecutive term).

The next claim is based upon someone's "personal vision":

> CLAIM 7. Fulfilled Daniel 9:27. Very early in the morning, on Thanksgiving Day, I could not get back to sleep...I was very, very confident that the Lord was giving me a BRAND NEW REVELATION, further confirmation that on OCT. 29, 2008, OBAMA CONFIRMED THE COVENANT OF DANIEL 9:27, thrusting the world into the Final Seven Years...The Lord had called me to be a watchman many years ago... We have in circulation almost 10,000,000 tracts...2520 days (360 days X 7 Jewish years), after the 30 MINUTES OF SILENCE IN HEAVEN on Oct. 29, 2008, is Feast of Atonement. This is by divine design, not happenstance, or coincidence...There may be a peace treaty with Israel and the Antichrist in the near future, but it will NOT be 7 years in length and it will NOT be the fulfillment of Daniel 9:27. THE FULFILLMENT OF DANIEL 9:27 HAS ALREADY HAPPENED ON OCT. 29, 2008, WITH THE CONFIRMING OF THE COVENANT. TRY CONVINCING ALL OF THAT AWESTRUCK AUDIENCE IN HEAVEN, WHO WERE COMPLETELY SILENT FOR EXACTLY 30 MINUTES AS OBAMA GAVE HIS HISTORIC SPEECH that this was not the confirming of the covenant of Daniel 9:27...[228]

Contrary to claims and visions, the deal in Daniel 9:27 has not been made (Barack Obama was not even elected president in October 2008). The deal will be confirmed by a European as even most Protestant commentators recognize. This deal still needs to be made. It should also be noted that the Day of Atonement in 2015 will be on September 23rd, and therefore not 2520 days after October 29 as the above person claimed. Hence, I would not wish to accept his vision as coming from God.

Barack Obama, contrary to various posts and emails floating around on the internet, is not the Antichrist.

The Names "Barack," "Hussein," "Obama," and Kenyan Prophecy?

Barack Hussein Obama's mother who was part Caucasian and part American Indian. His father was "a Luo from Nyang'oma Kogelo, Nyanza Province, Kenya."[229]

Here is some information on the Luo

> **Luo**...the Luo number over 3 million people, or about 13 percent of Kenya's total population...the Nomiya Luo Church, which started in 1912, was the first independent church in Kenya. The founder of this church, Johanwa Owalo, is believed to be a prophet similar to Jesus Christ and Muhammad. Owalo later teamed up with a Catholic priest and began teaching a new theology that rejected both the Pope and the doctrine of the trinity...[230]

Hence, there apparently is a Luo religion in Kenya, and there named Johanwa Owalo was associated with it and made some prophecies. Barack Obama is considered, by some at least, to be a Luo.

His first name, however, is Hebrew:

> The meaning of the name Barak is Lightning, Spark
>
> The origin of the name Barak is Hebrew[231]

There is a Barak mentioned in the Hebrew scriptures (Judges 4:6).
His middle name is Arabic:

> The meaning of the name Hussein is Handsome One
>
> The origin of the name Hussein is Arabic[232]

His last name seems to mean "slightly bent":

> The meaning of the name Obama is Slightly Bent
>
> The origin of the name Obama is African
>
> Notes: From a rare Luo (Kenyan) name, meaning a baby born with bent arm or leg or possibly a breech birth.[233]

While Obama is apparently a Luo Kenyan word, if it originally came from Hebrew, it most likely would have come from the word "Bama":

> The meaning of the name Bama is: **Son of prophecy**.[234]

So, combining the definitions above, the name Barak Hussein Bama could possibly literally mean the *handsome timid gleam, son of prophecy*.

Now, on the internet there is claimed to be a 1912 prophecy by Johanwa Owalo, the founder of Kenya's Nomiya Luo Church, about the United States:

So far have they [the United States] strayed into wickedness in those [future] times that their destruction has been sealed by my [father]. Their great cities will burn, their crops and cattle will suffer disease and death, their children will perish from diseases never seen upon this Earth, and I reveal to you the greatest [mystery] of all as I have been allowed to see that their [the United States] destruction will come about through the vengeful hands of one of our very own sons.[235]

Because Barack Obama's father is *ethnically* a Luo of Kenya, Barack Obama seems to meet the criteria above as being "one of our very sons." National Public Radio (and other sources) even refers to him as "the son of Kenya."[236]

Thus, in several senses, Barack Obama may be at least a "son of prophecy." Whether or not that Kenyan "prophecy" is legitimate and whether or not it applies to him, the timing of his election makes Barack Obama of prophetic interest.

Why is Barack Obama Apocalyptic?

The last book of the Bible is referred to as "Revelation" or the Apocalypse (the Greek term which means revealing). For purposes of this section, we will use the term "apocalyptic" to mean related to events that lead to the end-time events prophesied in the Bible.

Although Barack Obama is not, and will not, be the final Antichrist, there are reasons to believe that the rising of the prophesied final ten-horned beast power (Revelation 13:1) and the destruction of the United States will take place under the Obama administration if it lasts two full terms (eight years). And this destruction is likely to include terrorism and partial nuclear devastation.

Catholic Cardinal Stafford (who is head of the Apostolic

Penitentiary of the Holy See [237]) claimed that Barack Obama was "aggressive, disruptive, and apocalyptic." He specifically explained:

> My use of the word "apocalyptic" would be emphatically biblical, rooted in the understanding of the Book of the Apocalypse.[238]

Here are seven specific reasons indicating that President Barack Obama may be "apocalyptic":

> 1. The timing of his election. It may be that only two presidential terms are left before the start of the Great Tribulation and the fulfillment of related prophecies in the Book of Revelation (called the Apocalypse by most Catholics). Barack Obama's very presence (as well as his planned and unplanned actions) should be enough to enable the fulfillment of various end-time prophecies.
>
> 2. As one with a Luo Kenyan father, Barack Obama *may* be part of the fulfillment of Deuteronomy 28:43.
>
> 3. Since 1973, the U.S.A. switched from being a creditor nation and instead has become the greatest debtor nation in the history of humankind. Because the U.S.A. owes alien nations trillions of dollars, it appears that the curse in Deuteronomy 28:44 of having to borrow from aliens is happening to it now. President Barack Obama has put forth economic policies that will (for at least several years) greatly increase that debt. Yet, increasing national debt like this will lead to destruction at the appointed time of the end (Habakkuk 2:3, 6–8).

4. Barack Obama has pledged increased cooperation with the Europeans. And while cooperation is normally a good thing, this particular cooperation is likely to lead to the rise of the prophesied King of the North, who is to be the final leader of the Beast of Revelation (Revelation 13:1). Unlike previous U.S. administrations, President Obama's administration has declared that it will encourage and support increases in Europe's own military, far beyond what Presidents Bush or Clinton were willing to consider.[239] These policies will enable the rise of the King of the North.

5. Barack Obama has called for increased dialogue with those considered as enemies of the U.S.A. As mentioned earlier, even some Shi'ite Muslims believe that his presidency may lead to the rise of their Mahdi who seems to be the same person that the Bible calls the King of the South.

6. An increase of military action in Afghanistan, which President Obama has called for, may stretch U.S.A. military commitments. Because of domestic economic concerns and international pressures, Barack Obama is shifting priorities away from defense spending[240], while encouraging the Europeans to increase their military might. This will help lead to the destruction of the United States, when the Europeans are ready and the U.S.A. is not.

7. President Obama actually claimed, "the only measure of my success as president when people look back five years from now or nine years from now is going to be, did I get this economy fixed?...I'm going

to be judged on, have we pulled ourselves out of recession?"[241] As the God of the Bible expects leaders to encourage repentance and moral behaviors when they are subject to destructive punishment (cf. Jonah 3:6-9), and Barack Obama does not seem to believe that the U.S.A. needs to repent for its sins against God, his policies seem to be focused on not relying on God. Hence, without national repentance, the U.S.A. is doomed for destruction.

Habakkuk 2 makes clear that at the appointed time of the end, a great borrowing people will be destroyed (Habakkuk 2:3,6-8). Something similar is in Deuteronomy 28:42-51. No nation in the history of humankind has ever accumulated as much debt as the United States of America (because the U.K. may have the highest amount of per capita debt[242], its fate would seem to be similar). Yet, the relationship between debt accumulation and prophesied destruction remains unapparent to many.

And although President Obama inherited a debt-laden nation, his policies, according to his own public pronouncements, will lead to greatly increased U.S.A. debt for several years. These increases of debt are likely to go past the point of no return and become one of the final factors that will cause creditors to rise up and destroy the U.S.A.

It seems clear that during his presidency, Barack Obama will be an enabler in the sense that his policies will help lead to the rise of the prophesied final Kings of the North and South that Daniel 11 discusses. Nothing from his administration thus far suggests that he will call for meaningful massive repentance and turning back to God.

Therefore, President Obama (who should be U.S.A. President in 2012 and perhaps until 2017) is apocalyptic.

Of course, it is not only the United States that needs

repentance as God "now commands all men everywhere to repent" (Acts 17:30).

But because of biblical prophecy, and the fact that the Bible teaches that to "everyone to whom much is given, from him much will be required" (Luke 12:48), the U.S.A. is expected to be amongst the first to suffer from the Great Tribulation (Matthew 24:21). This period is also called the "time of Jacob's trouble" (Jeremiah 30:7).

For much more on the destruction of the United States and its Anglo-allies, please see Appendix B.

CHAPTER 9
DOES THE BIBLE POINT TO 2012? WHEN DOES THE 6,000 YEARS END?

Does the Bible itself give any hint about the time near 2012?

Actually, it does, though not necessarily specifically that year.

But before getting to specific years, it should be pointed out that there is a doctrine that was held by many early leaders who professed Christ, which has been held by some (as well as some Jewish leaders) throughout the ages. There was an early teaching that God had a plan that would result in humans being given 6,000 years to live on their own, with their own governments, and basically cut off from God.

At this point, it should be mentioned that the 6,000 years begins with humans starting with Adam and Eve leaving Eden.

Truly understanding what the Bible teaches may be helpful to *all* in these latter days—and not only those who base their beliefs on it.

Have People Long Believed in Six Thousand Years of Human Rule?

In the late 18th century, the historian Edward Gibbon documented certain facts regarding the first century

Christians:

> The ancient and popular doctrine of the Millennium was intimately connected with the second coming of Christ. As the works of the creation had been finished in six days, their duration in their present state, according to a tradition which was attributed to the prophet Elijah, was fixed to six thousand years. By the same analogy it was inferred that this long period of labor and contention, which was now almost elapsed, would be succeeded by a joyful Sabbath of a thousand years; and that Christ, with the triumphant band of the saints and the elect who had escaped death, or who had been miraculously revived, would reign upon earth till the time appointed for the last and general resurrection.[243]

While traditions should never supersede scripture, the above is certainly an interesting and ancient tradition, as it shows that the idea of a six-thousand-year plan, followed by Christ establishing His kingdom on the earth was a common teaching among those who professed Christ in the early days.

Here are specific Jewish traditions related to the millennium from the Talmud:

> *R. Kattina* said: Six thousand years shall the world exist, and one [thousand, the seventh], it shall be desolate, as it is written, And the Lord alone shall be exalted in that day {Isaiah 2:11}.
>
> *Abaye* said: it will be desolate two [thousand], as it is said, After two days will he revive us: in the third day, he will raise us up, and we shall live in his sight {Hosea 6:2}.

> It has been taught in accordance with R. Kattina: Just as the seventh year is one year of release in seven, so is the world: one thousand years out of seven shall be fallow, as it is written, And the Lord alone shall be exalted in that day,' and it is further said, A Psalm and song for the Sabbath day {Psalm 92:1}, meaning the day that is altogether Sabbath — and it is also said, For a thousand years in thy sight are but as yesterday when it is past {Psalm 90:4}.
>
> *The Tanna debe Eliyyahu* teaches: The world is to exist six thousand years. In the first two thousand there was desolation; two thousand years the Torah flourished; and the next two thousand years is the Messianic era.[244]

Note: I inserted the scriptures quoted or alluded to above within {}, as they are in the footnotes associated with the above.

And while there are some errors in that Talmudic understanding, it supports the idea that there is a six-thousand-year plan, that the current two thousand years essentially represents the Church/Messianic era, and that a one thousand year period remains. And apparently, according to those Jewish scholars, the 6,000 years would likely be over in the next decade or so, if Jesus was the Messiah (and, of course, He was).

Notice what the respected Protestant historian Johann Karl Ludwig Gieseler observed about the second century Christians:

> Jewish Christians...the *Nazarenes*... *the millenarianism* of the Jewish Christians...for which the reputation of John (Apoc. xx. 4-6; xxi.) and his peculiar followers,

afforded a warrant—this *millenarianism* became the general belief of the time, and met with almost no other opposition than that given by the Gnostics...The thousand years' reign was represented as the great Sabbath which should begin very soon, or as others supposed, after the lapse of the six thousand years of the world's age, with the first resurrection, and should afford great joys to the righteous. Till then the souls of the departed were kept in the underworld, and the opinion that they should be taken up to heaven immediately after death, was considered a gnostic heresy.[245]

Hence, it is known that the belief that the Judeo-Christians (the Nazarene sect) held on the millennium and six-thousand-year plan was adopted by all Christians in the second century—and that view was only challenged at that time by false "Christians," called Gnostics.

A Thousand Years is Like a Day to God

Some believe that because God made/recreated the world in six days and rested on the seventh day (Genesis 2:1-3), that humans will have 6,000 years to live on the earth under Satan's influence, but will have a 1,000 years to be under Christ's reign. (Some also believe that the original creation of the universe may have been billions of years earlier c.f. Genesis 1:2; Isaiah 45:18). The 6,000 plus 1,000 years equals God's seven thousand year plan.

Many have noted that a thousand years seems to be as one day to God. This is a concept from both the Old and New Testaments:

> [4] For a thousand years in Your sight Are like yesterday when it is past (Psalm 90:4).

> ⁸ But, beloved, do not forget this one thing, that with the Lord one day is as a thousand years, and a thousand years as one day (2 Peter 3:8).

Based upon certain calculations that have been proposed, it seems that Adam and Eve were created and/or apparently left the garden of Eden between 5,980 to 5,995 years ago (roughly 3974-3989 B.C.). This would mean that when Jesus began to preach (roughly 27 A.D., over four thousand year later) He was preaching in "thousand-year day five," as four of the seven "one thousand year days" would have been over before then.

Thus days five and six would have been considered as part of the "last days" by the early disciples.

That being so, this helps explain why some New Testament figures indicated that they were in the last days:

> But Peter, standing up with the eleven, raised his voice and said to them, "Men of Judea and all who dwell in Jerusalem, let this be known to you, and heed my words. For these are not drunk, as you suppose, since it is only the third hour of the day. But this is what was spoken by the prophet Joel: *'And it shall come to pass **in the last days**, says God, That I will pour out of My Spirit on all flesh* (Acts 2:14-17).

> God, who at various times and in various ways spoke in time past to the fathers by the prophets, has **in these last days** spoken to us by His Son, whom He has appointed heir of all things (Hebrews 1:1-2).

If there is no six-thousand-year plan of human rule followed by a one-thousand- year millennial reign, then the New Testament statements above about them being in the *last days* seem to make little sense. But, as God does apparently have a seven-thousand-year plan, these statements do make sense. That also explains why the end has not come yet—there is still a little more time in "the last days."

It should be pointed out that there are two types of *last days* referred to in the New Testament. When some were stating that they were in the last days, this indicates the latter days of the seven-thousand-year week. However in other places, New Testament writers sometimes refer to the time of the final generation before Jesus returns as being the last days, as they indicate that this is not the same time as when they were writing (cf. 2 Peter 3:3).

James Ussher's Calculations

Many believe that the 6,000 years are up because of some 17th century calculations a historian, James Ussher, made. James Ussher was then the Anglican Archbishop of Armagh (in what is now Northern Ireland).

Ussher primarily based his calculations upon the chronologies and reigns of kings in the Old Testament to conclude that the world was created in the Fall of 4004 B.C.

There are some problems that can arise from using James Ussher's method:

> 1) The first is that Ussher's method did not seem to take into account that sometimes a son began the reign in a kingdom before his father king died (which, for one example, seems to have started with Solomon, per 1 Kings 1:32-43), hence the official chronologies often counted both co-reigns. This could have contributed to possible over-counting by Ussher.
>
> 2) It is probable that the 6,000 years for humans to rule over themselves apart from direct contact with

God began after Adam and Eve sinned, and hence left the Garden of Eden. It could have taken them one day or twenty or more years to sin—the Bible is not specifically clear on this point.

3) James Ussher presumed that Solomon built the Jerusalem Temple in 1012 B.C., but it was likely built decades later.

4) Some claim he also made some biblical calculation errors.[246]

Therefore, people who rely on Ussher's 4004 B.C. calculations to claim that the 6,000 years are up are apparently relying on assumptions, as opposed to fact. But Ussher was somewhat close, and the 6,000 years is ending soon.

Did Second and Third Century Writers Teach the Six-Thousand-Year Plan?

The idea that God essentially had a 7,000 year plan, with 6,000 years for humans to rule themselves nearly cutoff from God's rule, followed by a one-thousand- year reign by Christ on the planet is found in several early post-New Testament writings.

Although most scholars do not consider that the so-called *Epistle of Barnabas* is divinely inspired, that writing does show that in the early second century, some did understand the idea of a six-thousand-year plan, followed by the thousand-year reign of Christ:

> Moreover concerning the Sabbath likewise it is written in the Ten Words, in which He spake to Moses face to face on Mount Sinai*And God made the works of His hands in six days, and He ended on the seventh day, and rested*

> *on it, and He hallowed it.* Give heed, children, what this meaneth; *He ended in six days.* He meaneth this, that in six thousand years the Lord shall bring all things to an end; for the day with Him signifyeth a thousand years; and this He himself beareth me witness, saying; *Behold, the day of the Lord shall be as a thousand years.* Therefore, children, in six days, that is in six thousand years, everything shall come to an end. *And He rested on the seventh day.* this He meaneth; when His Son shall come, and shall abolish the time of the Lawless One, and shall judge the ungodly, and shall change the sun and the moon and the stars, then shall he truly rest on the seventh day.[247]

Hence the above quote shows that there was a belief among those who professed Christianity that there would be a literal thousand-year reign of Christ on the Earth, and a six-thousand-year plan for humans prior to that.

Around the end of the second century, a follower of a heretical leader named Bardesan wrote the following:

> Bardesan, therefore, an aged man, and one celebrated for his knowledge of events, wrote, in a certain work which was composed by him, concerning the synchronisms with one another of the luminaries of heaven…And this, says he, "is one synchronism of them all; that is, the time of one such synchronism of them. So that from hence it appears that to complete too such synchronisms there will be required six thousands of years. Thus: 200 revolutions of Saturn, six thousands of years; 500 revolutions of Jupiter, 6 thousands of years; 4 thousand revolutions of Mars, 6 thousands of years; Six thousand revolutions of the Sun, 6 thousands of years. 7 thousand and 200

> revolutions of Venus, 6 thousands of years; 12 thousand revolutions of Mercury, 6 thousands of years. 72 thousand revolutions of the Moon, 6 thousands of years."
>
> These things did Bardesan thus compute when desiring to show that this world would stand only six thousands of years.[248]

Hence, Bardesan believed that the world would last 6,000 years.

Irenaeus, a Roman supporting leader that Roman Catholics consider a saint, claimed to have met the faithful Polycarp of Smyrna. Irenaeus wrote that human were given 6,000 years:

> Thus, then, the six hundred years of Noah, in whose time the deluge occurred because of the apostasy, and the number of the cubits of the image for which these just men were sent into the fiery furnace, do indicate the number of the name of that man in whom is concentrated the whole apostasy of six thousand years, and unrighteousness, and wickedness, and false prophecy, and deception.[249]

Hippolytus was, and is still considered to have been, "the most important theologian and the most prolific religious writer of the Roman Church in the pre-Constantinian era".[250]

Notice what he wrote:

> And 6, 000 years must needs be accomplished, in order that the Sabbath may come, the rest, the holy day "on which God rested from all His works." For the Sabbath is the type and emblem of the future kingdom of the saints, when they "shall reign with Christ," when He

comes from heaven, as John says in his Apocalypse: for "a day with the Lord is as a thousand years." Since, then, in six days God made all things, it follows that 6,000 years must be fulfilled.[251]

Notice therefore that **"the most important {Roman} theologian — in the pre-Constantinian era"** taught the seven-thousand-year plan (6,000 for humankind, followed by 1,000 from God).

Thus, certain second and third century leaders who professed Christ clearly believed in the teaching that there was a six-thousand-year plan.

When is the 6,000 Years Up?

According to some Roman Catholics, parts of this view have long been the belief of those who claim to believe at least part of the Bible:

> *E Culligan* (20th century): ...the time of the First Resurrection will end...It is the time when the Seventh Millennium will set in, and will be the day of Sabbath in the plan of creation...It has been the common opinion among Jews, Gentiles, and Latin and Greek Christians, that the present evil world will last no more than 6,000 years...Christians and Jews, from the beginning of Christianity, and before, have taught that 6,000 years after the creation of Adam and Eve, the consummation will occur. The period after the consummation is to be the seventh day of creation—the Sabbath...St. Jerome said, "It is a common belief that the world will last 6,000 years."[252]
>
> *Priest G. Rossi* (19th century): One day with the Lord, then, is as a thousand years, and a thousand years as

one day. It is the common interpretation that each of the six days of creation is equivalent to one thousand years for the future existence of human generations. Now God employed six days in the creation of this world; this world, then, shall last only six thousand years; the Sabbath, or seventh day, representing eternity.[253]

This six-thousand-year time period that some Catholics have held to throughout history, is almost up, and we are in the end times that are leading up to the millennium.

One Catholic monk, called "the venerable Bede," indicated that the creation was in 3952 B.C.[254] And thus, even with this date, the 6,000 years would be close to being up. Other Catholics have thought that the 6,000 years would have been up in the late twentieth century, even in a writing blessed by Pope Paul VI in 1966.[255]

However, after Cardinal Joseph Ratzinger became Prefect of the Congregation for the Doctrine of the Faith, formerly known as the Holy Office, the historical Inquisition, he took steps to stop the Catholic Church from endorsing any millennial teachings,[256] and the Church of Rome no longer teaches a six-thousand-year plan. Joseph Ratzinger is now known as Pope Benedict XVI.

But others, in other faiths, still have taught the 6,000 years of human rule.

For example, the late evangelist John Ogwyn indicated that the creation was approximately 3983 B.C. based upon his understanding of the Bible as follows:

> Do Genesis 5:3–29 and 7:11 show that 1,656 years transpired between the creation of Adam and the Flood of Noah's day? (Note: Genesis 5:3 shows that Adam was 130 when Seth was born. Add up the age of each patriarch at the birth of his son, plus the age of

Noah at the time of the Flood)...

Do Genesis 11:10-32 show that 427 years passed between the Flood and the death of Terah, which was the time that Abram left Haran (cf. Acts 7:4)? Was Abram 75 years of age when he left Haran? Genesis 12:4...

How old was Abraham when God made the covenant of circumcision with him? Genesis 17:1-10. Had 24 years passed since he left Haran? (Note: A careful comparison of Genesis 12:4 with Genesis 17:1 will reveal Abraham's age at the time of the covenant)...

According to Galatians 3:16-17, how many years passed between the time of the covenant with Abraham and the Sinai covenant, which was the year of the Exodus? (cf. Exodus 12:40)...

How many years were there between the Exodus and the fourth year of King Solomon when the temple was begun? 1 Kings 6:1. (By using secular records most scholars date the fourth year of Solomon to approximately 966 BC)...

If you add the numbers (1,656 + 427 + 24 + 430 + 480 + 966) what would have been the approximate year bc of Adam's creation?

Would this not prove that 6,000 years will soon have elapsed?[257]

Galatians 3:17, which is cited, but without showing the years above, shows four hundred and thirty years. 1 Kings

6:1 shows four hundred and eighty years from the time the children of Israel left Egypt until the fourth year of Solomon's reign. (For more explanation of Terah's age, please see the note related to Abraham[258].)

Therefore, if we add up 1,656 + 427 + 24 + 430 + 480 + 966, this suggests the creation of Adam was around 3983 B.C. Because years of life are not exact (since few people are born and die on the precisely same calendar date, and some of the calculation may suggest that, there could possibly be 10 additional years past 2018) this could be off somewhat–but it does give a biblical indication of when the end is coming.

Also, as the John Ogwyn writing indicated, it is partially dependent upon an estimate of scholars pointing to a 966 B.C. temple dedication—as the work of other scholars indicates that the separation of Israel from Judah was possibly 931 B.C. [259]. This separation happened shortly after (1 Kings 11:43; 12:1–20) Solomon's forty-year reign (1 Kings 11:42), therefore it would seem that one less year could be indicated (966+4-40=930 B.C. vs. 931 B.C.). However, if there were a co-regency of 3–4 years, it would be 2–3 years later than 3983.

And while 966 is an estimated temple date, there are several who believed Solomon's reign began in 970, hence would come up with a 966 date four years later. Here are other references:

> *Jesse Long*: Working back from these dates and the biblical references to the reigns of the kings of Israel and Judah (78 years from the death of Ahab in 853/852 BC) the Kingdom of Solomon was divided in 931/930 BC, at the ascension of Rehoboam to the throne of Israel following the death of Solomon. Since Solomon reigned forty years (v. 42), he must have ascended the throne in 971/970 B.C.[260]

Edwin Thiele: Rehoboam of Judah succeeded Solomon between Tishri 931 and Tishri 930.[261]

John Canning: SOLOMON (Reigned c. 970–c. 932 Bc)[262]

Leon Wood & David O'Brien: SOLOMON THE KING Solomon's reign was long, lasting forty years (970–931) as had his father's before him.[263]

Israel Finkelstein & Neil Silberman: Solomon 40 C. 970–931 BCE.[264]

But while there is some controversy related to particulars of any calculation, let's look at the 3983 B.C. date, while understanding it is likely to not be precisely accurate.

If one starts from the year 2009 A.D. and adds 3983 years, this adds up to 5992. However, because there was no year zero (for the transition between B.C. and A.D.), this make it year 5991. Thus, the 6,000 years may be up in about 8-9 years from 2009 (2009 plus 9 would be the year 2018).

However, it is important to note that the Bible shows that the days will apparently need to be shortened:

> And unless those days were shortened, no flesh would be saved; but for the elect's sake those days will be shortened (Matthew 24:22).

While 2018 may be the end of the 6,000 years, it is possible that it may be one or more years earlier or even ten or so years later. And the Great Tribulation may begin 3 1/2 years before then—thus the Great Tribulation may begin around 2013–2016—it cannot be before 2013, as the deal in Daniel 9:27 has not happened yet (but if the deal happened and was unannounced, then an earlier year could be possible).

Thus, according to a variety of sources, but mainly the Bible, the 6,000 years will be up in the twenty-first century—and probably the next decade. This will lead to the return of Jesus Christ and the real age of peace.

This timeframe is somewhat consistent (though not quite) with Mayan and other prophecies related to the year 2012. And somehow, the secret sect will need to succeed in proclaiming the gospel of the kingdom to the world as a witness before the end (Matthew 24:14) of the 6,000 years is here.

CHAPTER 10
THE NEW WORLD ORDER PROPHESIED FOR THE GREAT MONARCH AND AN ANTIPOPE

In the 21st century, many are looking forward to a time when a new ecumenical religious order will come on to the world scene. Many others, however, dread such an occurrence.

The Bible, in Daniel 11:38, mentions a new god honored by the King of the North. And this new god is apparently a sort of a new ecumenical religion.

This religion is related to, "a god which his fathers did not know."

This same religion seems to have a "foreign god," according to Daniel 11:39 (see also Revelation 13:15 and Appendix B):

> ^{38}—he {the King of the North} shall honor a god of fortresses; and a god which his fathers did not know he shall honor with gold and silver, with precious stones and pleasant things. ^{39} Thus he shall act against the strongest fortresses with a foreign god, which he shall acknowledge, and advance its glory (Daniel 11:38–39a).

What might this religion be?

While many Buddhists, as well as those in the New Age Movement, look forward to a peaceful religious leader, certain Catholic prophetic writings provide detailed clues to this.

The first is from a mystic nun:

> *Anne Catherine Emmerich* (19th Century): I saw the Church inspired by the Holy Spirit, introducing various changes in her discipline when devotion and veneration towards the blessed sacrament had grown weak...Incalculable graces were thereby bestowed upon the whole Church.[265]

The above suggests some major changes are to occur within the framework of the Catholic Church when it seems to be in a weakened condition.

The Catholic-writer Desmond Birch wrote the following (**bold italics** in the text):

> ...Francis {of Paula, 15th century} also speaks in a series of letters to Simeon de Limena, Count of Montalto in great detail of a future Great Monarch who will be a Roman Emperor. Limena was a great patron of St. Francis' order and also a great military protector of the Church...Several potentially confusing things are now told about this future Monarch. He is described as founding a new religious order. To the reader this may sound like he also becomes a priest. That is not the case. What happens is that he founds a religious order, part of which contains military men who take religious vows. He will be the head of the military arm of this order. In this sense it will be like the Knights Templar of the Middle Ages.
>
> > "***He shall be the founder of a new religious order different from all others***. He will divide it into three strata, namely military knights, solitary priests, and most pious hospitalliers.

> This shall be the last religious order in the Church, and it will do more good for our holy religion than all other religious institutions.
>
> "...These devout men will wear on their breasts... the cross...
>
> "He shall...destroy all tyrants and heresies. There will be one fold and one shepherd. He shall reign until the end of time. On the whole earth there will be twelve Kings, one Emperor and one Pope.[266]

Notice that Francis prophesied that there will be a new religious order (led by a militaristic leader) that will do more good for an ecumenical church than all other religious institutions, but that this ruler will destroy all heresies—which would suggest putting an end to all dissention from his new order. The Byzantine *Anonymou Paraphrasis* might also be predicting such an order.[267]

The following also may be related:

> *Priest Laurence Ricci, S.J.* (died 1775): **This great ruler... will,** with the aid of the Pope, **introduce new rules...** Everywhere there will be one fold and one shepherd.[268]

Priest Ricci talks about "new rules" with the "aid of a pope." This could be because the King of the North will work with the Pope to make the world apparently nominally "Catholic" (it will be a changed, more ecumenical in form, probably using the name Catholic).

A new religious order claiming to be "Catholic" seems to fit into Daniel's statement of "god which his fathers did not know" (see Appendix B).

An Antipope Is Prophesied to Implement a New Order

Furthermore, it appears that other Catholic writings suggest that it is an *antipope* who is involved in the imposition of a changed church:

> *Oba Prophecy*: It will come when the Church authorities issue directives to support a new cult, when priests are forbidden to celebrate in any other, when the highest positions in the Church are given to perjurers and hypocrites, when only the renegades are admitted to occupy those positions.

> *Nun Anna-Katarina Emmerick* (19th century): I saw again a new and odd-looking Church which they were trying to build. There was nothing holy about it...

> *Yves Dupont* (writer interpreting A. Emmerick above), They wanted to make a new Church, a Church of human manufacture, but God had other designs...The Holy Father shall have to leave Rome, and he shall die a cruel death. An anti-pope shall be set up in Rome.[269]

> *Jeanne le Royer* (died 1978): I see that when the Second Coming of Christ approaches a bad priest will do much harm to the Church.[270]

> *Yves Dupont* (reader and reporter of Catholic prophecies): prophecies are quite explicit about **the election of an anti-pope**...Many prophecies predict an anti-pope and a schism.[271]

> *Blessed Joachim* (died 1202): Towards the end of the world Antichrist will overthrow the Pope and usurp his See.[272]

Bl. Anna-Maria Taigi (19th century): After the three days of darkness...a new Pope...Christianity, then, will spread throughout the world...At the end, he will have the gift of miracles, and his name shall be praised over the whole earth.[273]

Ted and Maureen Flynn (20th century): Catholic prophecy warns us of severe problems facing the papacy in these end times...chaos will be within our midst. An Antipope will seize papal authority...It will be those who hold fast to the truths of the faith who will be labeled as the perpetrators of this horrible schism, according to some visionaries.[274]

C. Van Den Biesen (20th century): The beast from the land has two horns like a ram. Its power lies in its art of deceiving by means of tokens and miracles. Throughout the remainder of the book it is called the false prophet. Its office is to assist the beast from the sea, and to induce men to adore its image.[275]

Merlin (7th century): There will come a German Anti-Pope. Italy and Germany will be sorely troubled.[276]

St. Hildegard (died 1179): *But now you see her from the waist down; for you see her in her full dignity as the Church...And from her waist to the place that denotes the female, she has various scaly blemishes... ... And thus in the place where the female is recognized is a black and monstrous head.* For the son of perdition will come raging with the arts he first used to seduce...causing people to deny God and tainting their minds and tearing the Church with the greed of rapine.[277]

Comment by Barbara Newman (1998): But as early as Scivias, Hildegard shockingly portrayed Ecclesia {the Catholic Church} as giving birth to Antichrist himself... Some other early works of Hildegard's, written before 1159, show a similar sourness of tone with respect to the institutional church.[278]

Abbott Joachim (died 1202): A man of remarkable sanctity will be his successor in the Pontifical chair. Through him God will work so many prodigies that all men shall revere him.[279]

Saint Zenobius (died 285): Antichrist will work a thousand prodigies on earth.[280]

St. Hildegard (died 1179): When the great ruler exterminates the Turks almost entirely, one of the remaining Mohammedans will be converted... will kill the pope before he is crowned, through jealousy, he wishing to be pope himself; then when the other cardinals elect the next pope this cardinal will proclaim himself Anti-Pope, and two thirds of the Christians will go with him. He, also well as Antichrist, are descendants of Dan.[281]

Pope Gregory the Great (died 604): In those days, near the end, hardly a Bishop, but an army of priests and two-thirds of the Christians will join the Schism.[282]

Catechism of the Catholic Church (20th century): Before Christ's second coming the Church must pass through a trial that will shake the faith of many believers.[283]

St. Francis of Assisi (died 1226): There will be an

uncanonically elected pope who will cause a great Schism, there will be divers thoughts preached which will cause many, even those in the different orders to doubt, yea even agree with the heretics, which will cause my Order to divide.[284]

Priest Gaudentius Rossi (19th century): According to St. Malachy, then, only ten, or at most eleven, popes remain to be in future more or less legitimately elected. We say more or less legitimately elected, because out of those future popes it is to be feared that one or two will be unlawfully elected as anti-popes.[285]

Priest O'Connor (20th century?): **This final false prophet will be a bishop of the church and will lead all religions into becoming one.**[286]

Priest H. Kramer (20th century): In the vision of the Seer now appears a second beast rising out of the earth, having two horns like a lamb but speaking like a dragon...In other places he is called the false prophet... This prophet may re-establish the pagan Roman Empire and build the "Great Harlot", Babylon… The False Prophet...will persuade all infidels, apostates and apostate nations to worship and adore him...Antichrist "sitteth in the temple of God" (2 Thes. II. 4). This is not the ancient Temple in Jerusalem...this temple is shown to be a Catholic Church...The False Prophet will proclaim the resurrection of the Roman Empire.[287]

Thus, while some Catholic prophecies praise a new religious order, many others indicate that a new type of "Catholicism" will be false to that religion. This also seems to be consistent with an Orthodox understanding of the last false religious power coming from Rome:

> *Bishop Gerasimos of Abydos* (20th century): The army of Antichrist is made up of the worldly powers, mainly the Roman Empire, symbolized by the two beasts and the harlot woman (Rev. 11:7; 13:1-17; cf. Dan. 7:11-12)… The final confrontation with evil is presented in chapters 19 and 20…The war is waged by the beast and the false prophet. **Both of these are organs of Satan, representing the political and religious authority of Rome** (Rev. 13:1-18).[288]

Whatever new order that the Great Monarch (who is to be crowned the leader of the Roman Empire according to other writings) implements with Rome will not be faithful to the teachings of Christ or His original faithful followers.

Therefore a "false pope" is expected, and a great loss of Catholic members to his religion is prophesied.

A Spanish-influenced Mayan writing seems to warn against the rise of an Archbishop, who could possibly be considered as an antipope:

> *Chilam Balam* (16th century): There is no reason or necessity for you to submit to the Archbishop. When he comes, you go and hide yourselves in the forest. If you surrender yourselves, you shall follow Christ, when he shall come.[289]

The above also warns that the faithful will need to hide and follow Christ and not the Archbishop.

According to *The Catholic Almanac*, there have been thirty-seven "antipopes."[290] Thus, contrary to the views of many, it certainly makes sense that there could be one more, especially considering that the Malachy prophecies suggest the next pope is the last pope.

Notice the following two reports from another priest:

> *Priest Paul Kramer* (21st century): The errors of Orthodoxy and of Protestantism will be embraced by that false church, it will be an ecumenical church because the Anti-Pope will be recognized by the world—not by the faithful, but by the world—by the secular world and the secular governments.[291]
>
> *Priest Paul Kramer* (21st century): The Anti-Pope will be recognized as the legitimate Pope of the "church," and the legitimate head of the Vatican State. That "church" will be united with all the false religions. They will be united together under the universality of the Masonic umbrella. In that motley ecumenical union will be the established religion of the so-called civilized world. This is how we will get into the time of great persecution such as the world has never seen.[292]

Some Orthodox look forward to this, but also expect an antipope near then:

> *Helen Tzima Otto* (20th century): We have been told time and time again through the prophets that the Great Monarch and Papa Angelorum…will convene the 8th Ecumenical Council, which will reunify all Christians…The Emperor will spend three years waging wars against the non-Christian nations… {later will be} the end time schism of the Roman Catholic Church of the End Times and the rise of an antipope.[293]

Apparently the "non-Christian nations" will be those that

do not desire to be part of the ecumenical church that is to form.

Notice information from a Roman priest:

> Father O'Connor quotes from Holy Scripture, the stunning prophecies of St. Vincent Ferrer, Pope St. Pius X, St. Francis of Assisi, St. John Eudes, Sr. Lucy of Fatima, Pope Pius XII and Bishop Fulton J. Sheen. Father explains how **God will and is punishing the world for sin, and that the Fathers of the Church all wrote that the False Prophet would be a Catholic Bishop who will become an invalid anti-pope** while the real Pope dies a cruel death in exile.[294]

Another priest wrote:

> *Priest E. Sylvester Berry* (20th century) As indicated by the resemblance to a lamb, **the prophet will probably set himself up in Rome as a sort of antipope during the vacancy of the papal throne** . . . [295]

Thus, some Catholic writings suggest that this "new order" will result in the world becoming nominally Catholic. That is consistent with prophecies that indicate the entire world will tend to agree on worship (cf. Revelation 13:8). And it seems to have a European base.

Notice also the following:

> *Cardinal J.H. Newman* (19th century): Now let us recur to the ancient Fathers, and see whether their further anticipations do not run parallel to the events which have since happened. Antichrist, as they considered, will come out of the Roman Empire just upon its destruction;—that is, the Roman Empire

will in its last days divide itself into ten parts, and the Enemy will come up suddenly out of it upon these ten, and subdue three of them, or all of them perhaps...[296]

The above writing suggests that while there will be a resurrected Roman Empire, at first it will seem fine, but then it will change. This appears to be a prophecy about what will happen to the European Union in the future and seems to be consistent with Isaiah 10:5-11 where a power that does not mean to become militaristic does so.

Since the King of the North is going to nominally claim to be Catholic (see also Appendix B), having a newly claimed Catholic order would be the most logical "foreign god," as many may not see what is happening to that Church. Notice carefully the following Catholic prophecy:

> *Frederick William Faber* (died 1863):....**Antichrist**...Many believe in a demonical incarnation—this will not be so—but he will be utterly possessed...His **doctrine as apparent contradiction of no religion, yet a new religion**...He has an attending pontiff, so separating regal and prophetic office.[297]

That prophecy, which is in a book with an official imprimatur from a Catholic bishop (as well as others), confirms my basic point.

Which basic point?

The point that there soon may be a change to the "Catholic" religion that will make it the religion of an antipope.

This change will not seem to be a contradiction, but it will be a new religion—like a new order within the Catholic religion. This is something we should start to see rising near 2012, and the world needs to understand it today.

Catholics, Evangelicals, Orthodox, and Others Need to be Concerned

While some Catholics are concerned that a change to their faith will occur, even atheists, Protestants, Orthodox, and others should also be concerned about this.

Here is one reason why:

> *Venerable Bartholomew Holzhauser* (17th century): … **there will be an ecumenical council** which will be the greatest of all councils by the power of the Great Monarch, and by the authority of the Holy Pontiff, and by the union of the most devout princes, **atheism and every heresy will be banished from the earth**. The Council will…be believed and **accepted by everyone**.[298]

Hence, an ecumenical council is prophesied to eliminate atheists and others who will not believe in a religion that will use the power of some coming Great Monarch.

Various events around the globe suggest that people of many faiths are getting to the point where they are likely to accept some type of ecumenical religion.

Notice that one evangelical Protestant has predicted that there will be a collapse of evangelicals within a decade because of compromise and limited biblical confidence—and that many will join the Catholics and/or Orthodox:

> *Michael Spencer* (2009): We are on the verge—within 10 years—of a major collapse of evangelical Christianity. This breakdown will follow the deterioration of the mainline Protestant world and it will fundamentally alter the religious and cultural environment in the West… Millions of Evangelicals will quit…massive majorities of Evangelicals can't articulate the Gospel with any coherence…Even in areas where Evangelicals

> imagine themselves strong (like the Bible Belt), we will find a great inability to pass on to our children a vital evangelical confidence in the Bible and the importance of the faith… Two of the beneficiaries will be the Roman Catholic and Orthodox communions. Evangelicals have been entering these churches in recent decades and that trend will continue, with more efforts aimed at the "conversion" of Evangelicals to the Catholic and Orthodox traditions…[299]

And the above does not include the fact that those "Catholic and Orthodox communions" will themselves likely come together and change under the guise of the ecumenical movement that will strengthen in Europe—an ecumenical movement that news events show is occurring.

Perhaps this would be a good time to mention some of the differences between the Orthodox and the Church of Rome that one or both will have to compromise on for unity to occur. Here are ten such differences:

> 1. The Eastern Orthodox, like most Protestants, reject the Roman Catholic notion of purgatory.[300]

> 2. The Eastern Orthodox, like most evangelicals, number the ten commandments as they originally were[301] and not as the Roman Catholics number them. Those of Rome combine the first two, even though that is not what those such as Clement of Alexander (2nd century) did.[302]

> 3. The Eastern Orthodox, as do most evangelicals, believe in baptism by immersion.[303] The Roman Catholics usually employ sprinkling.

4. Most of the Eastern Orthodox (presuming no abortive devices are used), as do most Protestants, believe in "the responsible use of contraception within marriage."[304] The Roman Catholic position seems to be more limited.

5. The Eastern Orthodox, like most Protestants, reject "the dogma of the immaculate conception of the Virgin."[305] That is a Roman Catholic dogma.[306]

6. The Eastern Orthodox, like most Protestants, teach that presbyters (which they call "priests," but Protestants tend to call "ministers" or "elders") can be married.[307] The Roman Church requires celibacy for all presbyters, even though that was not its original position.[308]

7. The Eastern Orthodox, similar to most Protestants, teach that, "Christians must always be 'People of the Book.' "[309] Yet, throughout history, the Church of Rome has tended to place more emphasis on non-biblical sources for much of its doctrines—and this is likely to worsen greatly in the end, as the final faith called "Catholic" will change to be even more distant from the Bible.

8. The Eastern Orthodox, like most Protestants, do not observe Ash Wednesday. The Church of Rome admits that it added this observance in the Middle Ages from non-biblical sources.[310]

9. Neither the Orthodox nor Protestants believe that the jurisdiction of Rome has any real bearing on apostolic succession. Yet, the Roman Church has

officially claimed that apostolic succession was lost by the Orthodox and others when they stopped accepting the jurisdiction of Rome:

> Regarding the Greek Church, it is sufficient to note that it lost Apostolic succession by withdrawing from the jurisdiction of the lawful successors of St. Peter in the See of Rome. The same is to be said of the Anglican claims to continuity.[311]

It perhaps should be mentioned that many respected Roman Catholic scholars have admitted that Rome simply does not have provable "apostolic succession" itself. They also realize that Rome probably did not have its first "bishop" until the middle of the second century.[312] But the coming false Vatican leader will likely take a different position—thus those who compromise with him will also be compromising from the facts of history.

10. Neither the Orthodox nor Protestants believe in the concept of "papal infallibility." That concept became a dogma for the Church of Rome in the 19th century (at Vatican I).[313]

While there are certain ceremonial similarities (as well as differences) between the Roman Catholics and Eastern Orthodox, if people really wish to become "the people of the book" they need to reject all non-biblical doctrines and not enter into greater unity with Rome (as well as look into many of their own doctrines).

This is also true for evangelicals and any who believe that they should get their theological doctrines and practices from the Bible (*sola Scriptura*).

Notice what one mystic, when she was "in ecstasy," wrote about the Orthodox (called Greeks below):

> *Saint Brigata* (14th century): Concerning the Greeks, they know that all the Christians need to keep the only Catholic faith and to submit themselves to the Roman Church, they also know that the Sovereign Roman Pontiff, exercises the spiritual power over them…and they reject this spiritual subjection…So, they {sic} will be no mercy neither pardon in my court in their death.[314]

So, the position of one mystic who was receiving "a spiritual message" is that the Orthodox throughout history cannot be forgiven for not accepting Rome's authority for centuries. Even IF the Greeks should have accepted that authority (which the Bible does not indicate that they should have after the time of the Apostle Paul), not accepting Rome cannot be the unpardonable sin (which is biblically defined as "blasphemy against the Holy Spirit," Matthew 12:31-32), hence Brigata should not have said what she did.

It should be understood that most official reasons for the "great schism" between the Orthodox and the Church of Rome has to do with a doctrine known as the "Filioque clause" in a creed that the Catholics of Rome adopted.

Notice the following from *The Catholic Encyclopedia*:

> **Filioque is a theological formula of great dogmatic and historical importance**. On the one hand, it expresses the Procession of the Holy Ghost from both Father and Son as one Principle; on the other, it was the occasion of the Greek schism…

> The dogma of the double Procession of the Holy Ghost from Father and Son as one Principle is directly opposed to the error that the Holy Ghost proceeds from the Father, not from the Son...
>
> As to the Sacred scripture, the inspired writers call the holy Ghost the Spirit of the Son (Gal., iv, 6), the spirit of Christ (Rom., viii, 9), the Spirit of Jesus Christ (Phil., i, 19), just as they call Him the Spirit of the Father (Matt., x, 20) and the Spirit of God (I Cor., ii, 11). Hence they attribute to the Holy Ghost the same relation to the Son as to the Father. Again, according to Sacred Scripture, the Son sends the Holy Ghost (Luke, xxiv, 49; John, xv, 26; xvi, 7; xx, 22; Acts, ii, 33,; Tit., iii.6)...as the Father sends the Holy Ghost (John, xiv, 26).[315]

Now the Church of Rome is correct on this as the Bible clearly shows that the Holy Spirit proceeds from the Father and the Son.

It is not currently clear how many doctrines those claiming Rome will ultimately compromise on in order to attain unity with the Orthodox. But, I will tell all Catholics that when I was in Istanbul in May 2008, I was specifically told by a representative of the Ecumenical Patriarch of Constantinople that when Pope Benedict XVI visited there, a papal representative told the Patriarch that Rome would change all doctrines necessary to attain full unity with the Orthodox, if the Orthodox would accept papal authority. And this definitely included changing Rome's position on the Filioque clause. Hence, those associated with the Church of Rome need to understand that this means that the Vatican's current (and likely future) leadership is willing to compromise on something that it has long held as being of "great dogmatic and historical importance."

The Author Leaving the Ecumenical Patriarch of Constantinople's Administrative Building

Thus, this strongly suggests that those leading the Church of Rome have embarked on an ecumenical program of change such as the Bible and various Catholic prophecies have warned about.

It also needs to be understood that while some of the Eastern Orthodox are looking forward to a Roman Catholic Great Monarch to be the "King of the Romans and the Greeks,"[316] other Greek Orthodox believe that they only should follow a Greek Orthodox future monarch.[317] The Orthodox should definitely not follow a Roman Catholic Great Monarch if they wish to follow the teachings of the Bible.

Since Vatican II (a major Catholic ecumenical council that ran from 1962–1965), many Catholics have been justifiably concerned that doctrinal compromise for the sake of ecumenical unity with those outside of fellowship of Rome was inevitable.

The Orthodox have long taught that the Church of Rome (known sometimes as Latins) will change doctrines to those of the Orthodox. A document known as the *Anonymou Prophecy* of 1053 refers to this as the "Deferring of the Latins to the error-free faith of the Orthodox."[318]

Thus, the Orthodox expect Rome to change its doctrines.

Notice that according to another Byzantine prophet, the final (the Orthodox recognize seven previous ones) ecumenical council satisfies what "heretics" want:

> *Saint Nelios the Myrrh-Gusher* (died 1592): During that time the Eighth and last Ecumenical Synod will take place, which will satisfy the contentions of the heretics...[319]

By satisfying "heretics", clearly this council compromises and changes the religion, which will be called "Catholic".

A Catholic prophecy shows that after its church is changed (reformed below), the Orthodox will come back:

> *Roger Bacon* (died 1294): There shall arise a...priest to reform the Church. The Greeks will return (to the Church)...there will be one fold, one shepherd.[320]

Everyone (Catholic or otherwise) should be careful, compare their teachings with the Bible, pray to God, and not accept doctrines that are unbiblical for the sake of this coming ecumenical unity.

Might Some Type of a Cross Symbol Be Involved?

It is possible that a symbol common to the Catholics, Orthodox, Protestants, and other religions (a cross) might become used as a unifying factor for this ecumenical religion.

Popular authors J. Weidner and V. Bridges have claimed that when they have examined the St. Andrew's Cross, it somehow points to the year 2012.[321] They also claim that the cross is a symbol of the equinox.

And while it is tempting to ignore the idea that the cross may be a symbol associated with 2012 or a falsely believed "age of peace" before Christ's return, there are several

Catholic writings that indicate the coming world dictator may use some type of cross symbol.

But before getting to them, notice the following claims from J. Weidner and V. Bridges about the cross:

> As we have seen, the equinox mid-point is bracketed by celestial events on the solstice, the most prominent of which is the helical rising of the sun and the galactic center on the winter solstice of 2012. As this is the end date of both the Mayan calendar and the Tibetan Kalachra, its significance becomes even more profound. Yet it is the Cross, as a symbol and a metaphor, that has universally held man's attention.
>
> The INRI above the Starburst on the eastern face of the Cross demonstrates how closely Christianity is related to the mystery of the Last Judgment. However, given the interpretation for INRI of "Isis Naturae Regina Ineffabilis," or Isis, the Ineffable Queen of Nature, and Isis' close association with the center of the galaxy, then we might/should adjust our understanding of Christianity to reflect a more Egyptian perspective.[322]

Thus, those not associated with traditional Christianity are seemingly claiming that 2012 has to do with the cross, and that the cross should also be considered as a symbol for the "Queen of Nature." This also gives, at least the hint, that some may consider apparitions of Mary some manifestation of this "Queen of Nature." Mary has been called the "Queen of Heaven" as well as "Queen of Nature."[323]

Furthermore, lest we forget the lessons of history, not only did the "Crusaders" use a cross as a symbol, Adolph Hitler used the swastika form of a cross as his symbol. So, having seen some type of cross as a symbol for a militaristic power in the past, we should wake up to the fact that some version of it may be used again in the future.

Someone calling himself "Brother David Lopez," made the following claims about a message supposedly from Mary in August 1987:

> Before the great tribulation, there is going to be a sign. **We will see in the sky one great red cross** on a day of blue sky without clouds...This cross will be seen by everyone: Christians, pagans, atheists, etc., as well as all the prepared ones (understand for prepared ones not only the Christians, because there are people who have never heard the Gospel, but also for those who have the voice of God in the sanctuary of their consciences) who will be guided by God in the way of Christ. They will receive grace to interpret the significance of the cross.[324]

According to a recognized Catholic saint, the coming new order is expected to use some type of a cross as their symbol:

> *St. Francis de Paul* (1470):...the Great Monarch ... shall be a great captain and prince of holy men, who shall be called 'the holy Cross-bearers' ... on his breast wear a sign which you have seen at the beginning of this letter (a red Cross)...He will gather a grand army...
>
> This religious order shall be the last and best in the Church: it shall proceed with arms...Woe to tyrants, to heretics, and to infidels **to whom no pity will be shown**...An infinite number of wicked men shall perish through the hands of the Cross-bearers...most holy Crossbearers elected by the Most High, who, not succeeding in converting heretics with science, shall

make vigorous use of their arms...**These holy Cross-bearers shall reign and dominate holily over the whole world until the end of time...**

But when shall this take place? When crosses with the stigmas shall be seen, and the crucifix shall be carried as the standard. The time is coming when the Divine Majesty will visit the world with a new religious order of holy Cross-bearers, who will carry a crucifix, or the image of our crucified Lord, lifted up upon the principal standard in view of all...

He shall be the great founder of a new religious order different from all the others...This shall be the last religious order in the Church and shall do more good for our holy religion than all other religious institutes. By force of arms he shall take possession of a great kingdom.[325]

By using the cross as a symbol, many will believe that this order is on God's side. However, their harsh militaristic actions suggest otherwise.

It would seem that the use of some type of cross as a symbol will allow people to think (because they have generally been taught not to fear the cross) that this could not possibly be a symbol used by Antichrist. One of the best ways to deceive people is by using symbols they are comfortable with. Of course, there are divergent groups such as the Living Church of God, LDS—Mormons, Jehovah's Witnesses, and even some Protestants and Catholics that have suggested that a type of cross is a possible symbol of the beast, but they and their views have tended to be dismissed by the majority within the mainstream churches.

One Catholic mystic claimed that "the secret society"

would be attacked by some wearing a red cross:

> *Anne Catherine Emmerich* (19th century): **I saw the secret society...and...** citizens and peasants, many of whom were marked on the forehead with a **red cross**. As this army drew near, the captives and oppressed were delivered and swelled the ranks whilst **the demolishers and conspirators were put to flight** on all sides.[326]

Thus, the supporters of "the secret society" will apparently not be wearing red crosses. Since the army is marked by a red cross, some are likely to twist the meaning of scriptures such as Ezekiel 9:14 as justification for the use of a marking cross to distinguish themselves from the "secret sect".

There is a different Catholic writer who indicates that the image or perhaps mark of the beast may be something resembling a cross similar to the one the Emperor Constantine used:

> *Priest P. Huchedé* (19th century): What this sign shall be time alone will reveal. Yet there are some {Catholic} commentators of the Holt Writ, who, according to a special revelation, pretend to say that it shall be formed out of the Greek letters X and P, interlaced... which resembles the number of Christ. (Cornelius a Lapide in Epis. 2 to Thes.). No one can either buy or sell without that...[327]

Another priest stated:

> *Priest Lavinsky* (died 1708): ...the Cross, to the astonishment of all, will shine in double splendor through many lands because of the great ruler.[328]

So, it should be clear by now that certain predictions suggest that a violent leader, who imposes a new religious order, will use some type of cross as a symbol in the future (other cultures have also used it as a symbol, as shown in Appendix B).

Now, this book is not saying that, based upon Catholic and other private prophecies, that "the image of the beast" or the "mark of the beast" absolutely must be a cross of some type. But, if there is some accuracy in these "private prophecies," some type of cross would seem to be one of the major symbols for this coming ecumenical religion.

Some Clergy and Others Will Resist the New Order, but the Antipope Will Endorse It

It needs to be understood that before the new order's influence is fully accepted, some jostling for position may occur among the clergy of some who profess Christ. The "antipope" will endorse its militaristic leader, however:

> *D. Birch* (20th century): Many of the prophecies speak of the fact **that the Great King at first will not be well-liked, especially by the French clergy... The Great King will be crowned Holy Roman Emperor by the reigning Pope**...A man who will subsequently be known as a great saint will ultimately be elected pope near the end of the Chastisement...He will be heavily responsible for the French acceptance of a king to be their military and civil leader.[329]

> *Gameleo* (uncertain century): The Great Lion will arise when the Holy See has been moved to Mentz, and a Sabinian elected Pope. **There will have been much dissension among the cardinals.**[330]

Franciscan Friar (18th century): **All the religious orders will be suppressed, except one**, the rule of which will be as rigid and severe as that of the monks of the past. During these calamities the Pope will die. As a result, the most powerful anarchy will prevail within the Church. Three Popes will vie for the pontifical throne, one German, one Italian, and another Greek. They will all be installed by the armed might of three factions.[331]

Sister Rose Asdenti of Taggai (1847): During a frightful storm against the Church, all religious orders shall be abolished, except two.[332]

So, a change is expected. Is even the Church of Rome supposed to change doctrines?

Please pay attention to the fact that that the Bible teaches:

[8] Jesus Christ is the same yesterday, today, and forever. [9] Do not be carried about with various and strange doctrines (Hebrews 13:8-9).

According to the Bible, the true Church is not supposed to make significant doctrinal changes—and while that type of falling away has happened with many throughout history, it looks as if this will happen further to those who accept the new religious order.

CHAPTER 11
WHO IS 666?

A famous number in prophetic circles is 666.

Who or what is 666?

While many are aware of the expression 666 from the Bible, some do not know that this number appears only one time in scripture:

> **18**. Here is wisdom. He that hath understanding, let him count the number of the beast. For it is the number of a man: and the number of him is six hundred sixty six (Apocalypse 13:18, RNT).

So 666 is the number of a man. Notice that this is six HUNDRED, sixty, and six. Thus, this is not intentionally referring to someone whose first, middle, and last names have six letters in them. Hence, despite some people's views, Ronald Wilson Reagan and Barack Hussein Obama are not the 666.

The first early writing that has been found suggests that a Roman, or the Roman Empire, is 666, was by Irenaeus (who was likely influenced by Polycarp). In the 2nd century, Irenaeus wrote:

> Then also Lateinos (LATEINOS) has the number six hundred and sixty-six; and it is a very probable [solution], this being the name of the last kingdom [of

the four seen by Daniel].³³³

The late John Ogwyn wrote this about 666:

> The earliest proposed solution to the meaning of 666 is a tradition attributed to Polycarp, the disciple of the same Apostle John who wrote Revelation. This tradition is preserved in the second century writings of Irenaeus. The number 666 is "…contained in the Greek letters of Lateinos (L=30; A=1; T=300; E,=5; I=10; N=50; O=70; S=200)" (*Commentary on the Whole Bible, Jamieson, Fausset and Brown*). Lateinos is a Greek term referring to the Romans. Interestingly, the Greek expression meaning "the Latin kingdom" (h Latine Basileia) also has a numeric value of 666. Greek writers commonly referred to the Roman Empire in this way. The book of Revelation was originally written in Greek, as it was written to Greek-speaking churches in ancient Asia Minor…
>
> The founder of ancient Rome was Romulus, from whose name Rome and Roman are derived. The Latin name Romvlvs is written in Hebrew as Romiith. In the Hebrew language this also adds up to 666 (resh=200, vau=6, mem=40, yod=10, yod=10, tau=400). Thus, in both Greek and Hebrew, the two languages of the Bible, the number 666 is stamped upon the kingdom that derived from Rome

Thus, 666 will be the leader of the revived Roman Empire—an empire that seemed to suffer from a "deadly wound" (cf. Revelation 13:3) centuries ago, but that is now apparently in process of forming again.

The final religious leader of a revised "Holy Roman

Empire" will be ultimately demon-influenced. The Bible calls him false prophet (Revelation 16:13). He is apparently also an "antipope" (in the sense that Roman Catholics would consider a demon-influenced pontiff an antipope).

Specifically, 666 is the number of the first beast in Revelation 13. The Antichrist is the second beast—the two-horned beast found in the same chapter. And as Revelation 13 shows, the two-horned beast works with and promotes the seven-headed (and ten-horned) first beast in that chapter (Revelation 13:11-16).

Here is more of what the Bible teaches about the first beast:

> [4]...they worshiped the beast, saying, "Who is like the beast? Who is able to make war with him?" [7]...It was granted to him to make war with the saints and to overcome them. And authority was given him over every tribe, tongue, and nation (Revelation 13:4, 7).

> [19] And I saw the beast, the kings of the earth, and their armies, gathered together to make war against Him who sat on the horse and against His army (Revelation 19:19).

This first Beast, the leader of the ten-horned power, is the one the Bible warns against as 666. He is also apparently the one that certain "Catholic" prophets have called the Great Monarch or "great prince of the North." The 666 is also the one the Bible refers to as the King of the North (see Appendix B for more details).

CHAPTER 12
THE FOUR VERSES IN THE BIBLE THAT USE THE TERM "ANTICHRIST"

Antichrist is a term that brings some type of fear to many. But who is the Antichrist?

The terms 'antichrist' and 'antichrists' are only used in the Bible five times (four and one respectively), and are only found in four verses of the Bible—all written by the Apostle John.

Those verses are II John 7, I John 2:18, I John 2:22, and I John 4:3. As all of them discuss some aspect of theology, they suggest that the final Antichrist is mainly a religious figure.

The Four Verses

Let's examine the four verses that specifically mention "antichrist" starting with II John 2:

> [7] For many deceivers have gone out into the world who do not confess Jesus Christ as coming in the flesh. This is a deceiver and an antichrist (II John 7).

This scripture says that antichrist is a deceiver who does "not confess Jesus Christ as coming in the flesh."

Was John only trying to say that Antichrist will not acknowledge that there was a person named Jesus?

This seems highly unlikely, as even most atheists acknowledge there was one referred to as Jesus Christ who lived in the flesh.

The doctrines of Antichrist might have something to do with not actually believing a member of the Godhead actually emptied Himself of His divinity to become human (even though that is what happened according to Philippians 2:6-7) and/or not humbling oneself to truly accept Christ to live His life in their flesh.

John also wrote,

> [1] Beloved, do not believe every spirit, but test the spirits, whether they are of God; because many **false prophets** have gone out into the world. [2] By this you know the Spirit of God: Every spirit that confesses that Jesus Christ has come in the flesh is of God, and every spirit that does not confess that Jesus Christ has come in the flesh is not of God. [3] And this is the spirit of the **Antichrist**, which you have heard was coming, and is now already in the world (I John 4:1-3).

This scripture similarly states that the "spirit of Antichrist" is not confessing that Jesus Christ has come in the flesh. It also shows that apparently some of Antichrist's teachings began when John was still alive.

These verses specifically tie in the idea that false prophets have the spirit of Antichrist. Thus, it would seem consistent with these passages to conclude that the final Antichrist would be a false prophet (which is a term that John uses later in the Book of Revelation).

In addition, John also wrote,

> [18] Little children, it is the last hour; and as you have heard that the Antichrist is coming, even now many

antichrists have come, by which we know that it is the last hour. [19] They went out from us, but they were not of us; for if they had been of us, they would have continued with us; but they went out that they might be made manifest, that none of them were of us. [20] But you have an anointing from the Holy One, and you know all things. [21] I have not written to you because you do not know the truth, but because you know it, and that no lie is of the truth. [22] Who is a liar but he who denies that Jesus is the Christ? He is antichrist who denies the Father and the Son (I John 2:18–22).

These scriptures show that while there will be a final Antichrist, even since John's time, there have been pretended believers. These passages also state that if people were true believers, they would have continued with John's practices.

Thus, because the Nazarene Christians have continued with the practices of the Apostle John (like Passover), there is reason to believe that at the end, the final Antichrist will embrace some type of religion that is somehow against those Nazarene Christians who hold to some of John's practices.

Who is the Antichrist?

The first Beast, also known as 666, is not the Antichrist, because the first Beast of Revelation 13 is not mainly a religious leader.

The second beast in Revelation 13 is primarily a religious leader (even though he has political influence). He promotes religious worship and is also referred to in other scriptures as "the false prophet" (Revelation 16:13; 19:20; 20:10). He is likely to be considered a current or future saint by his followers.

It is he who is the final "Antichrist," as all the specific warnings mentioning "antichrist" in the Bible are discussing religious leaders.

Interestingly, there is a Chinese prophecy dating back to the Middle Ages that appears to somewhat warn against him, as it states:

> All negative forces are subservient...China now has a saint. Even if he is not that great a hero.[334]

The final Antichrist would also appear to be the one warned about as the antipope in various Catholic and Orthodox writings. Also, notice the following:

> *Priest Herman Kramer* (20th century): This false prophet possibly...usurps the papal supremacy...His assumed spiritual authority and supremacy over the Church would make him resemble the Bishop of Rome... He would be Pontifex Maximus, a title of pagan emperors, having spiritual and temporal authority. Assuming authority without having it makes him the False Prophet...**Though he poses as a lamb, his doctrines betray him...**His principles and dogmas to be accepted...**it will comprise emperor-worship**...with the persecution of true believers.[335]

> *Priest A. Maas* (20th century): Nearly all commentators find Antichrist mentioned in the Apocalypse... many scholars identify Antichrist with the beast which had "two horns, like a lamb" and spoke "as a dragon"... the Abbot really believes that Antichrist will overthrow the Pope and usurp his See...[336]

> *Helen Tzima Otto* (2000): The anti-pope – Episcopal of the Beast, alias the false prophet...[337]

Furthermore, notice that the commentators of the *Rheims*

New Testament seem to agree with my assessment:

> Antichrist, if he ever were of or in the Church, shall be an Apostate and a renegade out of the Church, and he shall usurp upon it by tyranny, and by challenging worship, religion, and government thereof, so that himself shall be adored in all the Churches of the world which he list to leave standing for his honor. And this is to sit in the temple or against the Temple of God, as some interpret. If any Pope did ever this, or shall do, then let the Adversaries call him Antichrist.[338]

Thus, from biblical and other perspectives, it appears that the false prophet/final Antichrist may be a future demon-influenced "pope."

The final Antichrist is likely to be one who changes, though he does not clearly seem to be changing, the "Catholic" religion. It seems that this is the individual who has been warned against in both biblical and private Catholic prophecies.

Pope Benedict XVI is Not the Antichrist.

There is one point that should be made clear at this stage. When this book is referring to the future that occurs starting with the fulfillment of the deal that begins the seven years of Daniel 9:27 and the future "Catholic" religion, it is not saying that all who are now Catholics are currently supportive of the final religion of the final Beast.

To the contrary, I believe that most Catholics, if they truly understood it, would oppose it, as well as other changes they have adopted to alter the original faith. Actually, that was my original motivation for this book. After a visit to Vatican City a few years back, I prayed about how I could help warn Catholics (then I later added everyone else) about those "things which must shortly take place" (Revelation 1:1).

I also want to make it clear that I do not believe that Pope Benedict XVI is the final prophesied Antichrist any more than Martin Luther was. Nor unless some bizarre supernatural event occurs, will Pope Benedict XVI become the final Antichrist.

However, Pope Benedict XVI has inadvertently pursued policies that likely will allow for the rise of an antipope. This "antipope" (who may or not be the next pontiff) may be the final Antichrist that the Bible warns about.

The Antichrist, along with the Beast of Revelation, will change the current Catholic faith into a persecuting ecumenical form that many (including most non-Catholics) will sadly follow.

There will, however, be a great multitude of people of all backgrounds that will decide to follow the teachings of the "secret sect" that the Beast and the Antichrist will warn against:

> [9] After these things I looked, and behold, a great multitude which no one could number, of all nations, tribes, peoples, and tongues, standing before the throne and before the Lamb, clothed with white robes, with palm branches in their hands, [10] and crying out with a loud voice, saying, "Salvation belongs to our God who sits on the throne, and to the Lamb!" (Revelation 7:9-10).

And it is my hope and prayer that this book will be one influence in encouraging every person in the world, irrespective of their current religious affiliation (or lack thereof), to at some time (now would be good) support the work of God as advocated by the most faithful Nazarene sect, and not follow the soon-coming final Antichrist.

CHAPTER 13
THERE WILL BE TWO WITNESSES: WILL YOU PAY ATTENTION?

God will raise up His Church to do a short work (Romans 9:28) that will proclaim "gospel of the kingdom…in all the world as a witness to all the nations, and then the end will come" (Matthew 24:14). Even during the Great Tribulation, God will not be done with His witness to the world.

God will raise up two witnesses (apparently from the "secret sect") to continue to preach His messages. This chapter will attempt to provide biblical and non-biblical information that seems to discuss those witnesses.

First From the Bible

The Bible teaches the following about the two witnesses,

> [3] And I will give power to my two witnesses, and they will prophesy one thousand two hundred and sixty days, clothed in sackcloth." [4] These are the two olive trees and the two lampstands standing before the God of the earth. [5] And if anyone wants to harm them, fire proceeds from their mouth and devours their enemies. And if anyone wants to harm them, he must be killed in this manner. [6] These have power to shut heaven, so that no rain falls in the days of their prophecy; and they have power over waters to turn them to blood,

and to strike the earth with all plagues, as often as they desire.

⁷ Now when they finish their testimony, the beast that ascends out of the bottomless pit will make war against them, overcome them, and kill them. ⁸ And their dead bodies will lie in the street of the great city which spiritually is called Sodom and Egypt, where also our Lord was crucified. ⁹ Then those from the peoples, tribes, tongues, and nations will see their dead bodies three-and-a-half days, and not allow their dead bodies to be put into graves. ¹⁰ And those who dwell on the earth will rejoice over them, make merry, and send gifts to one another, because these two prophets tormented those who dwell on the earth.

¹¹ Now after the three-and-a-half days the breath of life from God entered them, and they stood on their feet, and great fear fell on those who saw them. ¹² And they heard a loud voice from heaven saying to them, "Come up here." And they ascended to heaven in a cloud, and their enemies saw them. ¹³ In the same hour there was a great earthquake, and a tenth of the city fell. In the earthquake seven thousand men were killed, and the rest were afraid and gave glory to the God of heaven. ¹⁴ The second woe is past. Behold, the third woe is coming quickly.

¹⁵ Then the seventh angel sounded: And there were loud voices in heaven, saying, "The kingdoms of this world have become the kingdoms of our Lord and of His Christ, and He shall reign forever and ever!" (Revelation 11:3-15).

Notice that for one thousand two hundred and sixty days (about 42 months) God raises up two witnesses to prophecy. They will proclaim the good news of Christ and His coming kingdom.

They are referred to as "two olive trees" and "two lampstands." They are clothed in sackcloth and perform miracles. Some try to kill them. And although God allows miracles to protect them, God will ultimately allow them to be killed. Three- and-one-half days after they are killed, a major earthquake happens. And shortly thereafter, the kingdom of God is established.

Interestingly, the Book of Revelation refers to the seven Churches as lampstands (Revelation 1:20), and the two witnesses as "two lampstands," hence the two witnesses seem to represent the Church. Clearly their prophesying must include the good news of the soon-coming millennial kingdom of God—as that is some of what Jesus expected the Church to do before the end would come (Matthew 24:14).

Because God identifies the two witnesses as "two olive trees," we should look at another place in the Bible that also discusses "two olive trees." Notice (**bolding** mine):

> 4:1 Now the angel who talked with me came back and wakened me, as a man who is wakened out of his sleep. 2 And he said to me, "What do you see?" So I said, "I am looking, and **there is a lampstand** of solid gold with a bowl on top of it, and on the stand seven lamps with seven pipes to the seven lamps. 3 **Two olive trees are by it**, one at the right of the bowl and the other at its left." 4 So I answered and spoke to the angel who talked with me, saying, "What are these, my lord?" 5 Then the angel who talked with me answered and said to me, "Do you not know what these are?" And I said, "No, my lord."

⁶ So he answered and said to me: "This is the word of the LORD to Zerubbabel: 'Not by might nor by power, but by My Spirit, 'Says the LORD of hosts. ⁷ 'Who are you, O great mountain? Before Zerubbabel you shall become a plain! And he shall bring forth the capstone With shouts of "Grace, grace to it!" ' "

⁸ Moreover the word of the LORD came to me, saying: ⁹ "The hands of Zerubbabel Have laid the foundation of this temple; His hands shall also finish it. Then you will know That the LORD of hosts has sent Me to you. ¹⁰ For who has despised the day of small things? For these seven rejoice to see The plumb line in the hand of Zerubbabel. They are the eyes of the LORD, Which scan to and fro throughout the whole earth."

¹¹ Then I answered and said to him, **"What are these two olive trees—at the right of the lampstand and at its left?"** ¹² And I further answered and said to him, "What are these two olive branches that drip into the receptacles of the two gold pipes from which the golden oil drains?" ¹³ Then he answered me and said, "Do you not know what these are?" And I said, "No, my lord." ¹⁴ So he said, **"These are the two anointed ones, who stand beside the Lord of the whole earth"** (Zechariah 4:1-14).

Thus, it appears that the Hebrew scriptures support the concept that the two witnesses are two who stand by God ("anointed" is not in the Hebrew) and the faithful church (the lampstand, cf. Revelation 1:20;2:5). Because the above scripture is prophetic, it would seem that the "two olive trees...standing beside the Lord of the whole earth" are two men currently on earth who are supporting the work of God.

Enoch and Elijah or Possibly a Type of Moses and Elijah?

Many who have looked into who the two witnesses might be like have indicated that they either are like Enoch and Elijah, or they are like Moses and Elijah.

A third century Catholic saint named Victorinus mentions that several have been considered as the two witnesses, but that he seems to lean towards Elijah as one of them:

> "...I will give to my two witnesses, and they shall predict a thousand two hundred and threescore days clothed in sackcloth." That is, three years and six months: these make forty-two months. Therefore their preaching is three years and six months, and the kingdom of Antichrist as much again...Many think that there is Elisha, or Moses, with Elijah..."These are the two candlesticks standing before the Lord of the earth." These two candlesticks and two olive trees He has to this end spoken of, and admonished you that if, when you have read of them elsewhere, you have not understood, you may understand here. For in Zechariah, one of the twelve prophets, it is thus written: "These are the two olive trees and two candlesticks which stand in the presence of the Lord of the earth;" that is, they are in paradise. Also, in another sense, standing in the presence of the lord of the earth, that is, in the presence of Antichrist. Therefore they must be slain by Antichrist.[339]

In the fourth century Cyril of Jerusalem called Moses and Elias (Elijah) two witnesses of Christ, but not necessarily as the final two witnesses. Notice:

> Nay more, we produce two witnesses, those who stood before Lord on Mount Sinai: Moses was in a cleft

of the rock, and Elias was once in a cleft of the rock: they being present with Him at His Transfiguration on Mount Tabor.[340]

A 21st century Roman Catholic theologian, W. Kurz, also supports the position that the two witnesses are like Moses and Elijah:

> John then prophesies about two witnesses...They have much in common with the Old Testament prophets Moses and Elijah.[341]

Priest Kurz is correct on the above. And while it is likely that one or both of the two witnesses will have something in common with Enoch, Enoch will not literally be one of the two witnesses.

The two witnesses are to a degree *like* Moses and Elijah. As John the Baptist was a type of Elijah (Matthew 11:12–14; Luke 1:17), and there is an Elijah to come (Matthew 17:11; Malachi 4:4–6), it would seem that one of the witnesses would also come "in the Spirit and power of Elijah" (Luke 1:17).

But irrespective of who they may be most like, the fact is that God will raise up His two witnesses at the end.

Two Witnesses Will Be Against the False Prophet

The Bible, as quoted earlier, suggests that the two witnesses will be prophesying and apparently helping convert (Revelation 7:9-14) people during the time of the Beast and the False Prophet (cf. Revelation 11:7, 16:13). And they will tell the world that Jesus will be coming to reign on the earth.

Interestingly this is consistent with what some Catholic writers have also written:

> *Priest H. Kramer* (20th century): The Two Witnesses

in our text will have the function of restoring all things...Perhaps at the time of the Two Witnesses all governments will be hostile to the Church...**Their office**, symbolized by the sevenfold candlestick and the seven golden lampstands, **is to enlighten the Church and the world by preaching and example to restore God's kingdom on earth**...By their testimony the Two Witnesses will reap for themselves the hatred of Christ's enemies, for they will expose heresies and discredit them to absurdity and lead to the truth all who sincerely seek it...The False Prophet will even outdo the Two Prophets...[342]

Which church will governments be hostile to—the ecumenical one that the world will follow (Revelation 13:3-4) or a Nazarene one?

Obviously, the governments will be hostile to the church that the two witnesses come from.

Sadly, there are "Catholic" (and "Orthodox") writings that seem to warn against the two witnesses (sometimes more focused on one of them):

> *Catholic writer Desmond Birch* (20th century): "The "False Prophet" arrives — the Precursor of Antichrist. He will "ape" the role that John the Baptist performed in preparing the people for the arrival of the Messiah.[343]
>
> *St. Vincent Ferr* (15th century)..."In the days... —before the end of the world —Christians shall be so lax in their religion that they will refuse the sacrament of Confirmation, saying it is unnecessary. And **when the false prophet, the precursor of Antichrist, comes, all who are not confirmed will apostatize**, while those who are confirmed will stand fast in their faith, and

only a few will renounce Christ.[344]

Jeanne le Royer (18th century, Sister of the Nativity): One day the Lord said to me: 'A few years before the coming of my enemy, **Satan will raise up false prophets who will announce Antichrist as the true Messiah**, and they will try to destroy all our Christian beliefs. And I shall make the children and the old people prophesy. The closer we get to the reign of Antichrist, the more will the darkness of Satan spread over the earth, and the more will his satellites increase their efforts to trap the faithful in their nets.[345]

Blessed Hieronymus Agathaghelos (1279): And lo, an evil assembly of the crafty leader, dressed in black mourning apparel...those who were taking in a most hypocritical manner the most holy name of Christ... those were the most filthy citizens of Pentapolis...these are semi-godless men...they will have to pay the price before the public executioner of the Sabbatians.[346]

Because the Bible shows that the two witnesses preach (while wearing black sackcloth, a type of mourning apparel) prior to the coming of Jesus and it never teaches that the False Prophet comes a few years *before* Antichrist (in any significant way), then these writers have appeared to have condemned the ones that will be God's witnesses (who are both biblically referred to as prophets). (Note the translated term "Sabbatian" seems to refer to Christians with Nazarene practices, including their being condemned by Orthodox scholar H. Tzima Otto for "the excuse" their practices are "explicitly mentioned in the Scriptures",[347] hence this persecution by the public executioner is apparently not limited just to two witnesses.)

Christians, however, need to be prepared for this and listen to the real two witnesses—and not believe that they are actually false prophets.

How will you be able to tell?

The two witnesses will have miracles and specifically teach that the Great Monarch and Antipope are the Beast and the False Prophet that the Bible warns against (Revelation 16:13-14). They will point out that the Beast will destroy many nations. Will you listen to them before or after those nations are destroyed?

Will you support God's true witnesses or accept the ecumenical beast power? There really will be little other choice (though certain nations will ultimately revolt against the Beast).

The Little Black Man and Black Church

Oddly, there are some mystics who seem to indicate that the two witnesses themselves are against the final ecumenical "Catholic" faith.

The following is one of few places in "Catholic" prophecies that is an objection to *two* specific individuals towards the time of the end that seems to make reference to the two witnesses (it also refers to two others) (any **bolding** mine):

> *Anne Catherine Emmerich* (October 1, 1822): The Protestant doctrine, as also that of the Greeks, is spreading everywhere. **Two men** live at this time who long to ruin the Church, but they have lost one who used to help them with his pen. He was killed by a young man about a year ago, and one of the two men of whom I speak left Germany at the same time. They have their employees everywhere. **The little black man** in Rome, whom I see so often, has many working for him without their clearly knowing for what end.

> He has his agents in **the new black church** also. If the Pope leaves Rome, the enemies of the Church will get the upper hand. I see **the little black man** in his own country committing many thefts and falsifying things generally. Religion is there so skillfully undermined and stifled that there are scarcely one hundred faithful priests. I cannot say how it is, but I see fog and darkness increasing. There are however, three churches that they cannot seize: St. Peter's, St. Mary-Major's and St. Michael's. Although they are constantly trying to undermine them, they will not succeed. I help not. All must be rebuilt soon for every one, even ecclesiastics are laboring to destroy—ruin is at hand. **The two enemies of the Church** who have lost their accomplice are firmly resolved to destroy the pious and learned men that stand in their way.[348]

Notice that she is warning that during an apparently ecumenical time, a church will be affected by the Greeks (the Orthodox) and the Protestants. Hence during that time, she says two that are opposed to this ecumenical church system will rise up.

Now, the "little black man in Rome" (which is not "his own country") is probably not actually Negroid in race (at least two Catholic commentators indicated he was some type of Caucasian). This is because a dark/black church is spoken about there and in other places,[349] and the term *black* in some Catholic writings[350] appears to mean one contrary to or outside of the Roman Church. Furthermore because the two witnesses seem to wear some black cloth (as sackcloth is black per Isaiah 50:3) and certain Catholic "prophecies" warn against biblical events, it appears that the above is a warning against God's two witnesses.

But irrespective of why "black" is mentioned, notice that

Anne Catherine Emmerich warns about "two enemies of the Church." These would be enemies of the ecumenical church.

The term "little" could suggest relationship to the Philadelphia remnant church (as it has "a little strength," per Revelation 3:8), but possibly this suggests someone who is not portly in girth or tall in height. Therefore, at least one of the individuals that Nun Emmerich warns about is possibly short in stature. Another Catholic prophecy indicates that those who are "taller" are defenders of the Catholic Church and the successors of the apostles, hence "little" may be intended as a metaphor. [351]

As far as having their "employees everywhere" and having "agents," these "employees" may include some people recently converted into Christianity (possibly out of the ecumenical "Catholic" or other religions) or some Christian people who did not flee to protection with the Philadelphians. The term "the new black church" would possibly be some version of either the Philadelphians or the combination of those Christians who did not flee and those newly converted individuals (Revelation 7:9-14).

Of course, private Catholic prophecies cannot be completely relied upon. Even the Roman Catholic Church teaches that they generally do not have to be accepted by faithful Catholics, so perhaps no writer gets killed as the above passage from Nun Emmerich states, and perhaps other details will not be fulfilled in a manner anywhere near what is written.

However, it does seem that this is a warning against those who will be the actual two witnesses, as well as perhaps those who may assist them.

Because the Bible records that various prophets may have made statements that are not in the scriptures themselves, any potentially accurate predictions that "Catholic private prophecies" may contain probably came from a spirit entity with knowledge of those statements.

Nun Emmerich also claimed:

> I see the Church alone, forsaken by all and around her strife, misery, hatred, treason, resentment, total blindness. I see messengers sent on all sides from a dark central point that issue from their mouths like black vapor, enkindling in the breast of their hearers rage and hatred...The situation is terrible! May God have mercy! How much I have prayed! O city! O city, (*Rome*) with what art thou threatened! The storm approaches—be on thy guard![352]

So Nun Emmerich sees messengers with something like a black vapor from their mouths. This may be a reference to the two witnesses, as well as problems for the revised "Church of Rome."

She also claimed (**bolding** mine):

> If the wicked party knew their own great strength, they would even now make their attack. I fear that the Holy Father will suffer many tribulations before his death, for I see the **black counterfeit church** gaining ground, I see its fatal influence on the public.[353]

Hence there is prophesied to be a church that gains influence (some version of the secret sect) and that this causes distress at least to the Pope. It is called both black and counterfeit—this may be because the true two witnesses are objecting to the antipope (or possibly that she is warning against the final ecumenical church).

Other Writings that Suggest that the Two Witnesses are

Nazarene Christians

Nun Emmerich also claimed (the *italics* are in the text cited):

> I saw the *black fellow* plotting again, the destroyers attacking the Church of Peter, Mary standing with her mantle over it, and the enemies of God put to flight. I saw Sts. Peter and Paul laboring actively for the Church and their basilica greatly enlarged. Then I saw darkness spreading around and people no longer seeking the true Church...I saw over the city terrible evils from the north...
>
> I continued my journey eastward over the sea into a cold country...the inhabitants were all staunch Protestants...I saw *the fellow* lurking near the shining place.[354]
>
> Nov. 15, 1819...I saw many people in Rome deeply saddened by the intrigues of **the *black man*, who looks like a Jew**.[355]

Original Nazarene Christians tended to "look like a Jew" to various historical Catholic writers. Also, Catholic writers sometimes refer to modern Nazarene Christians as Protestant (even though they trace their history prior to the Protestant Reformation). Many Catholics tend to classify almost all who refuse to accept modern Catholic doctrine, yet profess Christ, as Protestant. Catholic writings tend to indicate that "the shining place" is their church—though it would likely be a modified church calling itself Catholic at that time.

Also, note the following odd statement about the two witnesses from a Protestant commentary:

> *Matthew Henry's Commentary*: **Some think two**

witnesses are Enoch and Elias, who are to return to the earth for a time: others, the church of the **believing Jews** and that of the Gentiles.[356]

So although it seems to be a stretch, it is possible that some Protestant commentator had some historical influence to suggest that the witnesses may be churches or individuals, like "believing Jews."

However, it is possible that one of the two witnesses will be a converted Gentile, while the other may be primarily of Israelite ethnicity who was brought up in a Nazarene church. Why might that be so?

Two reasons. First, recall that the Bible refers to the witnesses as two olive branches (Zechariah 4:12). And second, notice that the Apostle Paul discusses two different types of branches in the New Testament—converted Gentiles as well as Israelites who accepted Christ:

> [11] But through their fall, to provoke them to jealousy, salvation has come to the Gentiles...[16] For if the firstfruit is holy, the lump is also holy; and if the root is holy, so are the branches. [17] And if some of the branches were broken off, and you, being a wild olive tree, were grafted in among them, and with them became a partaker of the root and fatness of the olive tree, [18] do not boast against the branches. But if you do boast, remember that you do not support the root, but the root supports you. [19] You will say then, "Branches were broken off that I might be grafted in." [20] Well said. Because of unbelief they were broken off, and you stand by faith. Do not be haughty, but fear...[22] Otherwise you also will be cut off...[24] For if you were cut out of the olive tree which is wild by nature, and were grafted contrary to nature into a cultivated olive

tree, how much more will these, who are natural branches, be grafted into their own olive tree? ²⁵ For I do not desire, brethren, that you should be ignorant of this mystery, lest you should be wise in your own opinion, that blindness in part has happened to Israel until the fullness of the Gentiles has come in. ²⁶ And so all Israel will be saved (Romans 11:11,16–20,22,24–26).

Hence, because the two witnesses are referred to as two branches, and there are Gentile and Israelite branches in the true Church, it is possible that one of the two witnesses will be of predominantly Gentile stock who converted to biblical Christianity, while the other may be one of predominantly Israelite stock brought up in biblical Christianity. Although this is not absolutely certain, it seems to be a biblical possibility.

Furthermore, notice the following from the Bible that might give a clue about some of the clothing of the witnesses:

> ³ I clothe the heavens with blackness, And I make sackcloth their covering (Isaiah 50:3).
>
> ¹² I looked when He opened the sixth seal, and behold, there was a great earthquake; and the sun became black as sackcloth of hair, and the moon became like blood (Revelation 6:12).

The implication in the above scriptures is that biblical sackcloth is black—thus it seems that the two witnesses wear some cloth that is black. The implication from *Matthew Henry's Commentary* is that believing Jews may have something to do with the two witnesses. The implication from those sources, combined with the Catholic prophecies, may be that the "black man" is one of the two witnesses, or at least is one associated with the two witnesses and the Nazarene Christians.

God Will Raise Up Two Witnesses

God will raise up two witnesses. They will be those with the true Christian faith of the Apostles, such as John. They will apparently sometimes wear some black cloth, perform miracles, and preach that God will come and establish His kingdom on the earth.

There is a Chinese prophecy that according to Ruan Pui-Hua is expected to be fulfilled during the time of the Apocalypse. Because of that timing, it would seem to refer to one of the two witnesses. One witness may possibly spend more time in China than the other one:

> *Zhuge Liang* (3rd century): Rescuing others from disaster, is only a saint…From extreme disaster is born hope.[357]

A great multitude, made up of people of all nations (including the Chinese), will understand the messages of hope from the two witnesses.

The millennial hope will be one of the defining differences between the two witnesses and combined the Beast/Antichrist power during the 3 1/2 years that the two witnesses have been given the power from God.

The Beast and the False Prophet will oppose the two witnesses, and will have them killed. However, the witnesses will be publicly resurrected, and Jesus will return shortly thereafter.

Those who oppose the two witnesses will be opposing God's messengers. But sadly, many in the world who will follow the ecumenical religion will then be in opposition to them (Revelation 11:7-10).

You do not have to be in opposition, however, as many apparently will heed the message of the witnesses (cf. Revelation 7:2-10).

CHAPTER 14
THE GREAT TRIBULATION IS COMING

The last President of the United States, who possibly may be Barack Obama, will help to set the stage for the beginning of the Great Tribulation.

When it starts, it will not be a good time for the U.S.A., or for its Anglo-allies (nor the nation of Israel). Biblical ("sudden destruction" 1 Thessalonians 5:3), Hopi[358], and Kenyan[359] prophecies suggest possible nuclear devastation of at least some their lands.

Notice some of what Jesus taught:

> [21] For then there will be great tribulation, such as has not been since the beginning of the world until this time, no, nor ever shall be [22] **And unless those days were shortened, no flesh would be saved**; but for the elect's sake those days will be shortened (Matthew 24:21-22).

The Great Tribulation is further described in Revelation 6:9-11 (the fifth seal that seems to occur because the faithful church has suffered martyrdom), Lamentations, Daniel, and other parts of the Bible.

What is interesting about that is that if it were to begin shortly after 2012, the fifth seal would roughly correspond to the end of the fifth Mayan long-count calendar cycles, the beginning of the berserk time of beginning of the fifth world of the Hopis,[360] and the fifth epoch of time that is supposed to end when the Great Monarch rises up.[361]

Some Survive, While Others Are Targeted

It remains likely that many survivors of the tribulation (whether or not they believed in a pre-tribulation view of Christ's return) will be part of the great multitude of those converted during the tribulation (c.f. Revelation 7:9) through the message that will mainly then be brought to the world by the two witnesses.

Those who protest against the changes of the ecumenical religion are those most likely to be part of that great multitude.

But who is the target of the Great Tribulation? Here is what the late John Ogwyn wrote:

> Jesus warned us of the Great Tribulation—a time unique in all history (Matthew 24:21-22). The Great Tribulation begins shortly after the "abomination of desolation" (v. 15)…
>
> This future time of trouble will clearly be a time of intense religious persecution, when all will be forced to conform to false religious practices that will be portrayed as "Christian." All will be required to give their devotion to the great false church and its hierarchy, labeled in Revelation 13:15 the "image of the beast." An outward sign of conformity called the "mark of the beast" will identify those whom Scripture labels as the children of disobedience.
>
> There is another aspect of this coming Great Tribulation that is often overlooked. It is not only a

time of religious persecution but it is also identified as "the time of Jacob's trouble" in Jeremiah 30:7. We know that this is identical with the time of which Jesus spoke in Matthew 24:21, because in both places we are told that it is a unique time, a time such as never was before nor ever again shall be. *There cannot be two separate times like that!*[362]

Notice that it is not the world as a whole, but those now trying to be followers of Christ (the Laodiceans mainly) and those who are physical descendants of Israel who are the initial targets of the Great Tribulation. And notice that they are persecuted by the Beast power and those supporting him.

One friar seemed to look forward to the persecution of what would seem to include true Christian sects by the cross-bearers:

> *Friar Francis di Paula* (1495): O holy Cross-bearers…You shall destroy…all infidels of every kind and of every sect. You shall put an end to all the heresies of the world.[363]

Notice what the prophet Daniel wrote about the coming persecuting king:

> [24] The ten horns are ten kings
> Who shall arise from this kingdom.
> And another shall rise after them;
> He shall be different from the first ones,
> And shall subdue three kings.
> [25] He shall speak pompous words against the Most High, Shall persecute the saints of the Most High,
> And shall intend to change times and law.
> Then the saints shall be given into his hand

For a time and times and half a time (Daniel 7:24-25).

Thus the time of severe persecution, where "the saints shall be given into his hand" lasts 3 ½ years (1 time + 2 times + ½ time = 3 ½ times or years) occurs under some leader. This leader is the King of the North.

Some Catholic Scholars Have Changed Their View of the Great Tribulation

What do modern Catholics teach about the Great Tribulation?

First, it may be best to read what early supporters of the Greco-Romans taught. In the third century, Hippolytus wrote:

> [62] The Lord also says, "When you shall see the abomination of desolation stand in the holy place (whoso reads, let him understand), then let them which be in Judea flee into the mountains, and let him which is on the housetop not come down to take his clothes; neither let him which is in the field return back to take anything out of his house. And woe unto them that are with child, and to them that give suck, in those days! for then shall be great tribulation, such as was not since the beginning of the world. And except those days should be shortened, there should no flesh be saved."[364]

Now notice what Cyril of Jerusalem taught in the fourth century:

> [16]... stand fast: *for then shall be great tribulation, such as has not been from the beginning of the world until now, no, nor ever shall be.* But thanks be to God who has confined the greatness of that tribulation to a few days; for He

says, *But for the elect's sake those days shall be shortened* ; and Antichrist shall reign for three years and a half only. We speak not from apocryphal books, but from Daniel ; for he says, *And they shall be given into his hand until a time and times and half a time. A time* is the one year in which his coming shall for a while have increase; and *the times* are the remaining two years of iniquity, making up the sum of the three years; and *the half a time* is the six months. And again in another place Daniel says the same thing, *And he sware by Him that lives for ever that it shall be for a time , and times, and half a time*. And some peradventure have referred what follows also to this; namely , *a thousand two hundred and ninety days* ; and this, *Blessed is he that endures and comes to the thousand three hundred and five and thirty days*. For this cause we must hide ourselves and flee; for perhaps *we shall not have gone over the cities of Israel, till the Son of Man be come.*[365]

Yet, even though they consider Cyril to have been a saint, some associated with Rome now seem to teach that the Great Tribulation was over by the time that Cyril wrote what he did. Notice what two modern Catholic priests have written:

> *Priest W. Kurz* (21ˢᵗ century): …great tribulation… probably already a horrific past event by the time Matthew wrote down his gospel.[366]

> *Priest H.B. Kramer* (20ᵗʰ century): The "great tribulation" is a stereotyped phrase used often in the Apocalypse and elsewhere in the New Testament (Mt. XXIV. 21) for the Roman persecutions. (See VII. 14)....THE GREAT TRIBULATION. The definite article used refers to something which had been mentioned before and

was presumed to be known...This scene is then in the fourth century, when the Roman persecutions had been abolished. "The great tribulation" had passed away to return no more, and since then the Church had grown to grand proportions.[367]

So some "Catholics" claim that the Great Tribulation has already occurred. This is a change in prophetic understanding that is not consistent with the teachings of the Bible or the traditions of the early church. The fact is that much persecution against the faithful Nazarenes began after Constantine's edicts. In the fourth century, Constantine began persecutions against all who did not accept his militaristic view of Christianity.

But the doctrinal truth is that the Great Tribulation that the Bible speaks about is NOT over. Even the *Rheims* translation of the New Testament (the first major Catholic accepted translation into English) teaches:

> **20.** But pray that your flight be not in the winter, or on the sabbath.
>
> **21.** For there shall be then great tribulation, such as hath not been from the beginning of the world until now, neither shall be. (Matthew 24:20-21, RNT).
>
> **14.** And there were given to the woman two wings of a great eagle, that she might fly into the desert unto her place, where she is nourished for *v* time and times, and half a time, from the face of the serpent (Apocalypse 12:14, RNT).

Thus, the time of the "great tribulation" comes at a particular time of fleeing.

Notice that even the notes in the *Rheims New Testament* make it clear that this fleeing is future:

> *v* This often insinuateth that Anti-christ's reign shall be but three years and a half.[368]

The Antichrist's 3 ½ year "reign" has not yet begun (though he is likely to be alive now and may actually have a leadership position for longer than that).

This teaching that the Great Tribulation is past is another change that some who call themselves "Catholic" have made, which differs from early and correct traditional understandings. Some Protestants also erroneously claim that the Great Tribulation is past (though most evangelicals do believe that the Great Tribulation is still ahead).

CHAPTER 15
THE DAY OF THE LORD: WHO "WINS THE BATTLE OF ARMAGEDDON"?

Many who follow biblical prophecies are familiar with the concept of armies being staged in Armageddon at the time of the end and have heard of "the Day of the Lord."

But many do not understand that there is some confusion about the Day of Lord, as well as who will win this particular battle that occurs after Jesus returns to the earth.

The Day of the Lord is One Year Long

What or when is the "Day of the Lord"?

Certain Protestant scholars seem to confuse the "Day of the Lord" and the Great Tribulation. At least one book refers to the tribulation as "the terrible week of the Lord"[369]—an expression that is not in scripture—and also as the "Day of the Lord."

Dr. LaHaye, J. Jenkins,[370] and Dr. Walvoord[371] teach that the "Day of the Lord" occurs after their hoped-for pre-tribulation rapture.

Thus, in a sense, the Day of the Lord is something they and others of their view apparently look forward to.

Yet, the Bible teaches:

[18] Woe to you who desire the day of the LORD! For

what good is the day of the LORD to you? It will be darkness, and not light. ¹⁹ It will be as though a man fled from a lion, And a bear met him! Or as though he went into the house, Leaned his hand on the wall, And a serpent bit him! ²⁰ Is not the day of the LORD darkness, and not light? Is it not very dark, with no brightness in it? (Amos 5:18-20)

As the Day of the Lord basically is a time that pre-tribulation Protestant rapturist scholars look forward to, the above prophecy sadly, will most likely apply to many of them.

The Great Tribulation

The Great Tribulation starts with horrors for physical and spiritual Israel and is also referred to as the "time of Jacob's trouble (Jeremiah 30:7). Nearly two and one-half years after it starts, the Bible shows that there will be heavenly signs (Matthew 24:29) which are then followed by the "Day of the Lord—a time of wrath and anger (Isaiah 13:9). This affects the whole world (cf. Matthew 24:30-31, Zechariah 14:1-4).

While most Protestant scholars understand that the 1260 days and "the time, times, and half a time" refer to 3 ½ years, some (like Dr. Walvoord) wrongly teach that the "Day of the Lord" will apparently only "be a lengthened day."[372]

That position is wrong because "Day of the Lord" itself is shown to be a year long in Isaiah, where it is basically described as punishment for those who punished the church (sometimes represented as Zion; cf. Psalm 9:11; 69:35; 76:2; 87:2; 125:1; 149:2):

> ⁸ For it is the day of the LORD's vengeance, The year of recompense for the cause of Zion (Isaiah 34:8).

> ² To proclaim the acceptable year of the LORD, And

the day of vengeance of our God; To comfort all who mourn,³ To console those who mourn in Zion (Isaiah 61:2-3).

The entire time of the "hour of trial" lasts 3 ½ years. The Bible shows that the Beast power (also called the King of the North) will persecute the saints for 3 ½ years (Daniel 7:25), and portion known as the "Day of the Lord" lasts one year (Isaiah 34:8; 61:3).

The Sixth Seal

The "heavenly signs" of the "sixth seal" are described in Revelation 6:12-17, Matthew 24:29, and other parts of the Bible. Here are some comments by John Ogwyn on this matter:

> When the sixth seal is opened, John sees dramatic signs in the heavens. He describes great meteor showers—so intense that it appears that the very stars are falling out of the sky! He also describes events, resembling eclipses, involving the sun and the moon. The sun becomes dark, just as during a solar eclipse, and the moon takes on a reddish hue, just as it often does during a lunar eclipse. These dramatic and frightening events, accompanied by massive volcanic and earthquake activity (cf. Joel 2:30-31), are the prelude to the time of the Creator's intervention, called throughout Scripture "the Day of the Lord."
>
> At this point, there is a pause in the action before John sees the seventh seal opened. Revelation 7:1-4 makes plain that this pause is for a very specific purpose. Before the outpouring of God's wrath, 144,000 saints from the 12 tribes of Israel are to be sealed so that they might be spared from what God is preparing to pour

out on rebellious mankind.

> A parallel can be found in Ezekiel 9, where Ezekiel saw a vision about God's punishment on the rebellious people of Jerusalem. In the vision, he saw an angel clothed in linen with a writer's inkhorn by his side standing beside the altar in front of the temple. The angel was told to go throughout the city, putting a mark on the foreheads of those who "sighed and cried" for all of the abominations of Jerusalem. In the wake of the angel with the writer's inkhorn, the other angels were to go out as avenging angels to slay the rebellious and ungodly. In the same way, Revelation 7 describes that a remnant of Israel will respond to God's grace with repentance. They are servants of God, and are to be set apart so that they might be spared God's wrath that will be poured upon the children of disobedience during the coming Day of the Lord.[373]

The seven trumpets plagues of Revelation 8, 9, and 11, and the seven plagues of Revelation 16 essentially constitute much of what will happen in the "Day of the Lord"[374]—though certain events in Matthew 24, Zechariah 14, and other portions of the Bible are also fulfilled then.

In addition to the warnings given by His two witnesses for 3 ½ years (Revelation 11:3), God is going to provide a warning of repentance to the world by way of three angels:

> [6] Then I saw another angel flying in the midst of heaven, having the everlasting gospel to preach to those who dwell on the earth—to every nation, tribe, tongue, and people— [7] saying with a loud voice, "Fear God and give glory to Him, for the hour of His judgment has come; and worship Him who made

heaven and earth, the sea and springs of water." ⁸ And another angel followed, saying, "Babylon is fallen, is fallen, that great city, because she has made all nations drink of the wine of the wrath of her fornication." ⁹ Then a third angel followed them, saying with a loud voice, "If anyone worships the beast and his image, and receives his mark on his forehead or on his hand, ¹⁰ he himself shall also drink of the wine of the wrath of God, which is poured out full strength into the cup of His indignation. He shall be tormented with fire and brimstone in the presence of the holy angels and in the presence of the Lamb. ¹¹ And the smoke of their torment ascends forever and ever; and they have no rest day or night, who worship the beast and his image, and whoever receives the mark of his name" (Revelation 14:6-11).

God wants people to repent. Most will not listen in this age, but He still wants them to be warned.

Because many people believe the Great Tribulation will be especially tough on the entire world, they will not realize it is happening, because the Nazarene Christians, the Anglo-American powers, and some Middle Eastern/Northern African nations will bear the brunt of the horrors of this time. Actually, because much of the rest of the world will prosper at this time (cf. Revelation 18), they will not be aware that the "Day of the Lord" is about to come, even though they will have been warned. That is probably why the Bible teaches that "the day of the Lord will come as a thief" (2 Peter 3:10).

Regarding the "Day of the Lord" John Ogwyn wrote:

> John records a vision of seven angels, with seven golden bowls that pour out seven final plagues, one after another. This pouring occurs rather quickly, as

we see when we examine the nature of the plagues. If the second and third plagues, for instance, lasted more than a few days, all life would perish from the planet.

When the first bowl is poured out, a grievous sore comes upon those who had disregarded the third angel's message and were still loyal to the Beast system. Then, when the second angel pours out his bowl, **all the oceans** become like "the blood of a dead man" (16:3). All sea life dies. With the pouring out of the third bowl, **all the fresh water turns to blood,** and sources of drinking water are destroyed. Then, the fourth angel pours his bowl, and scorching heat from the sun punishes rebellious mankind. Next, great darkness comes upon Europe ("the seat of the Beast") and its people are in agonizing pain and heat, engulfed in total darkness and lacking usable water all at the same time. The darkness results from the bowl poured out by the fifth angel.

After this, John sees the sixth angel pour his bowl upon the Euphrates. Demon spirits go forth to bring all the armies together north of Jerusalem. The huge Asiatic army that had previously been massed on the east bank of the Euphrates pours into the land of Israel, and converges in the area of *Armageddon* (Hebrew for "mount of Megiddo"). Megiddo is a hill that stands overlooking the Valley of Jezreel, about 55 miles north of Jerusalem. When the final seventh bowl is poured out, there will be a tremendous earthquake so massive that the very topography of the earth itself will be altered (vv. 18–20). Very likely this earthquake is the same one that is described in Zechariah 14:4, when the feet of Jesus Christ finally stand once more upon the

Mount of Olives, located just east of Jerusalem...

> It is important that we realize now, and in the crucial years ahead, that **God's victory is certain**. This history has already been written *in advance*! Therefore, it is imperative that we *come out* of this world's Babylonish system (18:4), and give our total and true allegiance to Jesus Christ and the *message* that He taught![375]

There are many details, but basically, this "Day of the Lord" is God's punishment on the world for persecuting His people, not listening to the Bible, and not listening to His servants, including the two witnesses or the "three angels (discussed later)."

Whether or not one believes secular scientists who assert that humans are causing "global warming," and islands will be submerged,[376] the Bible is clear that a time of high heat will happen, probably worsened by a solar flare-up of some type. It also mentions the islands being gone:

> [8] Then the fourth angel poured out his bowl on the sun, and power was given to him to scorch men with fire. [9] And men were scorched with great heat, and they blasphemed the name of God who has power over these plagues; and they did not repent and give Him glory...every island fled away (Revelation 16:8-9, 20).

The signs will be powerful. And the Babylonian power will fall during the Day of the Lord (Revelation 18:2). Since the Babylon in the Book of Revelation is a city on seven hills (Revelation 17:5-9), this is referring to a city such as Rome according to Catholic scholars as ancient Babylon was on a flat plain.

Wall Tiles from Ancient Babylon (Istanbul, 2008)

Strangely, there are private prophecies, from Orthodox and Roman Catholic sources respectively, that look forward to the establishment of a new Babylon under the Great Monarch:

> *Monk Leontios* (died 543): Rejoice, oh most unhappy one, oh New Babylon!...You, who are the New Babylon rejoice now on behalf of Zion! New Babylon, dance, bounce and leap greatly, make known even those in Haydes what a Grace you have received. Because that peace which was yours to enjoy in times past, and which God has deprived you of in course of battles, receive it once more from the hand of an Angel...oh, the City of Seven Hills the dominion will be yours.[377]

> *Abbott Joachim* (died 1202)...A remarkable Pope will be seated on the pontifical throne, under special protection of the angels. Holy and full of gentleness, he shall undo all wrong, he shall recover the states of the Church, and reunite the exiled temporal powers. As the only Pastor, he shall reunite the Eastern to the Western Church...This holy Pope shall be both pastor and reformer. Through him the

East and West shall be in ever lasting concord. **The city of Babylon shall then be the head and guide of the world. Rome, weakened in temporal power, shall forever preserve her spiritual dominion**, and shall enjoy great peace...At the beginning, in order to bring these happy results, having need of a powerful assistance, this holy Pontiff will ask the cooperation of the generous monarch of France (Great Monarch).[378]

The Bible warns against being part of the new Babylon (Revelation 18:4), so, a reunification of the Eastern (Orthodox) and Western (Roman Catholic) Churches (likely through compromise on both sides), and the "Great Monarch's" subsequent influence on them should alarm people. On the other hand, one Pope (who may not have understood what he was saying) predicted the end of Babylon and spoke positively about a title (Church of God) that would be used by the "secret sect":

> *Pope John XXIII* (1410): XVI. But on a sudden this Babylon is fallen, and in her fall she is broken to pieces, said the Spirit.
>
> XVII. All this shall come to pass for the purification of the just, and for the destruction of the wicked ; in order to make men honor the Church of God, and fear and serve the Lord.[379]

Interestingly, there are writings that may indicate that towards the beginning of the end-time, the "antipope" (whose "reign" is shown to be for four years below) and the Great Monarch will turn the world into some type of "Catholic" faith, and then there will be problems, leading to destruction:

> *Monk Hilarion* (died 1476): Before the Christian churches are renovated and united, God will send the Eagle (Great Monarch) who will travel to Rome and bring much happiness and good. The Holy Man (Angelic Pastor?) will bring peace between the clergy and the Eagle and his reign will last for four years.[380]
>
> *St. Caesar of Arles* (6th Century): ...there will be a great Pope...This Pope shall have with him, the Great Monarch...This Great Monarch will assist the Pope in the reformation of the whole earth...All nations shall recognize the Holy See of Rome, and shall pay homage to the Pope. But after some considerable time fervor shall cool...which shall bring upon mankind the last and worse persecution of Anti-Christ...There shall be great carnage.[381]

It may be that the above "Catholic" prophecy is pointing to the Day of the Lord—an event that is likely to occur within the next decade or so.

When Does Jesus Return?

The Bible shows that Jesus will come shortly after earthquakes and famines, especially after the great earthquake that levels the mountains:

> [12] Then the sixth angel poured out his bowl on the great river Euphrates, and its water was dried up, so that the way of the kings from the east might be prepared...
>
> [17] Then the seventh angel poured out his bowl into

the air, and a loud voice came out of the temple of heaven, from the throne, saying, "It is done!"

¹⁸ And there were noises and thunderings and lightnings; and there was a great earthquake, such a mighty and great earthquake as had not occurred since men were on the earth. ¹⁹ Now the great city was divided into three parts, and the cities of the nations fell. And great Babylon was remembered before God, to give her the cup of the wine of the fierceness of His wrath. ²⁰ Then every island fled away, and the mountains were not found. ²¹ And great hail from heaven fell upon men, each hailstone about the weight of a talent. Men blasphemed God because of the plague of the hail, since that plague was exceedingly great (Revelation 16:12, 17-21).

Yet notice what a mystic has claimed:

Hildegard of Bingen (died 1179): Immediately preceding Antichrist, there will be starvation and earthquakes...Antichrist will make the earth move, level mountains, dry up rivers, produce thunder and lightenings and hail.[382]

Clearly, those who rely on the declarations of Hildegard over the Bible will confuse Christ and Antichrist.

Depiction of Hildegard Receiving a Vision

Notice that even the *Rheims New Testament* teaches:

> **12**. And the sixth Angel poured out his vial upon that great river Euphrates: and dried up the water thereof that a way might be prepared to the kings from the rising of the sun...
>
> **17**. And the seventh Angel poured out his vial upon the air, and there came forth a loud voice out of the temple from the throne, saying: It is done. **18**. And there were made lightenings, and voices, and thunders, and a great earthquake was made, such an one as never hath been since men were upon the earth, such an earthquake, so great.
>
> **19**. And the great city was made into three parts: and the cities of the Gentiles fell. And Babylon the great came into memory before God, to give her the cup of

wine of the indignation of his wrath.

> **20.** And every island fled, and mountains were not found. **21.** And great hail like a talent came down from heaven upon men: and men blasphemed God for the plague of the hail: because it was made exceeding great. (Apocalypse 16:12, 17-21, RNT).

So do dry rivers, thunder, lightening, earthquakes, the leveling of mountains, and great hail precede Christ or Antichrist? According to the Bible, they precede the return of Jesus Christ (the Antichrist is on the scene by Revelation 13).

Does the Antichrist or Jesus Win the Battle that is Staged in Armageddon?

Most people familiar with prophecy are familiar with a battle that will be staged in Megiddo, and although it is not actually fought there, it is normally called "the battle of Armageddon" (the hills of Megiddo/Mageddo).

Highway sign indicating the approach to Megiddo Junction, nearby Har Megiddo

Here is some of what the Bible teaches about it:

> [13] And I saw three unclean spirits like frogs coming out of the mouth of the dragon, out of the mouth of the

beast, and out of the mouth of the false prophet. ¹⁴ For they are spirits of demons, performing signs, which go out to the kings of the earth and of the whole world, to gather them to the battle of that great day of God Almighty. ¹⁵ Behold, I am coming as a thief. Blessed is he who watches, and keeps his garments, lest he walk naked and they see his shame." ¹⁶ And they gathered them together to the place called in Hebrew, Armageddon (Revelation 16:13-16).

Although the Bible shows that God will win the battle against those who stage their armies in Armageddon (cf. Revelation 19:19-20), a prophetess claimed:

> *Anne Catherine Emmerich* (died 1824)...Antichrist will fight a successful battle at Mageddo in Palestine after which seven rulers, from fear, will subject themselves to Antichrist and he will thereafter become lord of the world.[383]

Because the Bible shows that God will win the related battle (see Revelation 19:19-20), and the Bible never says that Antichrist wins any battle of Megiddo, Nun Emmerich apparently misidentified Jesus as Antichrist.

Another prophetess claimed:

> *Venerable Maria of Agreda* (died 1665)...the kings will send armies to the Holy Land, but the Antichrist will slay them all.[384]

Notice that the Bible shows that it is God and NOT Antichrist who wins the battle:

> ¹⁷ Then I saw an angel standing in the sun; and he cried

with a loud voice, saying to all the birds that fly in the midst of heaven, "Come and gather together for the supper of the great God, [18] that you may eat the flesh of kings, the flesh of captains, the flesh of mighty men, the flesh of horses and of those who sit on them, and the flesh of all people, free and slave, both small and great." [19] **And I saw the beast, the kings of the earth, and their armies, gathered together to make war against Him who sat on the horse and against His army.** [20] **Then the beast was captured, and with him the false prophet** who worked signs in his presence, by which he deceived those who received the mark of the beast and those who worshiped his image. These two were cast alive into the lake of fire burning with brimstone. [21] And the rest were killed with the sword which proceeded from the mouth of Him who sat on the horse. And all the birds were filled with their flesh (Revelation 19:17-21).

Notice that the Beast and the False Prophet both lose that battle.

Yet some writers have falsely claimed that after the Great Monarch (the Beast of Revelation) and Great Pontiff (likely an antipope who is the "false prophet" Antichrist) will come:

> *Venerable Bartholomew Holzhauser* (died 1658):...The Sixth Epoch from the Great Monarch until Antichrist. This Sixth Epoch of the Church—'the time of consolation'—begins with the Holy Pope and the Powerful Emperor, and terminates with the reign of Antichrist.[385]

Yet, the Bible shows that it is Jesus who comes after the Beast and False Prophet, not that "Antichrist" comes after some special monarch and a particular pope.

Jesus will return at the last (the seventh) trumpet blast:

> ¹⁶ For the Lord Himself will descend from heaven with a shout, with the voice of an archangel, and with the trumpet of God. And the dead in Christ will rise first. ¹⁷ Then we who are alive and remain shall be caught up together with them in the clouds to meet the Lord in the air. And thus we shall always be with the Lord. ¹⁸ Therefore comfort one another with these words (1 Thessalonians 4:16–18).

Jesus Christ will then establish His millennial kingdom on the earth. The "secret sect," having been raised up in its entirety (1 Thessalonians 4:16-17), will reign with Christ on the earth (Revelation 5:10) for a thousand years (Revelation 20:6).

This is the final and ultimate "rising up" of the "secret sect." But this rising up will not be for at least several years past 2012.

And 1000 years after this "first resurrection," God will raise up every one else (Revelation 20:5). Yet, one "Catholic" prophet claims that this will happen under Antichrist:

> *St. Hildegard* (died 1179): **Antichrist**...His doctrine of faith will be taken from the Jewish religion and seemingly will not differ much from the fundamental beliefs of Christianity, for he **will teach that there is one God** who created the world, who rewards the obeyers of his commands and trespassers he chastises, **who will raise all from the dead in due time**.[386]

Because the Bible shows that God will resurrect everyone else after the millennium, this is certainly something that we would expect Jesus to teach. This is *not* a doctrine or

Antichrist.

Catholics need to understand that some prophets who have called themselves Catholic (such as Hildegard) are really warning against the returning Jesus Christ, and are referring to Him as Antichrist. Please do not be taken in by that.

CHAPTER 16
PREDICTIONS WILL HAPPEN IN WHAT SEQUENCE?

Many predictions and prophecies have been included in this book. The following is a table that gives an idea of what order these events are likely to occur in. Some events may occur in a slightly different order than shown in these tables as the sequence of some of these events is not known yet for certain.

Table 1: Author's Interpretation Regarding the Order of Predictions from Selected Sources

Source of Prediction	Claim or Prediction	Biblical Parallel
Sibylline prophecies [387]	The "last generation" begins around 2000 A.D.	2 Timothy 3:1 Matthew 24:34
Mayan calendar ends [388] Mayan interpretation [389] I Ching calculation [390]	December 21, 2012 (*I Ching* calculation may be a month earlier); some scoff and claim nothing "prophetic" can ever happen, some look for a flood. These are the times, however, of the last days.	2 Peter 3:1–5

Tibetan prophecy [391] New Age hopes [392]	December 22, 2012. World does not end in destruction. There is no world-destroying flood. Dawn of age of peace hoped for.	Matthew 24:6 Genesis 9:11 Deuteronomy 18: 21–22
Catholic prophecy [393] Chinese prophecy[394] Islamic prophecy[395]	A false peace will be believed by many, while a bad leader starts to rise up.	Ezekiel 13:8–16
Various scientists and forecasters [396]	Odd weather patterns result in food shortages and natural disasters.	Matthew 24:7
Hopi prophecy [397] Hindu interpretation [398] Mayan interpretation [399] Byzantine prophecy[400]	The world is actually in a berserk transition, as the real age of peace is not yet here. It may be a period of chaos. It is the beginning of sorrows	Matthew 24:8
Catholic prophecy [401] Orthodox interpretation[402]	Civil unrest in Europe results in a military leader rising up, with various signs, who will appear to support an old and new religion (note this, and the next event and/or some others below and a couple above, may very well occur prior to 2012).	Daniel 11:27 Revelation 13:1–2 cf. 2 Thessalonians 2:9–10
Shi'ite Muslim prophecy [403]	The great Mahdi will rise up and possibly make some type of deal at first with the West after a "tall black man will assume the reins of government in the West."	Daniel 11:27 Psalm 83:2–8

PREDICTIONS WILL HAPPEN IN WHAT SEQUENCE?

Catholic prophecy[404] Byzantine prophecy[405]	Secret sect rises up powerfully and causes problems for the old/new ecumenical order.	Daniel 11:28–30
Catholic prophecy [406]	Possibly American and/or British ships put on a display of force in the Mediterranean.	Daniel 11:30
Catholic prophecy [407] Orthodox interpretation[408]	Forces of Great Monarch go to Jerusalem.	Daniel 11:31 Luke 21:20
Catholic prophecy [409] Greek prophecy [410] Orthodox interpretation[411]	Great Monarch tries crushing opposition as some listen to the now "strong" members of the secret sect. Some pretending to be part of the sect betray it.	Daniel 11:32–35
Hindu prophecy [412] Catholic prophecy[413] Mayan writing[414] Orthodox prophecy[415] Sibylline oracles[416]	Military leader promotes an ecumenical religious order. An antipope supports changes to the faith called "Catholic." Assyria-Babylon is established.	Daniel 11:36-38 Revelation 17:1–17
Catholic prophecy[417] Orthodox warning[418]	Apparitions claiming to be "Mary" and/or other wondrous signs proclaim that the ecumenical religion is valid.	cf. 2 Thessalonians 2:9–10
Catholic prophecy [419] Hindu prophecy [420] Mormon prophecy[421]	Some who oppose this order will be physically persecuted by the supporters of this ecumenical leader.	John 16:2–4

Catholic prophecy [422] Mayan writings [423] Byzantine prophecy [424] Orthodox interpretation [425]	The secret sect will be publicly perceived to have been crushed. It will flee to the wilderness and end up living in caves claiming that God is supporting them.	Revelation 12:14–16 Isaiah 16:1–4 Isaiah 33:15–16 Matthew 24:15–20
Catholic prophecy [426] Byzantine prophecy [427]	Two men rise up, and for years they cause trouble for the ecumenical religion; people all over the world respond, and some secretly support them.	Revelation 11:2–7 Revelation 7:9
Catholic prophecy [428] Hopi tradition [429] Kenyan prophecy [430]	The Great Monarch and his cross-bearing warriors will destroy the English-descended peoples. This destruction will apparently involve a nuclear attack and conventional warfare, combined with terrorism.	Daniel 11:39a 1 Thessalonians 5:3b cf. Psalm 83:4 cf. Leviticus 26:33
Russian prediction [431] Catholic prophecy [432] Sibylline oracles [433]	Land of U.S.A., U.K., etc. divided amongst various nations. Captives will go to Assyria, which has ties to "Babylon."	Daniel 11:39b Lamentations 4:16 Joel 3:2
Catholic prophecy [434] Hindu prophecy [435]	Asians and some Muslims accept the ecumenical religion. Some will consider this as a time of peace. Heretics and opponents are rendered inconsequential.	Revelation 13:3–8 Jeremiah 6:14–15a
Muslim declarations [436]	A great Islamic leader (the Mahdi) will push at the land of the crusaders.	Daniel 11:40

PREDICTIONS WILL HAPPEN IN WHAT SEQUENCE?

Catholic prophecy[437] Syriac document[438] Byzantine prophecy[439]	The prince of the North will invade the Muslim lands to the South and eliminate Arabic—Islam as a threat. He will amass gold.	Daniel 11:40–43
Catholic prophecy[440] Notorious demagogue [441]	The world will be ecumenically "Catholic." The time under the warring Great Monarch and wonder-performing "pope" (less than 4 years if attacks are not considered to be "peace") will be believed to be "an age of peace." Much of the world appears prosperous.	Daniel 7:23–25 Revelation 11:2; 18:3, 11–19 Jeremiah 8:11–12a
Buddhist tenant [442]	People need to decide whether they should support the way of peace or the warring ways. Some few do truly support peace, many don't.	Revelation 7:2–10; 13:7–17
Catholic prophecy [443] Russian prediction [444] Russian Orthodox prophecy[445]	There will troubles with those coming from Asia. Russia decides to deal with those who had earlier erected the disastrous abomination.	Daniel 11:44 Revelation 16:12; 13:13–17 Jeremiah 50:41–43
Talmud [446] Hebrew tradition [447]	The 6,000 years God has given humankind to rule itself is about up.	Bible verses are in Chapter 9 of this book.
Various scientists[448]	Solar outbursts. High temperatures will cause human suffering.	Revelation 16: 8-9

Various scientists [449] Catholic prophecy [450]	There is some kind of darkness. Islands are submerged. There is turmoil in the oceans.	Revelation 16:10,20 Luke 21:11,25–27
Catholic prophecy [451] Orthodox Interpretation[452]	Great Monarch and "pope" die, and their forces lose at Armageddon.	Revelation 16:16 19:19–21
Mayan Dresden Codex [453]	World is cleansed of two evil figures.	Revelation 19:20
Buddhist prophecy [454] Koran [455] Hebrew scriptures [456] Greek scriptures [457] Hindu prophecy [458] New Age hopes [459] Hopi prophecy [460]	Great leader comes to earth. After evil opposition is removed, a real age of peace ensues. A truly loving ecumenical religion is practiced all over the world. This is the "golden age of peace." Those who truly want peace win.	Isaiah 9:7; 26:12 1 Thessalonians 4:16–17 Revelation 20:1–4

Although there are some differences, is it not amazing to notice how so many predictions are similar, line up, and match others?

At this stage, if you believe the Bible, you might ask yourself, "I am only interested in what the Bible says, as many false prophets have and will rise up, so why bother with non-biblical sources?"

My answer to that would be to remind people that the Apostle Paul quoted Greek pagan poets (Acts 17:28) to get his points across. He also tailored his message as he stated:

> [22] I have become all things to all men, that I might by all means save some. [23] Now this I do for the gospel's sake (1 Corinthians 9:22-23).

Thus, showing how non-biblical predictions coincide with those of the Bible should improve the credibility of the Bible amongst those who do not rely on it. Those looking at the Bible alone may wish to understand that the one sometimes called the "Great Monarch" seems to be the same as the final one the Bible calls the "King of the North." Similarly, "the Mahdi" sounds like the one the Bible refers to as the final "King of the South."

On the other hand, you might be someone who does not rely on the Bible, or at least many of the predictions contained within it. And you might ask yourself, "I have heard a lot of false predictions supposedly based on the Bible, so why bother paying any attention to someone doing that now?"

My response would be to admit that many have misunderstood scripture. It would also be wise to point out, however, that it should be of some personal interest to realize that there will be a convergence of both biblical and certain non-biblical predictions that will likely happen within the next decade. So, do not rule out the biblical prophecies, as they truly contain "ancient wisdom" that is relevant today.

Now, getting to the Bible alone, the following contains a relatively brief end-time sequence based only upon scripture. Some items may not be in the strictly correct order, but it does give a reasonable order for many events. Although not identical, astute readers will notice how well this correlates with the selected predictions shown in Table 1:

Table 2: Possible Biblical Order of End-Time Events

Scripture	End-Time Prediction
Matthew 24:5–34	A generation will experience end-time events, beginning with "sorrows," including the great tribulation, heavenly signs, the Day of the Lord, and finally the return of Jesus Christ. That generation is here now, in the 21st century.
2 Peter 3:1–9,13	Non-believers will scoff that end-time events are prophesied or that Jesus can come back in this generation. But Christians will look forward to His return and the time of righteousness.
Matthew 24:6–8	"Beginning of sorrows:" Famines, earthquakes, troubles—but the end is not yet.
Daniel 9:26b–27	European "prince" confirms a seven-year (one "week") peace deal in Middle East that he will break in the middle.
Ezekiel 13:8–16	Many believe a false age of peace is dawning or is about to dawn. (Note: This could happen earlier in this sequence.)
Isaiah 10:24 Revelation 13:1–2 2 Thessalonians 2:3 Romans 9:28	The sect (Zion) is not to be afraid of this European (Assyria) power to be led by this "prince" (man of sin). Secret sect reveals this deal appears to fulfill Bible prophecy, and with major media attention begins to do the "short work" as a witness to the world.

PREDICTIONS WILL HAPPEN IN WHAT SEQUENCE?

Daniel 11:27 Psalm 83:2–8 Daniel 11:28	The "prince" is now a "king." The Arabs/North Africans also now have a king. These kings make a secret deal to destroy Israel, the U.S.A., and Anglo-allies. The King of the North profits from this deal. The secret sect indicates that the deal is not only financial, and will result in the destruction of the U.S.A., its Anglo-allies, and ultimately, the nation of Israel. This upsets the King of the North, who plots against the Nazarene sect.
Daniel 11:29	The King of the North returns to the Middle East in the South.
Daniel 11:30 Matthew 24:9–11 Daniel 7:25a Revelation 16:13	The U.S.A., now wary of the King of the North's power, sends warships in a show of strength. The secret sect indicates that Daniel 11:30 is being fulfilled. The King of the North is enraged and tries to flatter some who have fallen away, so they can help him ultimately take his vengeance against the secret sect. Limited persecution has begun. Various false prophets, including "the False Prophet" has risen up.
Romans 9:28 Matthew 24:13–14	The King of the North contacts the U.S.A. and its Anglo-descended allies, pretends that his intentions are peaceful, and demands that the secret sect be silenced. The secret sect is often blocked from electronic media. Persecution continues. God allows the short work to end. The truth about gospel of the kingdom of God has been proclaimed to the world as a witness, so the end is about to come.

Daniel 11:31 Matthew 24:15–20 Luke 21:20 Daniel 12:11 1 Thessalonians 5:2–3	It is approximately 3 ½ years after the seven-year deal began. The forces of the King of the North are in Jerusalem in violation of the intent of that deal. The abomination of desolation is present. Some people heed Jesus' words to flee. The secret sect begins to flee. The 1290 days of Daniel begins. Some claim this is peace, but sudden destruction is approaching for Israel, the U.S.A., and their Anglo-descended allies.
Daniel 11:32–34	God gives the secret sect some type of strong abilities to carry on. Persecution of the secret sect becomes more obvious.
Daniel 11:35 Daniel 12:1 Revelation 12:14–16	More in the secret sect are betrayed. The secret sect flees to a place in the wilderness. Allies of the King of the North attempt to destroy them. The Archangel Michael stands up and the secret sect goes to a place of protection for 3 ½ years.
Daniel 11:36–38 2 Thessalonians 2:9–10 Habakkuk 2:6–7a Revelation 11:2–6; 16:13–14	The King of the North exalts himself and his new ecumenical religion; signs and wonders accompany this. The creditors of the indebted Anglo-American nations decide to rise up. The Two Witnesses are given power by God. They confirm the message of the secret sect and warn the world about 666 and the Antichrist.

PREDICTIONS WILL HAPPEN IN WHAT SEQUENCE?

Matthew 24:21 Daniel 11:39 Jeremiah 30:7 Habakkuk 2:7b–8 Deuteronomy 28:42–52 cf. Ezekiel 5:1–4 Daniel 7:25b Revelation 12:17	The 42 months begins, as does the Great Tribulation. The U.S.A. and some of its Anglo-allies are invaded during this time of "Jacob's trouble." The King of the North and his allies win. The King of the North divides the Anglo-American lands for gain. The Anglo-American debtors are subject to death and slavery. Those Christians who are not part of the secret sect face a deathly persecution that Satan inspires the ecumenical supporters to carry out.
Revelation 13:3–5 2 Thessalonians 2:9–12 Jeremiah 6:14–15a	The whole world (other than the Nazarene Christians and their supporters) worships the religion of the Beast, the King of the North. A false age of peace is proclaimed by those who committed the abomination.
Revelation 13:11–17; 16:14	The False Prophet and the Beast (666) try to persuade all to worship the image of the Beast, by using miracles and economic blackmail.
Daniel 11:40–43 Revelation 13:7 Revelation 18:3	The King of the South decides this is too much, so he rebels. The King of the North responds and takes over many lands. This increases the prosperity the King of the North, who will have added enough gold and precious resources to make his empire the undisputed Babylonian power. The merchants of the world will want to trade with him, though this will not last.
Luke 21:23b Revelation 6:12–17	Disasters will occur around the world. There will be a frightening earthquake and signs in the heavens. Some people will realize that the Day of the Lord will begin.
Revelation 8:1	There will be silence in heaven.

Amos 5:18–19 Revelation 8 & 9	The year-long Day of the Lord will begin. There will be signs in the heavens and on the earth. People will fear.
Daniel 11:44 Jeremiah 50:41–43	The vast armies in Russia and the East will suspect that the King of the North and the Antichrist are not representing the real God and will turn on them
Revelation 16:2–11	Many people will get terrible sores. Waters will be turned to blood. People will be scorched with heat. Islands are gone. A time of darkness will occur. Most people will blaspheme God.
Revelation 16:12–16 Revelation 17:16–18	The Euphrates river will dry up. Satan will work with the Beast and False Prophet to persuade the vast Asian armies to gather at Armageddon. . The Beast will also turn on Rome.
Revelation 11:7–10	The Two Witnesses are killed. The supporters of the ecumenical false religion rejoice and celebrate.
Revelation 11:11–14	After 3 ½ days, the Two Witnesses are resurrected. A great earthquake will occur in Jerusalem, killing 7,000 people.
1 Thessalonians 4:16–17 Revelation 11:15–18; 19:1–21	Christ returns and Christians are resurrected. The armies of the world are destroyed. Christ throws the Beast and False Prophet into the lake of fire. Various judgments occur.
Revelation 20:1–4 Revelation 5:10	Satan is bound and the millennium begins. The saints reign with Christ on earth for a thousand years. The secret sect has won.

Various ancient and modern sources, indicate that we are about to enter a turbulent time. A true age of peace will eventually come, but first, an ecumenical, world-ruling religion will proclaim a militaristic "peace." Whether or not you believe any of these sources, you will be affected. If you doubt this, you are challenged to consider that many of the predictions line up very well (as shown in this book), and that is not likely a coincidence.

CHAPTER 17
2012 AND THE RISE OF THE SECRET SECT: YOU WILL BE AFFECTED

A most exciting and turbulent time is ahead.

Apparently in the next decade, there will be a massive convergence of prophecies from many sources. Your challenge is to determine which, if any, you will heed.

And whether or not you personally believe that the Mayan, Buddhist, Catholic, Chinese, Hopi Indian, Muslim, New Age, and/or biblical predictions have any relevance, because many people do, something is likely to happen in the next several years that is destined to completely alter your life. The world economy, to mention just one example, will be different than what people have been used to in the past.

People throughout history and across the planet have predicted, hoped, and looked for an age of peace. While a peaceful age will come, biblical and non-biblical sources are often in agreement that a terrible period of war will precede the peace that most people long for.

As noted in this book, a small, numerically insignificant "separatist" Nazarene sect with ties to Jesus and the original apostles, has existed since Jesus' time, but it has long been subject to both secular and religious persecutions.

And as both the Bible and other predictions indicate, this sect will rise up and become much more well-known in the

21st century. It will explain that while a true "age of peace" will come, war and destruction (and a false "age of peace") are destined to precede it.

This rising up of the secret sect may well become apparent to much of the world in 2012.

But What About the Mayan December 21, 2012 Date?

The Mayan 2012 calendar date correctly predicts an astronomical event. That is part of its value. And there may be a bit more to it.

There are basically four possibilities that most have considered about December 21, 2012:

> 2012 is or is not an astronomical event and nothing else. It means nothing. This is a real possibility.

> 2012 is an astronomical event that accelerates climatic changes—another real possibility.

> 2012 marks the end of civilization and the destruction of the world by flood. Biblically, that is not a possibility. The world will not end by flooding in 2012.

> 2012 marks the beginning of a new age of peace. While not an age of true peace, it could mark the time when the following prophecy is fulfilled:
>
>> "Because, indeed, because they have seduced My people, saying, 'Peace!' when there is no peace" (Ezekiel 13:10).

While some type of an astronomical event will occur (even if it is not a true alignment), weather patterns often change. Some will likely claim 2012 is the dawn of a time of peace, as highlighted in point four. The 2012 prophecies may also be part of a spiritual deception.

Of course, the Bible shows that even people like King David (1 Chronicles 21:1) and Apostle Peter (Matthew 16:23) can be moved by Satan.

While this book is not accusing the Mayans (nor most of the others cited in this book) of intentionally trying to serve evil demons (the Mayans were simply the world's leading calendar experts), the Dresden Codex and various writings may have been inadvertently produced to add further confusion to end-time prophecies just prior to the Great Tribulation.

There are many age-of-peace prophecies from others, such as the Hopis, some of the Hindus, some of the Buddhists, and certain Catholic sources. Some might refer to this as collective thought. However, even the often-accurate Catholic Malachy's prophecies contain some false elements. Hence, caution is advised with regard to putting full faith in these private prophecies.

While a true age of peace is coming, some might erroneously conclude that it starts in 2012 or 2013 or shortly later—but it will not. It cannot.

When the world does not end in a flood in 2012, many will likely discount not only the Mayan prophecies, but any that seem to be predicting any type of a "doomsday" scenario. Because of that, many will discount the warnings that will come from "the secret sect."

On the other hand, it is likely that leaders of various religious persuasions will point to signs, wonders, the stars, etcetera, as reasons to believe that the age of peace has arrived. They will use these as justification for ignoring the warnings from the secret sect.

But people will ignore the warnings at their own peril.

In the next decade, the small Nazarene "secret sect" will

rise up more and more in effectiveness to fulfill the prophecy Jesus gave, as recorded in Matthew 24:14. Ultimately, the world will hear the message of the good news of the coming Kingdom of God on earth, under the rule of Jesus Christ and His saints (which is the ultimate rising up of "the secret sect").

The world will then also be more clearly told the message that a new ecumenical religion, one that is destined to temporarily take over the earth, is in the process of rising up.

The small sect will point out the instigator of this new order of religion (the King of the North, 666). The sect will likely explain that he will ultimately plunge the planet into the Great Tribulation, destroy the U.S.A. and its Anglo-allies, will invade the Middle East, will attempt to destroy/takeover all other religions (Islam, Buddhism, Hinduism, etc.), and that he will want only his ecumenical religion served.

Because he will not like the Nazarene sect warning about his identity and his plan, he will develop a strategy to destroy that "secret sect," and eventually, also those whom it had successfully influenced.

Whether you believe any of this or not, *you* will be affected. Much of your nation will be destroyed, or there will be such devastation in your land, that you will wish you would have listened to the messages from the "secret sect." Times will get so bad that the Bible warns:

> [6] In those days men will seek death and will not find it; they will desire to die, and death will flee from them (Revelation 9:5-6).

We are living in times of major historical interest, as both the "secret" Nazarene sect and the coming anti-Nazarene ecumenical religion will soon face one another. The "secret sect" truly has been faithful to the practices of the original apostles, while the other religion will apparently become quite distanced from those beliefs, as God warns His people to come out of that other religious system (Revelation 18:4).

For a while, this great ecumenical "Beast power" (666) will to some extent take over the whole world.

Jesus Christ Will Return

But despite its influence, the militaristic power will lose. Christ will return. The two apparently most evil human leaders will be removed from this world. A thousand years of peace will ensue, and those who have died throughout history will stand before the Great White Throne (Revelation 20:11-12).

In the final ending after the prophecies have been fulfilled, the Bible shows that there will be two groups. It discusses both as follows:

> [14] Blessed are those who do His commandments, that they may have the right to the tree of life, and may enter through the gates into the city. [15] But outside are dogs and sorcerers and sexually immoral and murderers and idolaters, and whoever loves and practices a lie (Revelation 22:14-15).

A new peaceful and glorious permanent age is coming as the Hindus, Christians, Buddhists, Muslims, New Age supporters, and many others have expected.

Notice that the Bible records:

> [1] Now I saw a new heaven and a new earth, for the first heaven and the first earth had passed away. Also there was no more sea. [2] Then I, John, saw the holy city, New Jerusalem, coming down out of heaven from God, prepared as a bride adorned for her husband. [3] And I heard a loud voice from heaven saying, "Behold,

the tabernacle of God is with men, and He will dwell with them, and they shall be His people. God Himself will be with them and be their God. ⁴ And God will wipe away every tear from their eyes; there shall be no more death, nor sorrow, nor crying. There shall be no more pain, for the former things have passed away" (Revelation 21:1-4).

May God help all who ask to make the right choice about which group to follow when the secret sect rises up over the next decade and more effectively warns against the future militaristic ecumenical world religion.

Whether or not you believe any of the ancient texts, if you are around during the entire next decade, you will likely need to choose between that ecumenical religion and the secret sect.

APPENDIX A: PROBLEMS WITH THE PRE-TRIBULATION RAPTURE HYPOTHESIS

Because many (especially in America) believe the pre-tribulation rapture hypothesis, this appendix will attempt to explain some of the scriptural problems associated with it.

Many evangelicals believe they will be raptured away before the deal in Daniel 9:27 is made, hence they feel that those events will not concern them personally. This is a relatively new concept, as it was never clearly stated in early literature or even in the literature of those who professed Christ in the Middle Ages.

If the pre-tribulation rapturists are right, then there are no worries for those who would be thus raptured. If this is true, it will be great!

But, what if this pre-tribulation is not biblically required and does not occur? Will you have world events "come on you unexpectedly" (Luke 21:34)?

Contrary to scripture, certain theologians who hold the pre-tribulation rapture view claim that the Church is not mentioned in the Book of Revelation from Chapter 4 through Chapter 18, and that this is because of the rapture.

Because of those beliefs, it is my opinion that many have been misled and will ignore the warnings found in the Bible and in this book.

Those who do ignore the warnings place themselves in

APPENDIX A: PROBLEMS WITH THE PRE-TRIBULATION RAPTURE HYPOTHESIS

a highly dangerous situation. That is because the belief that there will be a pre-tribulation rapture and the claim that the church is not mentioned at all in Revelation Chapters 4 through 18 are both scripturally in error.

Second Coming: Does Jesus Return Once or Twice?

The New Testament is clear that there will be a second coming of Jesus (e.g. Acts 1:10).

However, pre-tribulation rapture proponents essentially teach that many of the verses referring to Christ's return cannot be referring to the same return. They believe that Christ will only *almost* return the next time He is seen (during their "rapture"), and then will return about seven years later.

Thus, some believe that the rapture hypothesis, with a later second coming, is the only biblically defensible position.

Notice what was written by Dr. LaHaye and J. Jenkins (authors of the popular *Left Behind* series of novels):

> There are far too many conflicting activities connected with His return to be merged into a single coming ...
>
> Since we know there are no contradictions in the Word of God, our Lord must be telling us something here.[461]

Between the two statements above in their book is a page listing 24 scriptural passages that they indicate support the pre-tribulation rapture and 22 passages supporting the second coming.[462] However in the book, the passages are not actually quoted, just listed.

To show that those supposed pre-tribulation rapture scriptures are *not* in conflict with a single return of Christ (at the risk of seeming redundant), the actual quotes from the 24 "Rapture Passages" are listed below, along with comments on each of them.

Furthermore, some passages that those authors left out are also quoted. And while it is true that the Lord is telling us something, this includes, amongst other things, the fact that He is returning one more time—not that He is returning twice.

The 24 "Rapture Passages"
The authors Tim LaHaye and Jerry Jenkins first listed John 14:1-3 under the title "Rapture Passages." Presumably, those verses and the other "Rapture Passages" are supposed to offer proof that there is a "rapture" prior to the second coming.

Those scriptures in John 14:1-3 state:

> [1] Let not your heart be troubled; you believe in God, believe also in Me. [2] In My Father's house are many mansions; if it were not so, I would have told you. I go to prepare a place for you. [3] And if I go and prepare a place for you, I will come again and receive you to Myself; that where I am, there you may be also.

The above passage simply states that Jesus has a place for His followers, that He will return, and that His followers will be with Him. This includes no discussion of when. Hence, it is not proof of the LaHaye/Jenkins position.

The next listed "Rapture" passage was Romans 8:19:

> [19] For the earnest expectation of the creation eagerly waits for the revealing of the sons of God.

The above does not mention any rapture and is not in conflict with the Second Coming. Actually, because the kingdom of God is established after Jesus returns, it makes much more sense that this is referring to a post-tribulation coming. The "creation" would not be looking forward to a seven-year reign of the Antichrist—which is what the pre-tribulation rapturists normally teach begins right after the rapture.[463]

The next listed "Rapture" passage was 1 Corinthians 1:7-8:

> [7] so that you come short in no gift, eagerly waiting for the revelation of our Lord Jesus Christ, [8] who will also confirm you to the end, that you may be blameless in the day of our Lord Jesus Christ.

The above does not prove a pre-tribulation rapture and is not in conflict with the Second Coming; it clearly is associated with the Second Coming.

The next listed "Rapture" passage was 1 Corinthians 15:51-53:

> [51] Behold, I tell you a mystery: We shall not all sleep, but we shall all be changed— [52] in a moment, in the twinkling of an eye, at the last trumpet. For the trumpet will sound, and the dead will be raised incorruptible, and we shall be changed. [53] For this corruptible must put on incorruption, and this mortal must put on immortality.

The above does not prove a pre-tribulation rapture and is not in conflict with the Second Coming. In fact, it clearly is associated with the Second Coming. Also notice that this occurs with *the last trumpet*. As there are many trumpets that blow during the last 3 1/2 years before Jesus returns (cf. Revelation 8:2-6), there is no possible way that the LAST TRUMPET can signal a pre-tribulation rapture.

The next listed "Rapture" passage was 1 Corinthians

16:22:

> [22] If anyone does not love the Lord Jesus Christ, let him be accursed. O Lord, come!

Again, above does not prove the LaHaye/Jenkins position. All Christians want Jesus to come.

The next listed "Rapture" passage was Philippians 3:20–21:

> [20] For our citizenship is in heaven, from which we also eagerly wait for the Savior, the Lord Jesus Christ, [21] who will transform our lowly body that it may be conformed to His glorious body, according to the working by which He is able even to subdue all things to Himself.

The above does not prove a pre-tribulation rapture and is not in conflict with the Second Coming, because this verse does refer to the Second Coming–for that is when He will "subdue all things to Himself."

The next listed "Rapture" passage was Philippians 4:5:

> [5] Let your gentleness be known to all men. The Lord is at hand.

Again, the above does not prove a pre-tribulation rapture and is not in conflict with the Second Coming. Actually, by not fighting/participating in the military and keeping the commandment against killing, even during the tribulation (Revelation 14:12), the true Christians will let their gentleness be known then.

This will be one way that people will be able to tell the difference between real Christians and the supporters of the

APPENDIX A: PROBLEMS WITH THE PRE-TRIBULATION RAPTURE HYPOTHESIS

Beast's religion during the Great Tribulation.

The next listed "Rapture" passage was Colossians 3:4:

> [4] When Christ who is our life appears, then you also will appear with Him in glory.

Again, the above does not prove a pre-tribulation rapture and is not in conflict with the Second Coming, because it clearly is associated with the Second Coming.

The next listed "Rapture" passage was 1 Thessalonians 1:10:

> [10] and to wait for His Son from heaven, whom He raised from the dead, even Jesus who delivers us from the wrath to come.

Finally, there is a verse that at least hints that it could support a "pre-tribulation rapture." But this passage is not actual proof, as it has a couple of viable alternative explanations.

The first is that while many throughout history have waited for Jesus' return (and long since died), Jesus will deliver them from the wrath to come.

Which wrath?

If we let the Bible interpret itself, it would help to see where this expression is also used in the New Testament. It is included in two passages where Jesus twice warned the Pharisees (all of whom have died) about the "wrath to come" (Matthew 2:7; Luke 3:7). This warns about the future wrath after the last resurrection (Revelation 20:13-15). 1 Thessalonians 1:10 does not need to be speaking of the Great Tribulation.

Secondly, even if it is possibly referring to the Great Tribulation, the Bible shows that the faithful Church will be protected in her place for "for a time and times and half a time, from the presence of the serpent" (Revelation 12:14) while they await Christ's Second Coming. Thus, 1 Thessalonians 1:10 is not a clear "Rapture" passage, as it does not have to be interpreted as a pre-tribulation rapture.

And thirdly, even if it is referring to the final time of Jesus' return, recall that Jesus taught that, "unless those days were shortened, no flesh would be saved; but for the elect's sake those days will be shortened" (Matthew 24:22). Hence, Jesus will stop the wrath of destroying all flesh from the earth because of the elect—not because of some pre-tribulation rapture that will apparently not happen.

The next listed "Rapture" passage was 1 Thessalonians 2:19:

> [19] For what is our hope, or joy, or crown of rejoicing? Is it not even you in the presence of our Lord Jesus Christ at His coming?

This does not prove a pre-tribulation rapture, and is not in conflict with the Second Coming. Real Christians will rejoice when Jesus returns.

The next listed "Rapture" passage was 1 Thessalonians 4:13-18:

> [13] But I do not want you to be ignorant, brethren, concerning those who have fallen asleep, lest you sorrow as others who have no hope. [14] For if we believe that Jesus died and rose again, even so God will bring with Him those who sleep in Jesus. [15] For this we say to you by the word of the Lord, that we who are alive and remain until the coming of the Lord will by no means precede those who are asleep. [16] For the Lord Himself will descend from heaven with a shout, with the voice

APPENDIX A: PROBLEMS WITH THE PRE-TRIBULATION RAPTURE HYPOTHESIS

of an archangel, and with the trumpet of God. And the dead in Christ will rise first. [17] Then we who are alive and remain shall be caught up together with them in the clouds to meet the Lord in the air. And thus we shall always be with the Lord. [18] Therefore comfort one another with these words.

The above is the "classic rapture" passage. And while it is comforting that Jesus will return, the above does not in any way prove a pre-tribulation rapture, as it is not in conflict with being associated with the Second Coming.

The fact that Christians will always be with the Lord does not prevent them from reigning with Christ for 1,000 years on the earth once He returns (Revelation 20:4). Furthermore, because the resurrection of the saints occurs then, *and* this is the same resurrection shown in 1 Corinthians 15:51-52 (which occurs at the "last trumpet") this *CANNOT POSSIBLY TAKE PLACE BEFORE THE GREAT TRIBULATION.*

The next listed "Rapture" passage was 1 Thessalonians 5:9, 23:

> [9] For God did not appoint us to wrath, but to obtain salvation through our Lord Jesus Christ...
>
> [23] Now may the God of peace Himself sanctify you completely; and may your whole spirit, soul, and body be preserved blameless at the coming of our Lord Jesus Christ.

The explanation after 1 Thessalonians 1:10 also applies here.

Furthermore, while the Greek term *orge*, translated as "wrath" is in one verse clearly associated with the tribulation (Luke 21:23), *orge* is most often used to refer to the end-time wrath/judgment (John 3:36; Romans 1:18, 2:5, 3:5–6, 5:9, 13:4–5; Ephesians 5:6; Colossians 3:6–7; Revelation 11:18, 14:10) of Revelation 20:13-15. It seems unwise to insist that the Great Tribulation is being referred to in 1 Thessalonians 5:9.

(It should be noted that there is another Greek term *thumos* sometimes translated into English as "wrath" (NKJV), but it does not seem to mean the same thing, as *orge* seems to be more destructive.)

The next listed "Rapture" passage was 2 Thessalonians 2:1. However, that LaHaye/Jenkins book left out the next three verses, which seem to actually *disprove* the "pre-tribulation rapture" position, so all four verses are shown below:

> [1] Now, brethren, concerning the coming of our Lord Jesus Christ and our gathering together to Him, we ask you, [2] not to be soon shaken in mind or troubled, either by spirit or by word or by letter, as if from us, as though the day of Christ had come. [3] Let no one deceive you by any means; for that Day will not come unless the falling away comes first, and the man of sin is revealed, the son of perdition, [4] who opposes and exalts himself above all that is called God or that is worshiped, so that he sits as God in the temple of God, showing himself that he is God.

Notice that above passage states that the man of sin is to be revealed BEFORE Jesus comes and our gathering together to Him. Thus, because the gathering of Christians takes place when Jesus returns (1 Thessalonians 4:13-18), there is no pre-tribulation rapture.

This also shows that the most faithful Christians will know who the man of sin is. Paul is warning Christians not to be deceived by others who teach otherwise. Hence this passage clearly disproves the pre-tribulation rapture position

APPENDIX A: PROBLEMS WITH THE PRE-TRIBULATION RAPTURE HYPOTHESIS

that the rapture is the next prophetic event that will occur. Obviously the revealing of the man of sin will occur before Jesus comes.

The next listed "Rapture" passage was 1 Timothy 6:14:

> [14] that you keep this commandment without spot, blameless until our Lord Jesus Christ's appearing,

The above does not mention any rapture and is not in conflict with occurring at the Second Coming (the "this commandment" essentially was to keep the faith in verse 12).

The next listed "Rapture" passage was 2 Timothy 4:1, 8:

> [1] I charge you therefore before God and the Lord Jesus Christ, who will judge the living and the dead at His appearing and His kingdom ...

> [8] Finally, there is laid up for me the crown of righteousness, which the Lord, the righteous Judge, will give to me on that Day, and not to me only but also to all who have loved His appearing.

Not only does the above not mention any rapture (nor is it in conflict with occurring at the Second Coming), it specifically refers to Christ judging at the appearance of His kingdom. Amazingly at least 3 of the "Second Coming Passages" that Dr. LaHaye lists[464] specifically refer to **judgment that occurs at the Second Coming** (2 Peter 3:1–14; Jude 1:14–15; 2 Thessalonians 1:6–10). Additionally, Jesus' kingdom begins at the beginning of the millennium, which is *after* the Great Tribulation.

Why "pre-tribulation rapturists" would list 2 Timothy 4:1, 8 as a pre-tribulation "Rapture" passage is perplexing, as it is in conflict with their position.

Do they really think that Jesus will only "judge" those who meet Him in the sky?

If 2 Timothy 4:1 is referring to the Second Coming (which it is), then this would show that Jesus will judge when He comes down to earth to establish His kingdom. This verse, like all those supposed "Rapture Passages," simply includes events that are associated with the Second Coming—not a pre-tribulation rapture "almost coming."

The next listed "Rapture" passage was Titus 2:13:

> [13] looking for the blessed hope and glorious appearing of our great God and Savior Jesus Christ,

The above does not prove a pre-tribulation rapture, and is not in conflict with the Second Coming, because Christians truly are looking forward to Christ's return—His "Second Coming."

The next listed "Rapture" passage was Hebrews 9:28, but Dr. LaHaye & J. Jenkins failed to list the preceding verse which I included below:

> [27] And as it is appointed for men to die once, but after this the judgment, [28] so Christ was offered once to bear the sins of many. To those who eagerly wait for Him He will appear a second time, apart from sin, for salvation.

Not only does the above not mention any rapture, nor is it in conflict with occurring at the Second Coming, but it specifically refers to Christ judging at the appearance of His kingdom. This is consistent with 2 Timothy 4:1, 8.

As Jesus' kingdom begins at the beginning of the millennium *and not* prior to the Great Tribulation, why the "pre-tribulation rapturists" would list this as a "Rapture

APPENDIX A: PROBLEMS WITH THE PRE-TRIBULATION RAPTURE HYPOTHESIS

Passage" is bizarre. It appears to be in conflict with their position.

The next listed "Rapture" passage was James 5:7-9:

> ⁷ Therefore be patient, brethren, until the coming of the Lord. See how the farmer waits for the precious fruit of the earth, waiting patiently for it until it receives the early and latter rain. ⁸ You also be patient. Establish your hearts, for the coming of the Lord is at hand. ⁹ Do not grumble against one another, brethren, lest you be condemned. Behold, the Judge is standing at the door!

Again, another judgment passage that not only fails to mention any rapture, but it is not it in conflict with occurring at the Second Coming—and can *only* occur then. The return occurs *after* the saints have patiently waited (cf. Daniel 12:12; Revelation 14:12-14). It makes more sense that this is a post-tribulation passage, as it would be more logical that Christians will need to patiently wait throughout the Great Tribulation and Day of the Lord, than it is for two billion "Christians" to be raptured, especially because most of them do not even believe in the rapture. If they do not believe they are waiting for the rapture, most cannot be patiently waiting for it.

The next listed "Rapture" passage was 1 Peter 1:7, 13:

> ⁷ that the genuineness of your faith, being much more precious than gold that perishes, though it is tested by fire, may be found to praise, honor, and glory at the revelation of Jesus Christ…

> ¹³ Therefore gird up the loins of your mind, be sober, and rest your hope fully upon the grace that is to be brought to you at the revelation of Jesus Christ;

The above does not mention any rapture, nor is it in conflict with occurring at the Second Coming. It specifically refers to faith being tested, which would clearly occur for those who make it through the Great Tribulation and Day of the Lord (whether specifically protected by God or not).

The next listed "Rapture" passage was 1 Peter 5:4:

> [4] and when the Chief Shepherd appears, you will receive the crown of glory that does not fade away.

Because the Bible clearly shows that Christians will reign with Christ for 1,000 years (Revelation 20:4), they do not need an actual crown *before* the Great Tribulation—but at the beginning of the millennium (Revelation 20:4). Thus, the above does not prove a pre-tribulation rapture, and is not in conflict with the Second Coming; it clearly is associated with the Second Coming.

The next listed "Rapture" passage was 1 John 2:28-3:2:

> [28] And now, little children, abide in Him, that when He appears, we may have confidence and not be ashamed before Him at His coming. [29] If you know that He is righteous, you know that everyone who practices righteousness is born of Him.
>
> [3:1] Behold what manner of love the Father has bestowed on us, that we should be called children of God! Therefore the world does not know us, because it did not know Him. [2] Beloved, now we are children of God; and it has not yet been revealed what we shall be, but we know that when He is revealed, we shall be like Him, for we shall see Him as He is.

Again, the above does not prove a pre-tribulation rapture,

APPENDIX A: PROBLEMS WITH THE PRE-TRIBULATION RAPTURE HYPOTHESIS

and is not in conflict with the Second Coming; it clearly is associated with Christ's Second Coming.

The next listed "Rapture" passage was Jude 1:21:

> [21] keep yourselves in the love of God, looking for the mercy of our Lord Jesus Christ unto eternal life.

Once again, the above does not prove a pre-tribulation rapture, and is not in conflict with the Second Coming. Christ will be merciful to His people when He returns.

The next listed "Rapture" passage was Revelation 2:25:
[25] But hold fast what you have till I come.

The passage above does not prove a pre-tribulation rapture will occur, and certainly refers to the Second Coming.

Dr. LaHaye and J. Jenkins listed Revelation 3:10 as the last "Rapture" passage in their list, but let us also look at verse 11, which they did not include:

> [10] Because you have kept My command to persevere, I also will keep you from the hour of trial which shall come upon the whole world, to test those who dwell on the earth. [11] Behold, I am coming quickly!

What the above passage shows is that Jesus will keep the Philadelphians (see verse 7) from the "hour of trial," and that Jesus is coming quickly. If the rapture were to come prior to the "hour of trial," Jesus would more likely have listed that He was first coming, and then He would keep them from the tribulation, but instead He listed the events in the opposite order.

It is shocking that these falsely labeled "Rapture Passages" are claimed to be in conflict with "Second Coming Passages," as they simply are not. And several of the passages frankly contradict the false "pre-tribulation rapture" hypothesis that the authors were attempting to support.

Instead of actually studying their Bibles to learn the truth, it appears that most who have accepted a pre-tribulation rapture simply hope certain verses prove it. And some people apparently hope that those verses truly differ from those that they believe are discussing Christ's Second Coming.

Notice the following about Christ's Second Coming:

> [11] "Men of Galilee, why do you stand gazing up into heaven? This same Jesus, who was taken up from you into heaven, will so come in like manner as you saw Him go into heaven." [12] Then they returned to Jerusalem from the mount called Olivet, which is near Jerusalem (Acts 1:11-12).

This passage shows that Jesus will end up on the Earth at the Mount of Olives (as does Zechariah 14:4) when He returns. That is not a position that those who hold to a pre-tribulation or mid-tribulation rapture seem to believe, as they think He will not come back to the earth when He next comes, but that He will do that in another return.

Although it was not in the LaHaye/Jenkins list, I saw Hal Lindsey (on his *Hal Lindsey Report* telecast) refer to another passage that he claimed proved that the rapture came before the great tribulation and the final return of Jesus Christ. Here is the passage:

> [37] But as the days of Noah were, so also will the coming of the Son of Man be. [38] For as in the days before the flood, they were eating and drinking, marrying and giving in marriage, until the day that Noah entered the ark, [39] and did not know until the flood came and took them all away, so also will the coming of the Son of Man be (Matthew 24:36–39).

APPENDIX A: PROBLEMS WITH THE PRE-TRIBULATION RAPTURE HYPOTHESIS

Hal Lindsey basically stated that because people would understand that the Great Tribulation has already begun, the above had to occur before the seven-year deal of Daniel 9:27.[465]

While on the surface Hal Lindsey's comments would seem to make some sense, it needs to be understood that most on the world will not know that the Great Tribulation has begun, according to the Bible.

Notice the following passage about God's two witnesses who preach for 3 ½ years, beginning close to the start of the Great Tribulation:

> [7] Now when they finish their testimony, the beast that ascends out of the bottomless pit will make war against them, overcome them, and kill them. [8] And their dead bodies will lie in the street of the great city which spiritually is called Sodom and Egypt, where also our Lord was crucified. [9] Then those from the peoples, tribes, tongues, and nations will see their dead bodies three-and-a-half days, and not allow their dead bodies to be put into graves. [10] And those who dwell on the earth will rejoice over them, make merry, and send gifts to one another, because these two prophets tormented those who dwell on the earth (Revelation 11:7-10).

Even though these witnesses have preached for 3 ½ years, people around the world will have a big party. People would not do this once God's two witnesses were killed if they understood that the Great Tribulation had occurred, and that they were God's true two witnesses.

Hence, as the Bible is clear that many will ignore even the most obvious signs, thus Matthew 24:36-39 does not prove that there must be a pre-tribulation rapture.

There are a few other scriptures that support this position.

Notice what Jesus taught in Luke:

> [25] "And there will be signs in the sun, in the moon, and in the stars; and on the earth distress of nations, with perplexity, the sea and the waves roaring; [26] men's hearts failing them from fear and the expectation of those things which are coming on the earth, for the powers of heaven will be shaken. [27] Then they will see the Son of Man coming in a cloud with power and great glory. [28] Now when these things begin to happen, look up and lift up your heads, because your redemption draws near"...
>
> [34] "But take heed to yourselves, lest your hearts be weighed down with carousing, drunkenness, and cares of this life, and that Day come on you unexpectedly. [35] For it will come as a snare on all those who dwell on the face of the whole earth. [36] Watch therefore, and pray always that you may be counted worthy to escape all these things that will come to pass, and to stand before the Son of Man." (Luke 21:25-28, 34-37).

Notice the following from the Book of Revelation:

> [12] I looked when He opened the sixth seal, and behold, there was a great earthquake; and the sun became black as sackcloth of hair, and the moon became like blood. [13] And the stars of heaven fell to the earth, as a fig tree drops its late figs when it is shaken by a mighty wind. [14] Then the sky receded as a scroll when it is rolled up, and every mountain and island was moved out of its place. [15] And the kings of the earth, the great men, the rich men, the commanders, the mighty men, every slave and every free man, hid themselves in the

caves and in the rocks of the mountains, ¹⁶ and said to the mountains and rocks, "Fall on us and hide us from the face of Him who sits on the throne and from the wrath of the Lamb! ¹⁷ For the great day of His wrath has come, and who is able to stand?" (Revelation 6:12–17)

As the heavens are shaken after the beginning of the Great Tribulation, and humans are fearful then (also the islands moved out of place would cause the roaring of the seas, possibly causing seriously rising sea levels), it should be clear that the events Jesus is discussing come prior to His real return, not as a pre-tribulation rapture.

Does the Church Exist During the Great Tribulation?

It may come as a surprise to people who have actually studied the Book of Revelation, but some Protestant pre-tribulation rapture proponents falsely claim that the church is not mentioned in Revelation from chapter 4 through chapter 18.

Based upon this assertion, they claim that this somehow proves that the "pre-tribulation rapture" is the only viable explanation. Here are such claims from Dr. LaHaye & J. Jenkins and Dr. Walvoord:

> The church is mentioned seventeen times in the first three chapters of Revelation, but after… chapter 4… the church is not mentioned or seen again until chapter 19…Why? The answer is obvious: *She isn't in the Tribulation*. She is raptured…[466]

> …Book of Revelation…The total absence of any reference to the church or any synonym of the church in chapters 4–18 is highly significant…[467]

But the position that the church does not exist during the tribulation is in extreme error in biblical interpretation.

The Book of Revelation most certainly does mention saints (those who make up the true Church per 1 Corinthians 1:2) in these chapters. Perhaps it would make sense to quote and comment on some of them.

Notice:

> [18] The nations were angry, and Your wrath has come,
> And the time of the dead, that they should be judged,
> And that You should reward Your servants the prophets and the saints,
> And those who fear Your name, small and great,
> And should destroy those who destroy the earth (Revelation 11:18).

The above passage clearly shows that the nations will be angry when Christ returns, and that they and the dead should be judged.

It also shows that this is the time when the saints receive their reward. It should be pointed out that pre-tribulation rapturists claim that the reward for the "prophets and saints" mainly comes at the rapture—yet this passage is pointing to sometime after the Great Tribulation begins.

Further, notice:

> [14] But the woman was given two wings of a great eagle, that she might fly into the wilderness to her place, where she is nourished for a time and times and half a time, from the presence of the serpent…[17] And the dragon was enraged with the woman, and he went to make war with the rest of her offspring, who keep the commandments of God and have the testimony of Jesus Christ (Revelation 12:14, 17).

> ⁷ It was granted to him to make war with the saints and to overcome them. And authority was given him over every tribe, tongue, and nation. ⁸ All who dwell on the earth will worship him, whose names have not been written in the Book of Life of the Lamb slain from the foundation of the world. ⁹ If anyone has an ear, let him hear. ¹⁰ He who leads into captivity shall go into captivity; he who kills with the sword must be killed with the sword. Here is the patience and the faith of the saints (Revelation 13:7–10).
>
> ¹² Here is the patience of the saints; here are those who keep the commandments of God and the faith of Jesus (Revelation 14:12).
>
> ⁶ I saw the woman, drunk with the blood of the saints and with the blood of the martyrs of Jesus (Revelation 17:6).

Notice that the above verses show that the dragon (identified as Satan in Revelation 20:2), causes the saints to suffer and some to be killed, while some are protected. And that this is during the 3 ½ year period of time ("a time, times and half a time") that begins with the Great Tribulation.

Of course, many Protestant theologians do understand that the Church is being spoken of in places such as Revelation 12:14. For one example, *Matthew Henry's Commentary* even calls this "a place of safety" for "the church."[468] And even the commentary in the *Geneva Study Bible* of 1599 understood that the church is being discussed in this same chapter.[469]

Notice just one such statement by Jamieson, Faussett, & Brown in their commentary:

> This episode (Revelation 12:1–15:8) describes *in detail*

the persecution of Israel and the elect Church by the beast, which had been *summarily* noticed.[470]

The pre-tribulation rapturists who claim that the church is not mentioned in Revelation Chapters 4–18 have clearly taken a position that is in biblical error. This interpretation is also in disagreement with many respected Protestant scholars.

Catholic scholars, though they have differing explanations, also do teach that Revelation 12 is discussing the church.[471]

Thus, there are Catholic and Protestant scholars who disagree with the assertions of Drs. LaHaye and Walvoord regarding the mentioning of the church in Revelation 4–18.

Additionally, notice what the Bible teaches in Daniel 7:25:

> [25] He shall speak pompous words against the Most High, Shall persecute the saints of the Most High,
>
> And shall intend to change times and law.
>
> Then the saints shall be given into his hand
>
> For a time and times and half a time.

Even pre-tribulation rapturists such as Dr. Walvoord admit that these passages in Daniel 7:25 are referring to "His saints" during the tribulation.[472]

Because these verses clearly are referring to true Christians, it should be clear to any with "eyes to see" that Christians, those who compose the Church, will be around throughout the entire 3 ½ years of the tribulation, shown as the time, times, and half a time in Revelation and Daniel.

Parts of the Church Will Go Through the Tribulation.

Additionally, the proponents of the pre-tribulation rapture

APPENDIX A: PROBLEMS WITH THE PRE-TRIBULATION RAPTURE HYPOTHESIS

do admit that the church is mentioned in Revelation 2 and 3. Yet, they apparently overlook passages in those chapters, as well as Revelation, 12 that show that some in the church *are* subject to the troubles of the Great Tribulation.

Notice what Revelation 12 shows:

> [13] Now when the dragon saw that he had been cast to the earth, he persecuted the woman who gave birth to the male Child. [14] But the woman was given two wings of a great eagle, that she might fly into the wilderness to her place, where she is nourished for a time and times and half a time, from the presence of the serpent. [15] So the serpent spewed water out of his mouth like a flood after the woman, that he might cause her to be carried away by the flood. [16] But the earth helped the woman, and the earth opened its mouth and swallowed up the flood which the dragon had spewed out of his mouth. [17] And the dragon was enraged with the woman, and he went to make war with the rest of her offspring, who keep the commandments of God and have the testimony of Jesus Christ (Revelation 12:13-17).

Thus, one group of Christians will initially be persecuted, but will flee and be protected in the wilderness for 3 ½ years. And another group of Christians that apparently was not subject to the first persecution will have to endure Satanically-inspired persecution for those 3 ½ years.

So which Christians are protected and which Christians are not?

Jesus mentioned two characteristics in the Book of Luke:

> [36] Watch therefore, and pray always that you may be counted worthy to escape all these things that will

come to pass, and to stand before the Son of Man (Luke 21:36).

Hence, only those who will watch and pray MAY be counted worthy to escape.
But who are they?
Jesus later made it clear in the Book of Revelation that it is the Philadelphian Christians that will be protected:

> [7] And to the angel of the church in Philadelphia write...[10] Because you have kept My command to persevere, I also will keep you from the hour of trial which shall come upon the whole world, to test those who dwell on the earth (Revelation 3:7).

But this promise to Philadelphia is not made to the rest of the end-time Christians. Notice further what the Bible teaches about the non-Philadelphia Christians:

> And to the angel of the church in Thyatira write...I will kill her children with death, and all the churches shall know that I am He who searches the minds and hearts. And I will give to each one of you according to your works. Now to you I say, and to the rest in Thyatira, as many as do not have this doctrine, who have not known the depths of Satan, as they say, I will put on you no other burden. But hold fast what you have till I come (Revelation 2:18, 23–25).

> And to the angel of the church in Sardis write... Remember therefore how you have received and heard; hold fast and repent. Therefore if you will not watch, I will come upon you as a thief, and you will not know what hour I will come upon you (Revelation

3:1, 3).

> And to the angel of the church of the Laodiceans write...Because you say, 'I am rich, have become wealthy, and have need of nothing'—and do not know that you are wretched, miserable, poor, blind, and naked...As many as I love, I rebuke and chasten (Revelation 3:14,17,19).

Only the Philadelphia portion of the church (that comes in-between Sardis and Laodicea) is specifically promised protection from the hour of trial which shall come upon the whole world. The three portions of the church shown above not only do not receive end-time protection from the Great Tribulation, they are told that they will go through problems that would be expected in the Great Tribulation. Apparently some from Thyatira and Sardis, and apparently all from Laodicea, will have to go through the tribulation. Hence, it should be clear that part of the church does go through the tribulation.

The "Pre-Tribulation Rapture" is a Relatively New Concept

The idea of a pre-tribulation rapture did not exist until relatively recently.

Notice the following from the Catholic writer Paul Thigpen:

> The secret rapture theory is a novel, eccentric teaching that appeared only late in Church history and has never been embraced by the majority of Christians, Catholic or otherwise. Neither ancient Christians, nor medieval Christians, nor even the leaders of the Protestant Reformation were familiar with the idea.

They never referred to the teaching in their writings, and when they commented on the biblical passages some Christians now cite as support for the rapture idea, these Christian teachers of the past clearly interpreted these passages in ways that contradict such a notion.

In the eighteenth century a couple {of} isolated Protestant American writers and a Jesuit from Chile proposed ideas similar to the secret rapture doctrine, but the idea gained popularity only in the nineteenth century. It spread from a small sectarian Protestant circle in England to fundamentalist revivalists in America, who helped to popularize the idea.

Scriptural texts that Protestant Reformer John Calvin interpreted as referring to the same event—Christ's final coming in glory, not a secret rapture: 2 Thessalonians 2:8; 1 Corinthians 15:20–28; 1 Thessalonians 4:13–18.[473]

John Calvin was correct that 2 Thessalonians 2:8, 1 Corinthians 15:20–28, and 1 Thessalonians 4:13–18 apply to the Second Coming. Martin Luther, also, did not teach a pre-tribulation rapture.

The rapture concept was popularized by a nineteenth century British preacher named John Nelson Darby, who began to promote it in the 1830s.

The plain truth is that the idea of a pre-tribulation "rapture" is a relatively modern invention.

APPENDIX A: PROBLEMS WITH THE PRE-TRIBULATION RAPTURE HYPOTHESIS

The Errors of the Pre-Tribulation Rapturists Will Mislead Many

Hopefully we all have now seen how the Bible teaches that the two primary pre-tribulation rapture arguments (that their "Rapture Passages" are in conflict with "Second Coming Passages," and that those in the Church are not mentioned in Revelation 4–18) are clearly in error. The idea of a pre-tribulation rapture is relatively new and was not believed by the early church.

Sadly, many millions seemingly have been misled by this false pre-tribulation rapture hypothesis. Because of this, many will not understand the prophetic events that will soon come to pass.

An Eastern Orthodox writer observed:

> *Priest Seraphim Rose* (21st century): Those who…preach that "Jesus is coming soon" without warning of the great deception that will precede His coming: are clearly prophets of antichrist.[474]

If there is a pre-tribulation rapture and you are taken away, you will not need to worry about many of the predictions that this book highlights.

But what if no such rapture occurs? How will you feel?

The Bible warned about this. Notice:

> [14] Your prophets have seen for you
>
> False and deceptive visions;
>
> They have not uncovered your iniquity,
>
> To bring back your captives,

But have envisioned for you false prophecies and delusions (Lamentations 2:14).

Sadly, those who have promoted the concept of a pre-tribulation rapture have inadvertently set the stage to fulfill that prophecy in Lamentations. Many other prophets mentioned in this book may have as well, even though they have nothing to do with "rapture prophecies."

The Bible teaches that those who value wisdom can be preserved by it (Proverbs 4:5–6). All will do well to realize that a non-occurring pre-tribulation rapture will not preserve anybody.

APPENDIX B: DANIEL 11: IS THE GREAT MONARCH THE KING OF THE NORTH?

Will the Great Monarch Destroy the United States and its Anglo-allies?

It was discussed in Chapter 5 that the Bible foretells the rise of a leader, who will first be considered as a "prince" (or rising leader), then eventually a "king." And this individual appears to be the same one that Daniel 11 refers to as the King of the North.

This section discusses additional private prophecies. It will also look into some details as to what the Daniel 11 teaches about the coming final King of the North.

Some Catholic Prophecies of the Great Monarch

The following "Catholic" private prophecies show that in the latter days some Catholics expect a future emperor of Europe, who with a major pope (possibly an antipope), will control the earth:

> *Capuchin Friar* (18th century): A scion of the Carlovingian race {a descendant of Charlemagne}, by all considered extinct, will come to Rome to behold and admire the piety and clemency of this Pontiff, who will crown him, and declare him to be the legitimate Emperor of

the Romans, and from the Chair of St. Peter, the Pope will life the standard, the crucifix, and will give it to the new emperor.[475]

Venerable Bartholomew Holzhauser (died 1658): There will rise a valiant monarch anointed by God. He will be Catholic…He will rule supreme in temporal matters. The pope will rule supreme in spiritual matters at the same time. The reign of the Great Ruler may be compared with that of Caesar Augustus who became Emperor after his victory over his enemies, thereby giving peace to the world, also with the reign of Emperor Constantine the Great, who was sent by God, after severe persecutions, to deliver both the Church and State. By his victories on water and land he brought the Roman empire under subjection, which he then ruled in peace…**The Great Monarch will** have the special help of God and **be unconquerable**… 'Golden crown' refers to his Holy Roman (German) Empire…[476]

St. Ephraem (5th century): Then the Lord from his glorious heaven shall set up his peace. And the kingdom of the Romans shall rise in place of this latter people, and establish dominion upon the earth, even to its ends, and there shall be no one who will resist it.

Comment on the above from Catholic writer Desmond Birch: He is talking about some future "Kingdom of the Romans" of a "latter people." [477]

Thus, some writers and mystics were foretelling of the rise of a future European emperor. History shows that European emperors who attempt to establish dominion upon the earth tend to do that through conquering.

Daniel 11:27–39

Chapter 11 of the Book of Daniel discusses various leaders, including those known as the King of the North and the King of the South.

In this Appendix, there will be a verse by verse discussion of the sequence from Daniel 11:27–39.

Why begin the verse by verse commentary of Daniel 11 with verse 27?

Because this book is focused on the rise of the secret sect in the end, and verse 27 is the first place in that chapter that the "appointed time" of "the end" is mentioned.

The "appointed time" and the "end" (in Hebrew transliterated as *mowed' qets*) are terms used elsewhere by Daniel (e.g. Daniel 8:19) to describe end-time events.

In Daniel 11, there is an "appointed time" (*mowed'* Strong's #4150) in vss. 27, 29, and 35 (which indicates the events being discussed are still all in the future) that appears to be for the same specific period of time (this term is also used, for apparently the same time, in Habakkuk 2:3 and Zephaniah 3:18).

The specific word translated as "the end" is the same word (*qets* Strong's 7093) in vss. 27, 40, and 45 (the same Hebrew word, for apparently the same time, is also used in Habakkuk 2:3, Amos 8:2, Ezekiel 7:2–6). Daniel 11:45 is where the King of the North comes to his final end (*qets* is also used in vs. 40 when the King of the North invades the King of the South, which is apparently the end of the King of the South).

Thus, these passages all refer to the same general time period at the end. They have not been completely fulfilled, and therefore these passages need to be understood now.

While Catholic, Protestant, and other scholars are correct that there was some semi-fulfillment of many of these verses by Antiochus Epiphanes and others, as there is a duality in some prophecies (cf. 1 Corinthians 15:45-47), and the final appointed time has not yet come, these verses specifically do have a final end-time fulfillment.

And the proper place to look for the final fulfillment to begin is no later than verse 27.

So beginning with Daniel 11:27 (with the scriptures in **bold**):

27 Both these kings' hearts *shall be* bent on evil, and they shall speak lies at the same table; but it shall not prosper, for the end *will* still *be* at the appointed time.

The "they" is referring to the kings of the North and South, as they are the kings both later and earlier mentioned in most of Daniel 11.

Verse 27 suggests that some type of deal is made between the two—this would seem to be the deal that leads to the fulfillment of Psalm 83. It is highly likely that this deal will be portrayed publicly as a peace deal. If this happens in conjunction with the deal in Daniel 9:27 and comes near 2012, it is likely to fulfill the warning in the Bible about a false peace being proclaimed (Ezekiel 13:8-10).

In his commentary related to this verse, the Catholic Saint Jerome stated his belief "that all these things refer to the Antichrist and to the king of Egypt."[478] Thus the idea that there is a future fulfillment of Daniel 11, starting no later than verse 27, is not simply a modern Nazarene concept.

It may be of current interest to realize that on July 13, 2008, an agreement began to get the Europeans and the Mediterranean Muslims to cooperate more.

> July 14, 2008 PARIS — Leaders of 43 nations with nearly 800 million inhabitants inaugurated a "Union for the Mediterranean" on Sunday, meant to bring **the**

APPENDIX B: DANIEL 11: IS THE GREAT MONARCH THE KING OF THE NORTH?

> **northern and southern countries** that ring the sea closer together through practical projects dealing with the environment, climate, transportation, immigration and policing...
>
> The union has northern and southern co-presidents — to start, Mr. Sarkozy and President Hosni Mubarak of Egypt...
>
> Chancellor Angela Merkel of Germany...called the session "a very, very good start for a new phase in the **cooperation" between Europe and the south.**[479]

This was a news event that for many has simply eluded their understanding of its end-time significance. This "Union for the Mediterranean" even has a president of the North and a president of the South, and while not quite the same titles as "king," the parallels are striking.

Thus, the Union for the Mediterranean States is likely a prelude that will ultimately lead to the deal in Daniel 11:27 and Psalm 83.

Some, including the Jehovah's Witnesses have correctly taught, "The designations 'the king of the north' and 'the king of the south' refer to kings north and south of Daniel's people ...{in} to the land of Judah."[480] Yet, despite the correct understanding of geography, some incorrectly teach that the United States and the United Kingdom became the King of the South.[481]

So let us look at what Psalm 83:3–8 states:

> [3] They have taken crafty counsel against Your people,
> And consulted together against Your sheltered ones.
> [4] They have said, "Come, and let us cut them off from being a nation, That the name of Israel may

be remembered no more." ⁵ For they have consulted together with one consent; They form a confederacy against You: ⁶ The tents of Edom and the Ishmaelites; Moab and the Hagrites; ⁷ Gebal, Ammon, and Amalek; Philistia with the inhabitants of Tyre; ⁸ Assyria also has joined with them; They have helped the children of Lot.

The peoples above are essentially the current Arab-Muslim peoples. Notice that Psalm 83 shows those peoples will have decided to destroy Israel and that Assyria will later decide to join them.

Other biblical prophecies indicate that "Israel" includes more than those in the modern nation of Israel (cf. Genesis 48, 49). For now, let us understand that prophetically it appears that an Arab-Muslim confederation wants to eliminate the descendants of Israel, perhaps through terrorism and warfare, and that the Assyrian (apparently European) power decides to join them in order for this to succeed.

Verse 27 likely also sets the stage for proposing that the Antichrist come to Jerusalem to eliminate Israeli control of that city, as well as to fulfill Daniel 11:31 and probably Daniel 11:39.

Notice that this deal in Daniel 11:27 will be based upon deceit but will result in the end coming **at the appointed time**. Thus, this deal apparently pertains to the appointed time of the end.

Because of that, the Bible clearly supports the idea that ***there must be a future fulfillment of verse 27 onwards***. And this deal, (most details of it will likely not be made public), may be the next major prophetic fulfillment and may happen about the same time as the covenant in Daniel 9:27, or possibly after it.

28 While returning to his land with great riches, his heart shall be *moved* against the holy covenant; so he shall do *damage* and return to his own land.

In addition to setting the stage for a prosperous King of the North (see also verse 36 below), the above specifically indicates that something will upset the King of the North, apparently during a visit to the Palestine/Israel area, and he will return to his land (Europe) upset with the holy covenant, probably spiritual Israel (Romans 9:6).

During the end times, Christians would seem to be the people of the holy covenant (see Matthew 26:28; Hebrews 8:6-13). Baptism (and receiving God's Holy Spirit) seems to be what makes one heirs of the "holy covenant" in the New Testament, (cf. Luke 1:72-73 & Galatians 3:26-29).

The reason that the King of the North may be *moved against* Christians is that the "secret sect" may be somewhat effectively reporting/broadcasting what this deal in verses 27-28 means—as well as what is expected to happen next. It may also have tried to expose the deal in Daniel 9:26-27 earlier as well.

By this time, the short work Paul mentioned in Romans 9:28 probably will have begun or be almost finished, as will the gospel preaching of Matthew 24:14 that Jesus spoke of. This is the rising up of the "secret sect" that various prophets have foretold and hence seems to be consistent with various end-time prophetic scriptures

What causes the northern king's heart to be against the holy covenant, and what he does then is not specified in Daniel's writings. The word "damage" is not in the original Hebrew.

Thus, the King of the North may simply say something publicly, such as threatening to affect the true Philadelphia Christians' ability to continue to broadcast messages such as the threatening the gospel of the kingdom (a message that is not popular, with many, such as the current Pope Benedict XVI, see Chapter 6). These Christians may have upset the King of the North by telling the world in general, and the Americans in particular, that he is apparently the prophesied King of the North, the Great Monarch of Catholic prophecy, and that he will soon invade and destroy the Israel and the Anglo-American nations.

Notice the following translation of verse 28 in the *Contemporary English Version* (CEV) that seems to support the view that the holy covenant could be the true Christians at the end, as Christianity, and not Judaism is now the "religion of God's people":

> [28] Then the king of the north will return to his country with great treasures. But on the way, he will attack the religion of God's people and do whatever else he pleases (CEV).

Hence, the idea that Daniel 11:28 supports the notion that the true church is the holy covenant has more than limited support. The following rendering of this verse from *The Message* (MSG) translation is also intriguing:

> [28] The king of the north will go home loaded down with plunder, but his mind will be set on destroying the holy covenant as he passes through the country on his way home (MSG).

There is something intriguing about the above rendering.

It suggests that the King of the North is shown to have made up his mind that it is time to destroy the holy covenant, at least the Christian message. He may have decided to begin persecution then, interfere with broadcasting abilities, or at least began to think of plans to affect these Christians. These actions are likely to begin no later than Daniel 11:30, if it does not begin in 11:28.

Regardless of the verse that shows when this persecution precisely begins, it is clear that specific persecution will happen through verse 35, and it may include all of the forty-five-day period (1335 days-1290 days), and part of the thirty-day-period (1290 days-1260 days), in Daniel 12:11-12.

This seems to be the time when Satan is cast to the earth. Let us again notice what Revelation 12:13-14 shows:

> [13] Now when the dragon saw that he had been cast to the earth, **he persecuted the woman** who gave birth to the male Child.
>
> [14] But the woman was given two wings of a great eagle, that she might fly into the wilderness to her place, where she is nourished for a time and times and half a time.

This persecution appears to mainly be a persecution against the Philadelphian Christians, as they are given protection shortly thereafter. Yet it needs to be understood that the woman is apparently still persecuted until verse 16 of Revelation 12, therefore, the persecutions of the Philadelphians apparently occurs until Daniel 11:35—when Michael may stand (Daniel 12:1) and the Philadelphians flee into the wilderness.

Even the *Book of Mormon* speaks of a time when a great kingdom will arise with a great church and persecute:

> And it came to pass that I saw among the nations of the Gentiles the formation of a great church...which is abominable...which slays the saints of God, yea and tortureth them...[482]

Also, notice that the Bible states:

> [6] "Flee from the land of the north," says the LORD...[7] Up Zion! Escape you that dwell with the daughter of Babylon (Zechariah 2:6, 7).

It may be that prior to going to a place of protection (cf. Revelation 12:13-14), some Christians will flee out of the lands dominated by the rising King of the North prior to him moving into Jerusalem, probably during verses 28-30 of Daniel 11, as this is when the King of the North begins his anger against God's most faithful. Since God's faithful will apparently understand these passages in Daniel 11 by then (cf. Daniel 12:10), some will not wait until verses 30 or 31 to flee from the north, and will most likely go to Judea.

29 "At the appointed time he shall return and go toward the south; but it shall not be like the former or the latter.

The 'he' is still the King of the North. This verse suggests that the "appointed time" is not only different than any before, but that **this is the specific appointed time that leads to the final end** of both the King of the North and the King of the South (cf. vs. 27).

Although he had other misunderstandings, even the Protestant commentator A. Faucett realized that the deal in Daniel 11:27 is related to the fulfillment in verse 29 as he wrote the following about Daniel 11:29:

> **29. At the time appointed**--"the time" spoken of in Daniel 11:27.[483]

Political interference, with perhaps bringing some troops on ships, is probably what is happening in verse 29 as ships come against the King of the North in the next verse.

APPENDIX B: DANIEL 11: IS THE GREAT MONARCH THE KING OF THE NORTH?

30a For ships from Cyprus shall come against him;

According to *Vine's Expository Reference*, the Hebrew term translated as Cyprus above, *kittim*, means "Western lands" [484], but it seems to come from a word apparently meaning "bruisers."[485]

Jerome wrote about this as follows:

> *"And his heart shall be against the holy covenant, and he shall succeed and return into his own land. At the time appointed he shall return and shall come to the South; but the latter time shall not be like the former. And the galleys shall come upon him, and the Romans, and he shall be dealt a heavy blow."* Or, as another has rendered it, *"... and they shall threaten him with attack."*[486]

Daniel 11:30 suggests that a major western naval power will put on a display of force and that will upset the south-heading King of the North, who will then decide to enter at least the area where Jews are making sacrifices (see next verse), perhaps in retaliation for that action and/or to satisfy the complaints of his King of the South allies (vs. 27).

It is of interest to note that the U.S.A. and its ships, from a Judean or European Union perspective, are from western lands.

Of course, it is also possible that the U.S.A. or some other country could have naval ships at the Turkish-dominated portion of Cyprus or some other western land. However, **no small country with a minor naval presence would be likely to stop the King of the North at that stage of history—thus the U.S.A. seems to be the only possible naval force mentioned here**.

Note: *Because Cyprus, and many other western European countries, are part of the European Union, we have to eliminate them as being part of the "Western lands" in Daniel 11 (and even if* they were not affiliated with a European confederation, they would not seem to be capable of having enough naval power to stop the powerful King of the North). And because the Kings of the East and North are not alluded to until Daniel 11:44, we have to eliminate Russia, China, India, and Japan as possible naval forces for verse 30 (plus, of course, they are east and north, not west of Jerusalem).

Furthermore, because the Arab nations would tend to be supporters of the King of the South, there is no nation in an actually "western" area that this could possibly refer to in the early 21st century other than the U.S.A., Canada, the Caribbean, or Latin America.

And neither Latin America, nor the non-Spanish Caribbean countries, seem capable (at this point) of having a naval force that would stop the King of the North. Thus watching and understanding current world events, as Jesus advised, (e.g. Mark 13:32) makes it clear that the naval power would have to be the U.S.A. and possibly also include its English-speaking allies.

Canadian and American Warships

For a slightly different view, here are the entire verses—30 from 3 different translations: the *Bible in Basic English* (BBE), GOD'S WORD® Translation ©1995 (GWT), and the CEV:

> For those who go out from the west will come against him, and he will be in fear and will go back, full of

APPENDIX B: DANIEL 11: IS THE GREAT MONARCH THE KING OF THE NORTH?

wrath against the holy agreement; and he will do his pleasure: and he will go back and be united with those who have given up the holy agreement (BBE).

Ships will come from the west to attack him, and he will be discouraged and turn back. Angry at the holy promise, he will return, take action, and favor those who abandon the holy promise (GWT).

Ships from the west will come to attack him, and he will be discouraged. Then he will start back to his own country and take out his anger on the religion of God's faithful people, while showing kindness to those who are unfaithful (CEV).

Notice that the ships, while they may come to attack, do not have to actually attack the King of the North at this time—and that they seem to come from "the west."

But also notice that instead of taking his anger out against the naval power that sends the ships, the King of the North takes out his anger against the religion of God's people!

It seems obvious that these are the faithful Christians who are doing the main specific end-time work of God at this time. And they will be explaining these prophecies to the world.

About five years after I first thought that Daniel 11:30 could be referring to United States warships, I came across the following in a book written about Catholic prophecies by Gerald Culleton:

> *Countess Francesca de Billiante* (died 1935): When the land with the great fleet enters the Mediterranean (England or the United States?) then Europe will tremble...God will save Rome...[487]

Note: The comments ( ) in are from the Catholic writer Gerald Culleton. And while he did not connect this Catholic prophecy to Daniel 11:30 in that writing, that passage certainly may be related.

Because the Bible shows that the spirit world has knowledge of scripture (Matthew 4:5-6), it would appear that some spirits, inspired this and certain private prophets to make a variety of statements throughout history to try to confuse people at the end. The statement from the Countess may have been intended to tell the Europeans that they should not be too afraid of the coming "American" ships.

When this event happens, all should realize that it is showing that Daniel 11:30 etcetera is being fulfilled.

30b therefore he shall be grieved, and return in rage against the holy covenant, and do *damage.*

Partially because the U.S. naval forces have stopped him AND the "secret sect" is causing the modified ecumenical religion problems (as the media is likely to report much more of the Philadelphia Church's message then), the King of the North will apparently decide to do something to the members of the true Church ("damage" is not in the Hebrew) after he returns (apparently from Europe). This is apparently because he is "in rage against **the holy covenant.**"

Around the late fourth century, Jerome taught that this portion of verse:

> ... foreshadows the Antichrist, who is to persecute the people of Christ.[488]

The King of the North will most likely try to stop the supporters of the true church from proclaiming the truth about his intentions and from proclaiming "the gospel of the kingdom" (cf. Matthew 24:14).

APPENDIX B: DANIEL 11: IS THE GREAT MONARCH THE KING OF THE NORTH?

The King of the North will probably attempt to learn more about how to eliminate them by being nice to apostate former Christians (those who "forsake the holy covenant," verse 30c). Apparently, he attempts to get them to betray the Nazarene Christians (cf. Matthew 24:10).

It continues to strike me as important that although a western naval power stops the King of the North momentarily, **the King of the North becomes apparently more enraged with the people of the holy covenant than with the naval power**. He wants to eliminate the rising up of the secret sect!

Why would this be?

Most likely this occurs because the people of the holy covenant are warning the world that the King of the North is fulfilling these prophecies in Daniel 11. This enrages the King of the North so much that he tries to eliminate these people. The King of the North simply does not want the small Church telling the world in general, or the Anglo-American nations in particular, what his plans really are.

Jesus clearly taught that persecution would affect His people just prior to the beginning of the Great Tribulation:

> [7] And there will be famines, pestilences, and earthquakes in various places. [8] All these are **the beginning of sorrows**. [9] Then **they will deliver you up to tribulation and kill you**, and you will be hated by all nations for My name's sake. [10] And then many will be offended, will betray one another, and will hate one another (Matthew 24:7-10).
>
> [14] And this gospel of the kingdom will be preached in all the world as a witness to all the nations, and then the end will come. [15] "Therefore when you see the 'abomination of desolation,' spoken of by Daniel the prophet, standing in the holy place" (whoever reads,

let him understand), [16] then let those who are in Judea flee to the mountains…[21] For **then there will be great tribulation** (Matthew 24:14-15:16;21).

So notice that after the beginning of sorrows, faithful Christians will be delivered up. Many will be killed, and many will be betrayed by those pretending to be Christians. Christ's "gospel of the kingdom is preached to the world as a witness,", then the GREAT tribulation will come shortly thereafter. This clearly ties in with the events of Daniel 11, as Jesus Himself seems to tie Daniel 11:31 into Matthew 24:15.

This may be precisely when God has the work of His Philadelphia remnant church, in an organized manner, stopped (Romans 9:28). However, at least parts of the message will apparently continue to go out by scattered and fleeing individuals, as well as the two witnesses. It may be (and this is certainly speculative) that the Americans agree to stop (or suspend on some pretext) the Nazarene church's ability to broadcast as part of the negotiations that certainly will be needed because of the encounter between the King of the North (Europe) and the naval forces of the West (America).

Part b of verse 30 certainly may parallel Matthew 24:9–10. This might indicate that some type of persecution of true Christians may begin before the "gospel of the kingdom" will have gone to the world as witness, as that is completed in Matthew 24:14. Notice that the end comes once the Christians have successfully proclaimed that "gospel of the kingdom."

It is possible that verse 30b is when the two witnesses appear (or perhaps in or between vss. 31–39), as they will undoubtedly enrage the King of the North—of course so will the faithful Christians who will do the work.

30c So he shall return and show regard for those who forsake the holy covenant.

APPENDIX B: DANIEL 11: IS THE GREAT MONARCH THE KING OF THE NORTH?

It is somewhat possible that "those who **forsake** the holy covenant" are former "Christians," who in that sense have actually forsaken the biblical covenant.

Perhaps this includes those involved in the falling away (see 2 Thessalonians 2:3). The reason that the King of the North may wish to show them some type of favor may be so the King can learn more about the Christians to better be able to identify/eliminate/persecute its followers.

Here is what Jerome taught about the fulfillment of this portion of the verse:

> ...this is to be more amply fulfilled under the Antichrist, for he shall become angered at the covenant of God and devise plans against those whom he wishes to forsake the law of God.[489]

Notice that Jesus listed betrayal just before the abomination of Daniel is mentioned:

> [12] Now brother will betray brother to death, and a father his child; and children will rise up against parents and cause them to be put to death. [13] And you will be hated by all men for My name's sake. But he who endures to the end shall be saved.
>
> [14] "So when you see the 'abomination of desolation,' spoken of by Daniel the prophet, standing where it ought not" (let the reader understand), "then let those who are in Judea flee to the mountains" (Mark 13:12-14).

Thus, it appears that Daniel is referring to a betrayal—a deliverance to persecuting authorities—by supposed believers and/or the members of their physical family (see also Matthew 24:10 where Jesus makes a similar warning).

31 And forces shall be mustered by him, and they shall defile the sanctuary fortress; then they shall take away the daily *sacrifices,* **and place** *there* **the abomination of desolation.**

The above verse shows that the forces of the King of the North will stop the daily sacrifices. Of course for the daily sacrifices to stop, they will have had to start—thus this is a prophetic event that one can watch for (cf. Matthew 24:15; Luke 21:20).

Interestingly, this starting of sacrifices in Israel might be perceived as the terrible crime that a Catholic long ago prophesied would lead to some type of destruction:

> *Abbot Herman of Lehnin* (died 1300). Towards the end of the world "Israel will commit a terrible crime for which it will suffer death."[490]

Unlike in Daniel 11:30, the King of the North meets no strong naval resistance in verse 31. This may be because he negotiated something with the U.S.A. to allow him and/or (possibly an "antipope," see Chapter 10) to go to Jerusalem to broker "peace in the Middle East." Yet, it is likely that the King of the North does things that he had not told the U.S.A. he would do (such as go after some of the Nazarene Christians and interfere with Jewish practices/politics).

This may inflame the U.S.A. enough that it may be one of the reasons that the King of the North decides on a "blitzkrieg" invasion of the U.S.A. and/or its British-descended allies 30 days after stopping the daily sacrifices. The fact that the Europeans may be controlling the U.S.A.'s global positioning capabilities next decade[491] may be enough to embolden the King.

The King of the North will probably proclaim "peace and safety" while plotting for the sudden destruction of those opposing him (1 Thessalonians 5:2-3). This would be a second false proclamation of peace. The sudden destruction is likely to include a nuclear attack, and could possibly happen in conjunction with a NATO exercise that would catch the U.S.A. and its Anglo-allies off guard (other nations are likely to also be involved).

While the term "sacrifices" is not in the original Hebrew, Daniel 9:27 mentions what appears to be the same desolate abominations, and also that the same sacrifices and offerings will be stopped. It may be that part of the reason the King of the North will give for going into Jerusalem with armies is to stop extremists from having daily sacrifices that may provoke the Muslims and others.

The Great Monarch, apparently with his forces, is expected to go to Jerusalem toward the beginning and end of his reign and fight:

> *Y. Dupont* (20th century): The Great King will be of Frankish descent, although his actual nationality is uncertain...It seems that he will travel twice to Jerusalem, once at the beginning of his reign...and again at the end to fight... and be killed...[492]
>
> *Helen Otto Tzima* (2000): Jerusalem will be invaded in WWIII and finally liberated by the Great Monarch.[493]

Interestingly, a pope that does miracles and who works with the Great Monarch is expected to "recover the kingdom of Jerusalem" according to a 12th century Catholic prophecy.[494] If the final Antichrist, probably some type antipope, moves to Jerusalem to aid "world peace" (such as the Jewish/Palestinian situation), it would seem to make sense that he comes to Jerusalem prior to the King of the South fighting the King of the North (Daniel 11:40). This move may give the Arab world major cause for concern. Jesus warned of a coming time when Jerusalem would be "surrounded by armies" (Luke 21:20) and "trampled by Gentiles" (vs.24), which parallels a similar warning in Revelation 11:2.

Daniel 11:31, then is also just before the Philadelphians would flee as per Jesus' comments in Matthew 24:15-16 and Revelation 3:10.

Even *The Catholic Encyclopedia* seems to tie Jesus' statements in Matthew 24:15 to Daniel 11:31. However, it is somewhat unclear about what it actually means.[495]

32 Those who do wickedly against the covenant he shall corrupt with flattery; but the people who know their God shall be strong, and carry out *great exploits*.

Those who do wickedly against the covenant would appear to be those who persecute the faithful church (those of "the covenant"), the other nations that support the King of the North—possibly former Christians who forsook the truth—or perhaps the Laodiceans (if so, this would represent a major separation between the Philadelphians and the Laodiceans, a lukewarm group of Christians, per Revelation 3:14-16—which must happen close to that time). It may be all of them.

Here is the *Douay Old Testament* (DOT) translation and related comments on this verse:

> [32] And the impious against the testament shall dissemble fraudulently: but (m) the people that knoweth their God, shall obtain, and shall doe.
>
> (m) even in the hottest persecution of Antiochus, Nero or Antichrist some shall constantly confess true religion.[496]

It is likely that the Philadelphians are the ones who are

strong and will carry out something important.

Adam Clark in his commentary identifies the people as follows:

> ***But the people that do know their God***
> The genuine Christians.
>
> ***Shall be strong***
> Shall be strengthened by his grace and Spirit.[497]

The words *great exploits* in the NKJV do not literally appear in the Hebrew text; but perhaps these faithful Christians have the types of signs that Jesus mentioned in Mark 16:15-18. These people apparently know their God, kept the word of Christ, and have works that are approved, because the Bible states of the Philadelphians:

> [8] I know your works. See, I have set before you an open door, and no one can shut it; for you have a little strength, have kept My word, and have not denied My name (Revelation 3:8).

Joel 2:28-31 also suggests a future fulfillment of Daniel 11:32 as those prophesying then may be part of those who are strong and who carry out the exploits and these may occur when the Philadelphians are somewhat fleeing (cf. Revelation 12:14-17).

11:33 And those of the people who understand shall instruct many; yet *for many* days they shall fall by sword and flame, by captivity and plundering.

Those who understand and instruct many are those who faithfully do the work of God. This would seem to have to be the Philadelphia portion of the Church. Apparently, some will be killed and will also possibly have their houses or other buildings burned down.

This may occur for a relatively short period of time. It needs to be understood that the expression "for many" is not in the Hebrew before the word "days."

The MKJV (Modern King James Version), the LITV (Literal Translation of the Holy Bible), and even Douay OT did a better job with this verse as shown below:

> [33] And those who understand among the people shall teach many; yet they shall fall by the sword, and by flame, by exile, and spoil, for days. (Daniel 11:33, MKJV).
>
> [33] And those who understand among *the* people will instruct many, yet they will stumble by the sword and by flame, by exile and spoil *for* days (Daniel 11:33, LITV).
>
> [33] And the learned in the people shall teach very many: and they shall fall by sword, and by flame, and by captivity, and by spoil of days (Daniel 11:33, DOT).

Thus, there will be some **days** where intense persecution of the Philadelphian Christians will occur before they flee and receive supernatural protection.

Regarding falling by the flame, there is a Catholic prophecy that indicates members of a small sect will be burnt, possibly in fulfillment of this verse. For details see Chapter 6.

34 Now when they fall, they shall be aided with a little help; but many shall join with them by intrigue.

Verse 34 further suggests that some Philadelphians will suffer, as it is the Philadelphians that should be those of high understanding.

It should be pointed out that those suffering *may* be the Philadelphians (and/or other Christians) in areas controlled or influenced by the King of the North, specifically Europe. It possibly also includes Latin America. It may be that there will be a religious resurgence (cf. Revelation 13:4) that leads to some of God's people being killed in those lands, and even the U.S.A., etcetera, by self-appointed vigilantes calling themselves "Catholic" (such as one who actually called for a real crusade to begin in the 21st century). [498]

Those who join the Philadelphia Christians by intrigue may include those having fallen away or others pretending to assist the Christians, yet secretly really supporting the King of the North. Orthodox scholar H. Tzima Otto believes that some claiming Philadelphia Christian practices are going to betray genuine Philadelphians in the future and support the Great Monarch.[499]

Daniel 11:34 is a warning to the end-time Christians that while some will actually help them then, they will need to be quite cautious, as problems are likely with "many."

35 And some of those of understanding shall fall, to refine them, purify them, and make them white, until the time of the end; because it is still for the appointed time.

Verse 35 further shows problems for many of the most faithful in the Church. Because not even the faithful are perfect, some apparently will fall and/or be persecuted, so that they can be refined.

But Daniel 12:1 shows that this specific persecution will probably end in, or shortly after, verse 35. Then, probably by the beginning of Daniel 11:39 at the latest, the tribulation will begin.

Why?

The expression translated as "the appointed time" in

verse 35 is from the Hebrew word transliterated into English as `eth.[500] It is used in both Daniel 12:1 and 11:35.

The same Hebrew word (`eth) is translated as "the set time" in Psalm 102:13:

> [13] You will arise and have mercy on Zion; For the time to favor her, Yes, the set time, has come.

This seems to suggest that these verses (Daniel 11:35 and Psalm 102:13) are for the same time. If so, this is the time when God distinguishes between the truly faithful Church (Zion), and those outside the most faithful Church. Perhaps this is a parallel to when God no longer had the children of Israel experience the plagues in Egypt, Exodus 8:22.

However, one thing that is critical to notice is that verse 35 specifically shows that its activities go "until the time of the end"—**thus there must be a future fulfillment of vs. 35. And this may be a key verse to tie in with Daniel 12:1**.

The Wycliffe Bible Commentary states (bolding in original):

> Dan 12:1
>
> **At that time** (cf. on Dan 11:36). At the same time as the events of 11:36-45. **Michael.** See Rev 12:7; cf. Josh 5:13-15; 2 Kings 6:15-17; Isa 37:35-36; Matt 26:53. This is Israel's time of trouble. Every reference to it uses superlative language (cf. also Matt 24:21).[501]

Yet, the above from *The Wycliffe Bible Commentary* may be off a little bit.

Why?

Because the same Hebrew expression for "at that time" (`eth) occurs in verse 35, *not* verse 36. Therefore, somewhere between verse 35 and 39 is apparently when Michael stands up and begins to protect the Philadelphians.

The Philadelphians apparently will flee during vs. 35, as Jesus said that His people would flee just prior to the great tribulation in Matthew 24:20-21. Jesus specified that they would escape in Luke 21:36. Jesus stated that it would be the Philadelphians who would be kept "from the hour of trial which shall come upon the whole world" in Revelation 3:10.

The Bible shows that persecution will accompany this fleeing (Revelation 12:13-15), but that those fleeing are helped (vs. 16).

Because of the successful fleeing, the King of the North will stop his direct pursuit of them. They will no longer be proclaiming the gospel through any major organized media effort. The rising up of the "secret sect" will have ended.

A "Catholic" prophecy seems to possibly foretell of this time as the Philadelphian "sect" will likely perceived to be the enemy of the Great Monarch and the antipope:

> *David Poreus* (17th century): The Great Monarch...will crush the enemies of the Pope...[502]

Thus, as far as most will be concerned, the secret sect will have been "crushed."

The Faithful Philadelphians May Dwell in Caves

Many theologians have considered that part of the true Church would flee into the wilderness during this time [503]; and others specifically believe that this place has caves. [504] Tim LaHaye refers to a mountainous cave-filled place in Jordan called Petra and the people who flee as "believing Jews."[505] It would seem that those called "believing Jews" (historically known as Nazarene Christians) represent the "secret sect" that certain mystics have warned about.

However, at least one mystic warned in the 12th century that while those in caves seemed to be good, they really were not:

> *Hildegard of Bingen* (12th century): And fly from those who linger in caves and are cloistered supporters of the Devil. Woe to them, woe to them who remain thus! They are the Devil's very viscera, and the advance guard of the son of perdition.
>
> Therefore, O you My beloved children, avoid them with all devotion and with all the strength of your souls and bodies. For the ancient serpent feeds and clothes them by his arts, and they worship him as God and trust in his false deceptions...Because they are afraid of My people, they do not openly resist these institutions of Mine, but in their hearts and their deeds they hold them as nothing. By devilish illusion, they pretend to have sanctity; but they are deceived by the Devil, for if he were to show himself to them openly they would understand him and flee him…But because the Devil knows he has only a short time for his error, he is not hastening to perfect infidelity in his members; you, you evil deceivers, who labor to subvert the Catholic faith.[506]

It would appear that the mystic was demonically-influenced as she is actually warning against supporting the true Philadelphian pacifist Christians (something that may happen, as some might try to join them per Isaiah 56:8). It is the Philadelphians who will be protected, yet she seems to be claiming that they are the "supporters of the Devil" (probably because they will oppose the final revised ecumenical church and because that church will have persecuted them). Because she calls them "the advanced guard of the son of perdition," she apparently refers to a group of people who will be protected in caves just before Christ returns.

Notice also that she specifically warns against religious people in caves who are miraculously fed.

Yet she must not have realized that the Bible indicates that those who receive God's protection in the wilderness during the end time (Revelation 12:14–16), and are in caves (Jeremiah 48:28), are His people (Isaiah 16:1–4 in Sela/Petra), will be religious (Revelation 14:12), and will be miraculously fed (Isaiah 33:15-16). Hence, the above vision does indicate that even the demons have known about a place of protection where some people will be miraculously fed, for quite some time.

However, those associated with the King of the North will then turn their attention to the rest of her seed, the non-Philadelphian Christians (which will be a "secret sect," but will try to remain hidden, most likely, to avoid this persecution).

Even a commentator's note in the *Rheims New Testament* agrees that the Church goes to a wilderness location:

> The Church shall flee as to a desert in Antichrist's time, but not decay or be unknown, no not for so short a time. [507]

Early Catholic leaders such as Irenaeus,[508] Hippolytus,[509] and Cyril [510] also believed this. Hence Hildegard is once again not even faithful to Catholic positions on prophetic matters.

Furthermore, notice:

> *Bishop St. Victorinus* (2nd century): But the woman fled into the wilderness, and there were given to her two great eagle's wings…to that…church…let them go to that place which they have ready, and let them be supported there for three years and six months from

the presence of the devil.[511]

Thus, the idea of true Christians fleeing, being supported, and being away from the devil for 3 ½ years is consistent with both biblical and certain Catholic teachings. No one should rely on Hildegard's false admonition. The Greek Orthodox tend to believe that the faithful will flee to caves in the desert/wilderness for 3 ½ years.[512]

Now, it should be understood that the Bible shows that those who do not flee will be persecuted:

> [17] And the dragon was enraged with the woman, and he went to make war with the rest of her offspring, who keep the commandments of God and have the testimony of Jesus Christ (Revelation 12:17).

Thus, we see several parallels in Daniel 11:29-35 and Revelation 12:13-17. We specifically see that some will be persecuted, will flee to the wilderness, will be helped, but that Satan is not yet through (as Daniel 11:36-44 also seem to show).

The Spanish-influenced 16th century *Chilam Balam* also seems to warn those associated with the true church to be in a cave:

> Son, where is the cenote? All are drenched <with> its water. There is no gravel on its bottom; a bow is inserted over its entrance. <It is> the church.[513]

The 1933 compiler of the above (J. José Hoíl) added a note stating "Evidently a reference to a cave type of cenote".[514]

Thus this Mayan writing is showing the church being in a cave and being drenched with water in a manner similar to the concept of fleeing to a wilderness and avoiding the flood

APPENDIX B: DANIEL 11: IS THE GREAT MONARCH THE KING OF THE NORTH?

shown in Revelation 12:14-16.

36 "Then the king shall do according to his own will: he shall exalt and magnify himself above every god, shall speak blasphemies against the God of gods, and shall prosper till the wrath has been accomplished; for what has been determined shall be done.

The King of the North will prosper and honor his own god, but himself the most. Although there have been partial fulfillments in the past, **this would have to be at the time of the end.**

The prospering in Daniel 11:36 may also be related to Ezekiel 27. If so, this would suggest that that the European Union will start prospering through trading before it begins to prosper through military conquest. Notice that John Ogwyn also wrote:

> This European union of church and state will promise universal prosperity and will exercise worldwide economic dominance for a short while. Ezekiel 27, using the figure of the ancient commercial city of Tyre, speaks of this global economic combine which will include nations of Europe, Africa, Latin America, and Asia along with Israel and Judah (v. 17). Portions of Ezekiel 27 are paraphrased or quoted in Revelation 18 where the end-time system, called Babylon the Great, is described.

> The English-speaking nations will not prosper for long in connection with this system, however. In fact, they will ultimately be overpowered and destroyed by it militarily. Prior to military attack and occupation, devastating weather problems, combined with internal civil strife ("tumults in the midst" cf. Amos 3:9) will

bring our nations to the point of internal collapse.[515]

Thus a major trading power will prosper. Even today, the European Union is a major trading power.

It should be noted that the term translated as "Then" in vs. 36 (and the "Thus" in vs. 39) is the Hebrew word `asah which according to the *Interlinear Transliterated Bible* actually means "And shall do." [516] Therefore, it may be that every act listed is not necessarily consecutive, as some (from vs. 31 to 39) may be fairly concurrent.

37 He shall regard neither the God of his fathers nor the desire of women, nor regard any god; for he shall exalt himself above *them* all.

38 But in their place he shall honor a god of fortresses; and a god which his fathers did not know he shall honor with gold and silver, with precious stones and pleasant things.

Notice that the King of the North, the ten-horned beast, will really worship himself, but will outwardly honor some type of god.

Regarding "any god" in verse 37, it will probably be that the King of the North will pretend to be some type of "Catholic" until it is no longer convenient. The Beast will turn on an unfaithful church later as shown in Revelation 17:16–17.

Let us look at the original KJV here, as it seems a bit more true to the Hebrew intent. The NKJV gives a different impression:

> [37] Neither shall he regard the God of his fathers, nor the desire of women, nor regard any god: for he shall magnify himself above all. [38] But in his estate shall he honour the God of forces: and a god whom his fathers knew not shall he honour with gold, and silver, and

with precious stones, and pleasant things (Daniel 11:37-38, KJV).

The word translated both times as "regard" in 11:37 is the Hebrew word *biyn*, which essentially means to have intellectual understanding/perception of.[517] Essentially, the King of the North will probably consider that the Catholic religion should not be taken seriously internally, although, he will at first honor many Catholic beliefs publicly. Like Emperor Constantine, he will probably understand that religion may be useful for political purposes, including, at first, keeping the revised Holy Roman Empire united.

Verse 38 seems to be referring to two gods. The god that his fathers did not know (possibly called the foreign god of the next verse) and the god of fortresses. It would seem that those who believe that those who profess Christ, but endorse Christians fighting in carnal warfare, are in a sense honoring the "god of fortresses." Yet, this is something that the Nazarene Christians and their true spiritual descendants have never done. Others will likely have other opinions.

39 Thus he shall act against the strongest fortresses with a foreign god, which he shall acknowledge, and advance its glory; and he shall cause them to rule over many, and divide the land for gain.

The two Hebrew words translated as "the strongest fortresses" in verse 39 do not appear together anywhere else in the Bible.

Something is, thus, unique here.

Who has the strongest fortresses?

Looking down in this chapter further, we must eliminate the King of the South, because that king is not attacked until the next verse. We must also eliminate those in the North and East, as they do not get involved until verse 44.

Neither the rest of Africa nor Latin America has anything resembling "the strongest fortresses." The strongest fortresses belong to the United States, and to a much lesser degree, its English-speaking allies.

Thus, Daniel 11:39 is describing when the Anglo-English nations are destroyed.

Catholic Prophecies about the Destruction of the English Peoples

Interestingly, there seem to be several Catholic private prophecies that also foretell the destruction of the English-speaking peoples.

It should be noted, however, that many of the older Roman Catholic prophecies that mention the English were written before that area actually was called England, but was made up of territories of Anglo-Saxon peoples. Of course, if any apply to the U.S.A., Canada, Australia, and/or New Zealand, they were not formed as we now understand them until several centuries after some of the Roman Catholic prophecies were first written. Hence, although there are these are errors/distortions in translations, they do seem to somehow refer to the British-descended peoples. It would seem that many of them were intended to refer to the Anglo-American powers in the 21 century.

The following Catholic private prophecies appear to predict the destruction of the English:

> *St. Columbkille* (597): English nobility shall sink into horrible life—wars shall be proclaimed against them, by means of which the frantically proud race shall be subdued, and will be harassed from every quarter. **The English shall dwindle into disreputable people and shall forever be deprived of power**".[518]

...the English shall be defeated...they shall be harassed by every quarter; like a fawn surrounded by a pack of voracious hounds, shall be the position of the English amidst their enemies. The English afterwards shall dwindle down to a disreputable people.[519]

Mother Shipton (died 1551): The time will come when England shall tremble and quake...**London shall be destroyed forever after** . . . and then York shall be London and the Kingdom governed by three Lords appointed by a Royal Great monarch...who will set England right and drive out heresy.[520]

Saint Edward (died 1066): **The extreme corruption and wickedness of the English nation has provoked the just anger of God**. When malice shall have reached the fullness of its measure, God will, in His wrath, send to the English people wicked spirits, who will punish and afflict them with great severity...[521]

Saint Malachy (12th century): ...the English in turn must suffer severe chastisement. Ireland, however, will be instrumental in bringing back the English to the unity of Faith.[522]

Saint Cataldus of Tarentino (c. 500): **The Great Monarch** will be in war till he is forty years of age.......he will assemble great armies and expel tyrants from his empire. He **will conquer England** and other island empires.[523]

Franciscan Friar of Mount Sinai (died 1840): England will become the scene of the greatest cruelties. **Ireland and Scotland will invade England and destroy it.**

The royal family will be driven out and half of the population murdered.[524]

D.A. Birch (20th century Catholic writer): It is interesting to note that the National (Government) of England is foretold to have no role in the return of England to Roman allegiance. As a matter of fact, a number of prophecies specifically state that England will be reevangelized by the French and Irish **after England has suffered a terrible and specific chastisement.**[525]

Werdin d' Otrante (13th century): "The Great Monarch and the Great Pope will precede Antichrist...**All the sects will vanish. The capital of the world will fall**... The Great Monarch will come and restore peace and the Pope will share in the victory.[526]

In a sense, the capital of the world is the United States. Hence it seems to be the U.S.A. that Werdin d' Otrante was referring to. Thus, certain Catholic prophecies appear to be foretelling the destruction of the Anglo-American powers, apparently by their Great Monarch.

But it is interesting to notice that the Catholic Saint Edward specifically states that demons will be used to punish the English peoples (whether the majority of Scots, etc, will be specifically involved or not can be debated). This would suggest, that presuming that the Great Monarch attacks them, the Great Monarch is on the side of demons. And while this is consistent with scriptures that show that the final ten-horned beast leader is influenced by demons (Revelation 16:13-14), it should give all who call themselves Catholic pause to NOT support someone who is on the side of demons.

A Greek Orthodox document known as the *Anonymou Prophecy* of 1053 also seems to foretell of a time that the Anglos will no longer be in the area of England,[527] but that nation was not known by that name at that time so it is not clear what is meant by it.

Notice also the following (bolding in the original):

> Our blessed Mother through Father Gobbi of the Marion Movement...provided several messages...
>
> On November 15, 1990: **Mary spoke about the great trial coming to the United States and for all humanity. The Blessed Mother specifically mentions the United States will know the hour of weakness and of poverty as well as "the hour of suffering and defeat." The thunder of God's justice will have arrived**... America will know poverty and defeat! [528]

The "hour of trial" that the Bible speaks of (Revelation 3:10) seems to begin with the Great Tribulation, which is likely to begin sometime next decade.

There also was a prophecy from a famous stigmatic (a mystic with blood wounds supposedly reflective of those that Jesus suffered when nailed to the stake):

> *Therese Neumann* (20th century): ... at the end of this century America will be destroyed economically by natural disasters. [529]

Although the date of the last prophecy was false, it should be clear according to a variety of sources claiming Catholicism, the United States and the other English-descended peoples are facing disaster—and apparently relatively soon.

It should be noted that many evangelical Protestants correctly teach that the U.S.A. will be gone before Jesus' second coming (i.e. Hal Lindsey), but they generally do not seem to understand how that will happen nor what scripture refers to this.[530]

Why America and its Anglo-Allies?

Why would Europe ultimately destroy the U.S.A. and its Anglo-allies?

Because it is the nominally Protestant (as well as religiously diverse) U.S.A. that most stands in the way of the goals of a future single ecumenical religion in Europe to dominate the world.

Only by eliminating the vast bastions of Protestantism and other "heresies" (which several other "Catholic" prophecies seem to show is a goal) that are present in the U.S.A. and its Anglo-allies, can such an ecumenical domination be attained in those lands.

Notice what one "Catholic" has written:

> *Priest G. Rossi* (19th century): But boastful pride and presumption always go before a fall. With her large share of guilt, America cannot avoid her due share of punishment…If the world is not yet entirely converted to Christianity, the blame is not on the head nor in the conscience of the Catholic Church… Ah ! wretched Protestantism shall have to answer for the loss of faith… English schism and heresy have squandered their treasures and abused their great temporal power, not only in persecuting-the faith in Great Britain and Ireland, but also in banishing the true religion of Jesus Christ from their vast American possessions…Their long-deserved punishment, however, is approaching from the North![531]

So, at least one respected Catholic priest published that a northern power will punish Britain, and its descendants, including the U.S.A. and Canada, for their "pride" and Protestantism.

But why would God allow some of these nations be destroyed, given that the Anglo-Americans have been in the forefront of distributing Bibles, helping in humanitarian matters, assisting with international disasters, etcetera?

Because the New Testament clearly teaches:

> For everyone to whom much is given, from him much will be required (Luke 12:48).

The Bible also teaches that the Assyrians will be used to punish an hypocritical nation (or hypocritical people, as the Hebrew can be translated):

> ⁵ O Assyrian, the rod of mine anger, and the staff in their hand is mine indignation. ⁶ I will send him against an hypocritical nation (Isaiah 10:5–6, KJV).

Christians all need to recall that when Jesus came, He clearly condemned the hypocritical religious leaders of His day (e.g. Luke 11:44), more directly than he condemned the more obvious sinners (Matthew 9:10-13). This is not to say that non-Anglo peoples do not have sin or that they will not be punished. The European Assyrians will clearly also be punished, per Isaiah 10:12, but the **punishment will begin first** on those who should have known better. That is, the punishment will begin on those who have claimed to live by the Bible, but have repeatedly failed to do so.

While the gospel warning message will be made fairly clear to the English-speaking peoples by the "secret-sect," prior to Daniel 11:39, because the Anglo-American nations are not likely to heed that warning, they will have to answer for their relative lack of response (cf. Ezekiel 33:7-9) and their survivors will be taken captive (cf. Habakkuk 2:7).

Notice something from the Sibylline oracle, followed by a comment by one who translated the passages:

> But then as time rolled around there rose
>
> The Egyptian kingdom, then that of the Persians
>
> And of the Medes and Ethiopians,
>
> And of Assyria and Babylon…
>
> For he who rules in heaven completed earth
>
> To be a common property for all,
> And in all bosoms placed he noblest thought.
>
> To them alone the bounteous field yields fruit,
>
> A hundred-fold from one, and thus completes
>
> God's measure. But to them shall also come
>
> Misfortune, nor will they escape all plague.
>
> And even thou, forsaking thy fair shrine,
>
> Shalt flee away when it becomes thy lot
>
> To leave the holy ground, and thou shalt be
>
> Carried to the Assyrians, and shalt see
>
> Wives and young children serving hostile men.

APPENDIX B: DANIEL 11: IS THE GREAT MONARCH THE KING OF THE NORTH?

> Comment by *Milton Spenser Terry* (19th century): *Assyrians.*—Assyria and Babylon seem to have been often confounded together by the Sibylline authors.[532]

Thus, even the Sibyl may be warning that some peoples will be taken away and held captive by the Assyrians, who have a relationship with Babylon (typifying a false religious system). This seems to be consistent with biblical prophecies. And while some may feel this has been fulfilled, according to the Bible, it will happen in the future.

More about Verse 39

If the Great Monarch is the King of the North, then the many ruled over in Daniel 11:39 would seem to be those in the U.S., United Kingdom, Canada, Australia, and New Zealand.

Furthermore, the dividing of the land of the United States, etcetera, for gain, will in no small way help prosper the King of the North. Many others may assist in this attack outside of those in Psalm 83. Mexico, who wants its lost land back, comes to mind.

Because of its debts, a Russian professor named Igor Panarin has predicted that the Europeans, Russians, Mexicans, and Asians may divide the land of the U.S.A. in the 21st century.[533] And a Catholic prophecy (previously cited [534]) shows that the U.K. will be divided. (There is also an ancient Chinese prophecy that *might* hint that areas like Australia and/or New Zealand could end up as part of China.[535]) Perhaps it should be mentioned that the dividing of the conquered lands also seems to be foretold in the Bible in Lamentations 4:16 and Joel 3:2.

Yet, instead of being worried about this coming Beast power, the United States and some of the other Anglo-powers, seem to be encouraging the development of a major power in Europe.[536] This is something that the Anglo-American peoples will come to later regret.

Unless the English-speaking peoples soon repent of their sins, which is very unlikely, the Bible indicates that their nations will be destroyed relatively soon (see also Hosea 8:1-13).

The Catholics also have this prophecy:

> *Balthassar Mas* (17th century): I saw a land swallowed up by the sea and covered with water. But afterwards, I saw that the sea receded little by little and the land could be seen again. The tops of the towers in the city rose again above the water and appeared more beautiful than before, and I was told that this land was England.[537]

The above may have several interpretations. Figuratively, it may mean that Protestant England is to be destroyed and will become "Catholic." Or it may simply mean some type of tsunami will affect England. It probably is not related to the prophecy in Revelation about islands, as Revelation 16:20 discusses all islands, whereas this prophecy is specific to England.

Also notice this Catholic prophecy:

> *Venerable Bartholomew Holzhauser* (died 1658): England shall suffer much. The king shall be killed. After desolation has reached its peak in England peace will be restored and England will return to the Catholic faith with greater fervor than before. The Great Monarch will have the special help from God and be unconquerable.[538]

The Bible shows that the Beast will have special help from "unclean spirits" (Revelation 16:13) and will be considered to be unconquerable (Revelation 13:4).

Here is one of Nostradamus' prophecies involving Germany and England.

> *Nostradamus* (died 1566) Although nations talk peace, troubles brew everywhere. Militaristic parties rise in Germany and pagan cults revive. Opinions are not free and the people are not enriched. The heir to the London government is overthrown for having made too many peace protests.[539]

While many may believe that World War II fulfilled the above, it looks a bit more likely to be related to the next war as "opinions" are less free now than the were several decades ago—and "the heir to the London government" was not truly overthrown then (though some may debate that).

Thus, both biblical and certain "Catholic" prophecies seem to point to the destruction of the English-speaking peoples by a Great Monarch.

If you are in the Anglo-American countries (because you did not flee with "the secret sect"), and you see them destroyed, will you repent then? If not, what will it take? If you are in the Arabic lands, will you repent then, or will you wait until your great leader is destroyed shortly thereafter (Daniel 11:40-43)?

If you are elsewhere in the world, will you repent then? If not, how much will it take for you to understand that these events are truly coming to pass?

Who is the Foreign God?

Notice that verse 39 also mentions a "foreign god" that the King of the North will acknowledge, and advance its glory. What god might that be?

It is remotely possible that the "foreign god" in Daniel 11:39

could be some new-age god that he, the King of the North, believes in—such as one in which demons provide him with certain direct assistance.

But more likely, this god will simply be something acceptable to the new ecumenical "Catholicism" that the King of the North will publicly promote and acknowledge.

This "new religion" will have some type image associated with it that people will be told to worship:

> [15] He was granted power to give breath to the image of the beast, that the image of the beast should both speak and cause as many as would not worship the image of the beast to be killed (Revelation 13:15).

As mentioned in the other chapters, the idea of this being a new religious order claiming to be within Catholicism fits verses 38 & 39 by allowing two "gods" in a manner that would not be totally alien to some Catholic practice (there have historically been many religious orders, as well as many different type of statues, within "Catholicism").

Various Catholic writers have suggested, some type of cross might be associated with this religion and/or its image. This is interesting, as some versions of crosses have long been used in other religious traditions such as Hinduism, Buddhism, and Jainism. Here is one related reference:

> Leaving Africa, and proceeding to Asia, we find, in India, the cross bearing the same meaning as in Egypt. When with four equal arms it signifies the four elements, which cross the Hindoos consider as eternal, and the component parts with a cross upon his breast. The cross is also found in the hands of Siva, Brahma, Vishnu, and Tvashtri...To this day, in Northern India, the cross is used to mark the jars of

sacred water taken from the Indus and Ganges, as in the northeastern parts of Africa the women impress this sign as a mark of possession upon their vessels of grain, etc. In Southern India the cross is used as an emblem of disembodied Jaina saints. The worshippers of Brahma and Buddha outnumber those of Christ; and the symbol, identified as that of our Master, was revered by the East Indians—their Lao Tse, centuries before our Lord appeared upon earth.[540]

I personally have seen Hindu and Buddhist temples with crosses of various types, and have noticed that large crosses are sometimes built within them. The Angkor Wat temple in Cambodia, to cite one specific example, has several.

Hence, Islam notwithstanding, the cross seems to be an international religious symbol.

Thus, because the whole world will tend to accept this religion (Revelation 13:3-4), some type of ecumenical religious order, possibly using some type of a cross as a symbol, would seem to appeal to "foreigners" of all types. Thus, this may be what the "foreign god" will represent.

As Islam is opposed to icons, and especially any type of cross as a symbol (the Crusaders invaded them centuries ago), Muslims will strongly question where all of this is leading.

Once the U.S.A. and its Anglo-allies are out of the way, the King of the North will likely declare that a new world order of peace has been ushered in (consistent with Jeremiah 6:14-15a, which is a warning about peace statements from one associated with abomination).

This may be a third false proclamation of peace.

An ancient Chinese prophecy states:

> Beautiful people come from the West. Korea, China and Japan are gradually at peace.[541]

This seems to indicate that many Asians will accept a type of peace that will be related to a Western (European) power.

According to one only identified as the "notorious demagogue" in the 19th century "if you tell a lie often enough, the people will ultimately believe it."[542] Many will believe that it is a time of peace then, but some will correctly doubt it.

The distrust of the proclamations by the "crusaders," combined with the prevalence of crosses being displayed, may be part of what triggers the prophesied attack from the Islamic King of the South.

40 "At the time of the end the king of the South shall attack him; and the king of the North shall come against him like a whirlwind, with chariots, horsemen, and with many ships; and he shall enter the countries, overwhelm them, and pass through."

The one called the King of the South in the above passage may be one with the title "Mahdi." And while Shi'ite (and some other Muslims) consider that he will be "a saviour" and establish an Islamic world, the Bible clearly shows that the King of the North will defeat him (see also Daniel 11:41-43).

Hence, all Muslims need to be on their guard and *not* accept any pan-Islamic militaristic leader—especially one who might rise up in the next decade. He will not be God's representative, and he will lose.

Presuming that the republics of the U.S.A. and its allies are taken over in verse 39, there are several reasons why the King of the South may decide to launch his major attack shortly thereafter:

> 1) The fact that "the Great Satan," a term that certain Moslems call the U.S.A., has been eliminated, the King of the South will realize that the deals made (Daniel 11:27; Psalm 83) with the Assyrian King of the North

are of little or no value anymore.

2) Next, without the nominally Protestant U.S.A. in its way, the King of the North will try to impose its non-Moslem religion on more and more of the world. As many Arabs tend to be more devoutly religious than the Chinese and Russians, they are more likely to get upset with this before the Kings of the East and North-East do (which occurs in Daniel 11:44).

3) Because the Arab confederation wanted to eliminate Israel (Psalm 83 most likely refers to the nation of Israel as well as the U.S.A. and any other serious Israeli allies), it probably will think that its actions greatly helped the Europeans accomplish this. Because of this thinking, the King of the South may become emboldened.

4) It is also likely that the King of the South will feel that the conquest of the U.S.A. and its allies will strain the military of the King of the North. The King of the South may believe it is an ideal time to strike. This is likely, as one of the reasons that the U.S.A. may be so easy to take over is because its own military has been strained, given that the U.S.A. has been spreading its military strength quite thin in the 21st century.

5) Increasing displays of crosses, combined with people following wonders (such as perhaps including apparitions claiming to be Mary), will get many in the Arab lands to remember the Crusades. Enough will hold to some version of Islam that they will fear an attack must be made or Islam will be defeated.

6) Finally, as many of the Arab economies are

dependent upon oil revenues, and most oil fields will have passed their halfway point of production by that stage (and many of its weapons will be of Anglo-American origins), the King of the South may decide that there is no better time to attack.

Also note that this attack against the King of the South occurs "at the time of the end." Thus, even if this had some fulfillment with Benito Mussolini or previous leaders, as has been suggested, it also has a future final fulfillment at the end.

But although the King of the North is also not "a savior" for "Catholics," notice what a prophecy, previously cited, states:

> *Rudolph Gekner* (died 1675): **A great prince of the North with a most powerful army will traverse all Europe, uproot all republics, and exterminate all rebels.** His sword moved by Divine power will most valiantly defend the Church of Jesus Christ. He will combat on behalf of the true orthodox faith, and shall subdue to his dominion the Mahometan Empire. A new pastor of the universal church will come from the shore (of Dalmatia) through a celestial prodigy, and in simplicity of heart adorned with the doctrines of Jesus Christ. Peace will come to the world.[543]

If there were much accuracy in the above private prophecy, it would also show that all republics are to be uprooted before the Moslem King of the South is invaded.

And here two similar, possibly related, private prophecies (the first is from a Syriac document):

> *Pseudo-Methodius* (7th century): This new Muslim

> invasion will be a punishment without limit and mercy...In France, people of Christians will fight and kill them...At that same time the Muslims will be killed and they will know the tribulation...The Lord will give them to the powers of the Christians whose empire will be elevated above all empires...The Roman King (Great Monarch) will show a great indignation against those who will have denied Christ in Egypt or in Arabia.[544]

> *Anonymou Paraphrasis* (10th century): However, in the End Times...this King...will march to fight against the Ishmaelites. And he will conquer them...[545]

> *St. Francis de Paul* (1470):...From your lordship shall be born the great leader of the holy militia...These devout men shall wear on their breasts, and much more in their hearts, the sign of the living God, namely the cross... members of this holy order......the Great Monarch... will destroy the Mahometan sect and the rest of the infidels.[546]

Many "Catholics" will apparently be so misled by these and similar prophecies that they will not recognize that the "great prince of the North" seems to fulfill Daniel 11:40. Note the term *Ishmaelites* is a term that has been used by the Catholics and Orthodox to describe Arabs, but also has been used by them to mean all Muslims.[547]

Those who profess Catholicism may wish to consider what their Saint Jerome taught about Daniel 11:40-43:

> ...those of our viewpoint refer these details also to the Antichrist, asserting that he shall first fight against the king of the South, or Egypt, and shall afterwards

conquer Libya and Ethiopia.[548]

Hence, the idea that it is an evil power that will invade the Middle East is an older tradition than the private prophecies that some may become misled into believing.

41 He shall also enter the Glorious Land, and many countries shall be overthrown; but these shall escape from his hand: Edom, Moab, and the prominent people of Ammon.
42 He shall stretch out his hand against the countries, and the land of Egypt shall not escape.
43 He shall have power over the treasures of gold and silver, and over all the precious things of Egypt; also the Libyans and Ethiopians *shall follow* **at his heels.**

The "he" is the King of the North. Most scholars seem to have concluded that the Glorious Land is physical Israel.

All the nations specifically mentioned in these verses are in Africa or the Middle East. (Note: the term translated as "Ethiopians" is the plural of the word Hebrew *Kuwshiy*, which, according to *Biblesoft's New Exhaustive Strong's Numbers and Concordance with Expanded Greek-Hebrew Dictionary*, means "descendants of Cush." The Nubian Cushites are normally Moslems and have dwelled with the Arabs for so long, that some consider themselves to have been "Arabized."[549]) Thus other than Israel, this appears to be a taking over of Islamic lands.

Perhaps some of the peoples who are spared, are spared to run oil production or other activities that the Europeans believe will benefit them.

The fact that the King of the North will accumulate gold is consistent with several Byzantine ("Greek" Orthodox) prophecies of their expected Great Monarch:

APPENDIX B: DANIEL 11: IS THE GREAT MONARCH THE KING OF THE NORTH?

> *Emperor Leo the Philosopher* (died 912): You will amass gold…And you will be the leader of the surrounding nations…
>
> *Addressed to Emperor Manuel II Palaeogous* (died 1425): The Emperor…will discover gold and silver…
>
> *Saint Andrew Fool-for-Christ* (c. 4th century): God will reveal to this king all the gold wherever it happen to lay concealed from view…[550]

One side note is that, in Egypt, major gold deposits were found in 2006.[551] This is relevant for a couple of reasons, including that it does prove that Egypt now does have enough gold that some foreign power would be interested in taking/using it (and in that respect is a fulfillment of biblical prophecy). It also suggests that gold will still be a valuable item into the Great Tribulation (though near/during the Day of the Lord it will become less than worthless, see Ezekiel 7:19).

It would seem that once the U.S. dollar totally collapses people all around the world will consider that even if the Euro is strong, having a more gold-backed currency would be safer. Having the European power acquiring a lot more gold to back the Euro (even if the backing is only implied) or possibly other future European currency (that might potentially replace the Euro) may greatly increase European credibility, prosperity, and influence around the globe.

Because it was the King of the North who was provoked by the forces of the King of the South, it would seem that once the northern king wins, he will proclaim peace. This will be the fourth major false proclamation of an age of peace (Jeremiah 8:11-12a). Sometime after this, the Bible shows that those of Asia and Russia will decide to turn against this northern king (which is consistent with Jeremiah 6;15b; 8:12b).

44 But news from the east and the north shall trouble him; therefore he shall go out with great fury to destroy and annihilate many.
45 And he shall plant the tents of his palace between the seas and the glorious holy mountain; yet he shall come to his end, and no one will help him."

A mystic nun wrote:

> *Blessed Anna-Maria Taigi* (19th century): Whole nations will come back to the Church and the face of the earth will be renewed. Russia, England, and China will come into the Church.[552]

But, even though many in Russia and China (as well as others in Asia, such as India, Japan, Korea, etc.) will temporarily somewhat accept this ecumenical religion (though they should not), it is clear from Daniel 11:44 and other scriptures that they are discerning enough to be amongst the first to rise up against it (after the Arabs and their allies).

Two Catholic prophecies also suggest this:

> *Countess Francesca de Brillante* (20th Century). "I see yellow warriors and red warriors marching against Europe. Europe will be completely covered with a yellow fog that will kill the cattle in the fields. Those nations that rebelled against the law of Christ will perish by fire. [553]

> *Nostradamus* (16th century): Meanwhile the great Asiatic Empire will spread across the sea and continents to destroy the Christian world.[554]

APPENDIX B: DANIEL 11: IS THE GREAT MONARCH THE KING OF THE NORTH?

Daniel 11:44 is also consistent with Revelation 16:12 where "the kings of the east" are associated with the sixth angel pouring out his bowl. It is also consistent with the military force that can field a 200 million man army, as shown in Revelation 9:16.

Notice a declaration made by the Russian scientist Mendeleyeff as reported in the *New York Times* in 1907:

> ...one of the causes which will eventually lead to a regenerated China attacking Europe will be the predominance of males over females in the Celestial Kingdom...for China is bound to make a memorable appearance on the world's stage, and it is indispensable that Russia bind herself in close unison with China until China "overflows her shores and pours down in a torrent on Europe."[555]

China's one-child policy may be supportive of the Russian prediction as that policy has resulted in a higher relative number of males in China.

Only the Asians appear capable of fielding a 200 million man army that is mentioned in the Bible. As it has only recently been that any area of the world was capable of producing an army of this size, this is another indication that the end can occur fairly soon. It simply could not have occurred centuries ago.

Daniel 11:44, it shows those from the east and north will somehow battle the King of the North. And Jeremiah 50:41-43 indicates that this troubles the "daughter of Babylon."

So combining, Jeremiah 50:41-43, Revelation 16:12, and Daniel 11:44 together indicates that northern, eastern, and/or north-eastern powers will fight the King of the North.

Based upon their physical location, this would seem to be the Russians, Chinese, Indians, and/or other Asians. It would not be a surprise if Bangladesh, Bhutan, Cambodia, Indonesia, Korea, Laos, Myanmar, Nepal, Pakistan, Singapore, Sri Lanka, Thailand, Vietnam, the Tibeto-Burman peoples, and/or the Tai peoples were also involved.

There is a Byzantine Orthodox prophecy that suggests that the Russians will turn on the City (probably "new Babylon", a term that some Orthodox tie with Constantinople[555] and some fewer, Rome):

> *Orthodox Saint Andrew Fool-for-Christ* (4th century): I personally believe that some day the City will be invaded by the Blond Nation, whose name begins with the 17th letter of the Alphabet (P). Well, the Blond Nation will enter the City and it will cut down its inhabitants.[557]

The 17th letter of that alphabet, "P", is the Greek letter "rho"--it makes an "r" sound. Hence, this might suggest that at least one Orthodox prophet believed that the Russians would turn against the coming Beast power, which is likely to be allied with Constantinople at the end.

An interesting "Russian Orthodox" prophecy suggests that Russia will decide to deal with those who committed the abomination:

> *Vassula Ryden* (December 13, 1993): Russia…will glorify me in the end…When in the last days nation after nation will decline and pervert itself for having erected the disastrous abomination in the Holy Place… Russia…will preserve her integrity…[558]

Hence the above is a reference to that abomination in Daniel 11:31, which clearly involves the King of the North.

Now that vs. 45 of Daniel 11 shows that King of the

APPENDIX B: DANIEL 11: IS THE GREAT MONARCH THE KING OF THE NORTH?

North comes to his end at the *appointed time*, which is what is prophesied in verse 27. This is also consistent with Revelation 16:19, where Babylon is divided, and the great cities fall at the seventh angel's bowl, apparently, toward the end of the Day of the Lord. This is also consistent with certain private prophecies about the fall of the Great Monarch.

As this book goes to press, it is obvious that the King of the North has not clearly risen up yet, but he is very likely alive now and will likely rise up next decade. But the Bible shows that troubles are expected before he fully does rise up. He will likely adopt the term "Catholic" for his religion, and change it for the worse.

No one should look forward to this "Great Monarch." And although some "Catholic" writers have longed for him, many others have warned about one coming with a change to their religion.[559]

And although this "King of the North" will be a problem for the world, Jesus will return and His kingdom will be established (Revelation 19 and 20), and those who follow Him will be rewarded (Revelation 22:14-15).

You can wait until these things happen to decide what to do, but as for me and my household, we expect to remain supportive of the secret sect. We would not want to support a lie (the emerging ecumenical religious power), nor would you.

2012 AND THE RISE OF THE SECRET SECT

APPENDIX C: ENDNOTES

1. G. Jeffrey MacDonald. Does Maya calendar predict 2012 apocalypse? USA Today. http://www.usatoday.com/tech/science/2007-03-27-maya-2012_n.htm viewed 01/14/08
2. Joseph LE. Apocalypse 2012: An Investigation into Civilization's End. Broadway, 2008, p. 15
3. Mayan Doomsday Prophecy, Decoding the Past. The History Channel. Original air date 08/03/06. Frank Joseph reached similar conclusions regarding the Aztecs and their calendar in his *Discovering the mysteries of ancient America: lost history and legends, unearthed and explored.* Publisher Career Press, 2006 pp. 68-82
4. Pinchbeck, Daniel. 2012 The Return of Quetzalcoatl. Jeremy P. Tarcher/Penguin, NY, 2007, p. 381
5. Pui-Hua R. Ancient Chinese Prophecies Till the End of the World. AuthorHouse, Bloomington (IN), 2008, p.83. Specifically it foretell that, "Yin and Yang are reversed."
6. Geryl P. The Orion Prophecy: Will the World Be Destroyed in 2012. Adventures Unlimited Press, 2002, pp. 35-38
7. José Hoíl J, Roys R. The Book of Chilam Balam of Chumayel. Roys Publisher, 1933. Reprint Forgotten Books, 1967, p. 62
8. As cited in Miller L. 2012: A Y2K for the New Age. Newsweek, Published May 2, 2009, from the magazine issue dated May 18, 2009 . http://www.newsweek.com/id/195688 viewed 06/27/09
9. http://www.upi.com/Odd_News/2008/06/23/Many_Dutch_prepare_for_2012_apocalypse/UPI-40461214263554/
10. José Hoíl, pp. 78, 111
11. José Hoíl, p. 228
12. José Hoíl, p. 261
13. Crowley, Phil. 2012, Decoding the Past. The History Channel. Original air date 03/01/07
14. December 21, 2012 7 Prophecies Of Doom. Posted March 4, 2008. http://www.aprogrammingpro.com/2008/03/04/december-21-2012-7-prophecies-of-doom/ viewed 04/21/09
15. The Sibylline Oracles, Book VIII, verses 247-259: translated from

	the Greek into English blank verse by Milton Spenser Terry. Hunt & Eaton, 1890, Original from the University of Michigan, Digitized Apr 15, 2008, p. 184
16	Hopi Civilization. http://2012wiki.com/index.php?title=Hopi_Civilization viewed 01/14/08
17	Survive 2012. http://survive2012.com/why_2012_fractal.php viewed 04/12/08
18	Braden G. The Mystery of 2012: Predictions, Prophecies and Possibilities. Sounds True, Incorporated, 2009, p. 330
19	Baldwin C. Holes in Earth's magnetic cloak let the sun in. Reuters, December 16, 2008. http://www.reuters.com/article/scienceNews/idUSTRE4BF79220081216 viewed 03/23/09
20	Phillips, Tony. Solar Storm Warning. NASA. http://science.nasa.gov/headlines/y2006/10mar_stormwarning.htm viewed 04/22/09
21	Brooks, Michael. Space storm alert: 90 seconds from catastrophe. New Scientist Monday, March 23, 2009. http://www.newscientist.com/article/mg20127001.300-space-storm-alert-90-seconds-from-catastrophe.html?full=true viewed 03/23/09
22	New Solar Cycle Prediction. Red Orbit, May 29, 2009 www.redorbit.com/news/space/1697053/new_solar_cycle-predictor/ viewed 06/09/09
23	Joseph, p. 16
24	José Hoíl, p. 112
25	José Hoíl, p. 115
26	Eusebius. The History of the Church History, Book III, Chapter V, Verses 2,3. Translated by A. Cushman McGiffert. Digireads.com Publishing, Stilwell (KS), 2005, p. 45
27	Gibbon E. Decline and Fall of the Roman Empire, Volume I. ca. 1776-1788. The Modern Library, NY, pp. 389-391
28	Dameron, J.P. Spiritism: The Origin of All Religions. Published by The author, 1885. Original from the University of California. Digitized Mar 25, 2008, p. 88
29	Lewis, Harve Spencer. The Mystical Life of Jesus. Published by Rosicrucian press, AMORC college, 1929. Original from the University of California. Digitized Dec 3, 2007, p. 61
30	Irenaeus. Adv. Her. III, 4:3
31	Hoffman , David. Chronicles from Cartaphilus: The Wandering Jew. Published by , 1853. Original from the University of Michigan. Digitized Sep 7, 2007, p. 636 and Pritz R. Nazarene Jewish Christianity. Magnes Press, Jerusalem, 1988, p. 75

APPENDIX C: ENDNOTES

32 Bagatti B. The Church from the Gentiles in Palestine, Part 1, Chapter 1, pp. 18-19 and Stewart-Sykes A. Melito of Sardis On Pascha. St. Vladimir's Seminary Press, Crestwood (NY), 2001, p. 72
33 Thiel B. Nazarene Christianity: Were the Original Christians Nazarenes? Should Christians be Nazarenes today? http://www.cogwriter.com/Nazarene.htm viewed 05/19/09
34 Fanning S. Mystics of the Christian Tradition. Routeldge, New York. 2001, reprinted 2006, pp. 219-220
35 Irenaeus. Adversus Haeres. Book III, Chapter 3, Verse 4
36 Tertullian. The Prescription Against Heretics. Chapter 36. Translated by Peter Holmes. Excerpted from Ante-Nicene Fathers, Volume 3. Edited by Alexander Roberts and James Donaldson. 1885. Hendrickson Publishers, Peabody (MA), 1999 printing, p. 260
37 Fanning, pp. 219-220
38 Eusebius. The Life of Constantine, Book I, Chapters 28,30,31
39 Lewis, Joe E., editor. A Documentary History of Human Rights: A Record of the Events, Documents and Speeches That Shaped Our World. Published by Carroll & Graf Publishers, 2003, p. 115
40 Wilhelm, Joseph. "Heresy." The Catholic Encyclopedia. Vol. 7. Nihil Obstat. June 1, 1910. Remy Lafort, S.T.D., Censor. Imprimatur. +John Cardinal Farley, Archbishop of New York. New York: Robert Appleton Company, 1910. 13 May 2009 <http://www.newadvent.org/cathen/07256b.htm>
41 Bagatti. The Church from the Gentiles in Palestine, pp. 47-48
42 Eusebius of Caesarea. The Life of the Blessed Emperor Constantine, Book III, Chapters LXIV, LXV.—Constantine's Edict against the Heretics. Volume I, Nicene and Post-Nicene Fathers, 2nd Series, ed. P. Schaff and H. Wace, (Edinburgh: repr. Grand Rapids MI: Wm. B. Eerdmans, 1955; the digital version is by The Electronic Bible Society, Dallas
43 Bagatti, Bellarmino. Translated by Eugene Hoade. The Church from the Gentiles in Palestine. Nihil obstat: Ignatius Mancini, 1 Februari 1970. Imprimi potest: Herminius Roncari, 26 Februari 1970. Imprimatur: +Albertus Gori, die 28 Februarii 1970. Franciscan Printing Press, Jerusalem, 1971, pp. 13-14
44 Braun J. Transcribed by Michael T. Barrett. Vestments. The Catholic Encyclopedia, Volume XV. Published 1912. New York: Robert Appleton Company. Nihil Obstat, October 1, 1912. Remy Lafort, S.T.D., Censor. Imprimatur. +John Cardinal Farley, Arch-

bishop of New York
45 Pines, p.31
46 Gibbon E. Decline and Fall of the Roman Empire, Volume III, Chapter XXVII. ca. 1776-1788. The Modern Library, NY
47 Eusebius. The History of the Church, Book V, Chapter XXIV, Verses 2-7, p. 114
48 Fortescue, Adrian. "Theodosius I." The Catholic Encyclopedia. Vol. 14. Nihil Obstat. July 1, 1912. Remy Lafort, S.T.D., Censor. Imprimatur. +John Cardinal Farley, Archbishop of New York. New York: Robert Appleton Company, 1912. 3 Feb. 2009 <http://www.newadvent.org/cathen/14577d.htm>
49 Hurlbut JL. The Story of the Christian Church. Zondervan, 1967, pp. 58,62
50 Elowsky, Joel. Ancient Christian Commentary on Current Events: What Is War Good For? Christianity Today, posted October 28, 2003 and De Rosa, Peter. Vicars of Christ. Poolberg Press, Dublin, 2000, p. 156 and Latourette K.S. A History of Christianity, Volume 1, Beginnings to 1500. Harper, San Francisco, 1975, p. 89
51 Bede (Monk), first written ca. early 8th century. Edited by Judith McClure and Roger Collins. The Ecclesiastical History of the English People. Oxford University Press, NY, 1999, pp. 156-157. Bede wrote, "John…literally observed the decrees of the Mosaic law when the Church was still Jewish in many respects…"
52 Jerome. Translated by J.G. Cunningham, M.A. From Jerome to Augustine (A.D. 404); LETTER 75 (AUGUSTINE) OR 112 (JEROME). Excerpted from Nicene and Post-Nicene Fathers, Series One, Volume 1, Chapter 13. Edited by Philip Schaff, D.D., LL.D. 1886. Hendrickson Publishers, Peabody (MA), 1999 printing, p. 339
53 Epiphanius. Panarion 29 as cited in Pritz. Nazarene Jewish Christianity. Magnas, Jerusalem, 1988, p. 35
54 Jerome. De Viris Illustribus (On Illustrious Men), Chapter 18. Copyright © 2008 by Kevin Knight
55 Schaff, Philip, History of the Christian Church, (Oak Harbor, WA: Logos Research Systems, Inc.) 1997. This material has been carefully compared, corrected, and emended (according to the 1910 edition of Charles Scribner's Sons) by The Electronic Bible Society, Dallas, TX, 1998
56 Pritz R. Nazarene Jewish Christianity. Magnas, Jerusalem, 1988, p. 75

57 Bagatti, Bellarmino. Translated by Eugene Hoade. The Church from the Circumcision. Nihil obstat: Marcus Adinolfi, 13 Maii 1970. Imprimi potest: Herminius Roncari, 14 Junii 1970. Imprimatur: +Albertus Gori, die 26 Junii 1970. Franciscan Printing Press, Jerusalem, 1971, p. 35

58 Kramer H.B. L. The Book of Destiny. Nihil Obstat: J.S. Considine, O.P., Censor Deputatus. Imprimatur: +Joseph M. Mueller, Bishop of Sioux City, Iowa, January 26, 1956. Reprint TAN Books, Rockford (IL), p. 165

59 Shahan TJ. Transcribed by Sean Hyland. First Council of Constantinople. The Catholic Encyclopedia, Volume IV. Published 1908. New York: Robert Appleton Company. Nihil Obstat. Remy Lafort, Censor. Imprimatur. +John M. Farley, Archbishop of New York

60 Bagatti. The Church from the Circumcision, p.2

61 Pines S. The Jewish Christians of the Early Centuries of Christianity according to a New Source. Proceedings of the Israel Academy of Sciences and Humanities II, No.13; 1966. Jerusalem, pp. 38-39

62 Lewis, p. 61

63 Pines, pp. 38-39

64 The Original And True Rheims New Testament Of Anno Domini 1582. Prepared and Edited by Dr. William von Peters, Ph.D.Copyright © 1998, Dr. William G. von Peters. Ph.D. 2004, copyright assigned to VSC Corp., pp. 556-557

65 Third Lateran Council, Canon 27. 1179 A.D. Translation taken from Decrees of the Ecumenical Councils, ed. Norman P. Tanner

66 Pinay, Maurice. The Plot Against the Church, Part Four Chapter One. Translated from the German and Spanish editions of the same work. 1962

67 Hastings J, Selbie A, Lambert JC. Dictionary of the apostolic church. C. Scribner's sons, 1915, pp-207-208

68 The Confession of Faith: Which Was Submitted to His Imperial Majesty Charles V. At the Diet of Augsburg in the Year 1530. by Philip Melanchthon, 1497-1560. Translated by F. Bente and W. H. T. Dau. Published in: Triglot Concordia: The Symbolical Books of the Ev. Lutheran Church. St. Louis: Concordia Publishing House, 1921, p. 95

69 Davis, Tamar. A General History of the Sabbatarian Churches. 1851; Reprinted 1995 by Commonwealth Publishing, Salt Lake City, p. 106

70 Thiel B. The Beginning and the End of the Christian Church Era: An Alternative View of Church History by One Who Actually Believes the Bible. Nazarene Books, in press 2009. www.nazarenebooks.com
71 Ogwyn J. God's Church through the Ages. LCG booklet.
72 Devine, Arthur. Transcribed by Marie Jutras. Prophecy. The Catholic Encyclopedia, Volume XII. Published 1911. New York: Robert Appleton Company. Nihil Obstat, June 1, 1911. Remy Lafort, S.T.D., Censor. Imprimatur. +John Cardinal Farley, Archbishop of New York
73 Culligan E. The Last World War and the End of Time. The book was blessed by Pope Paul VI, 1966. TAN Books, Rockford (IL), Pp. 130-131
74 Culligan, pp. 100-101
75 Dupont, Yves. Catholic Prophecy: The Coming Chastisement. TAN Books, Rockford (IL), 1973, p. 23
76 Araujo, p. 59
77 Flynn T & M. The Thunder of Justice. Maxkol Communications, Sterling (VA), 1993, p. 20
78 Flynn, pp. 4-5
79 The Vision Of Pope Leo XIII, October 13, 1884 http://www.stjosephschurch.net/leoxiii.htm viewed 02/25/09
80 Tzima Otto, H. The Great Monarch and WWIII in Orthodox, Roman Catholic and Scriptural Prophecies. Verenikia Press, Rock Hill (SC), 2000, pp. xxii, 471
81 Culleton, R. Gerald. The Prophets and Our Times. Nihil Obstat: L. Arvin. Imprimatur: Philip G. Scher, Bishop of Monterey-Fresno, November 15, 1941. Reprint 1974, TAN Books, Rockford (IL), p.139
82 Birch, DA. Trial, Tribulation & Triumph: Before During and After Antichrist. Queenship Publishing Company, Goleta (CA), 1996, pp. 317,326
83 Emmerich AC. The Life of Lord Jesus Christ and Biblical Revelations. Schmöger edition, Vol. IV. Nihil Obstat: D. Jaegher, 14 Februari 1914. Imprimatur: A.C. De Schrevel, Brugis, 14 Februari 1914. Reprint TAN Books, Rockford (IL), 2004: pp. 353-354
84 Ogwyn, God's Church through the Ages.
85 Dupont, p. 113
86 Mother Shipton's Prophecies. http://www.crystalinks.com/shipton.html 08/26/08
87 Araujo, pp. 80-81

APPENDIX C: ENDNOTES

88   Dupont, p.37
89   Culleton, The Reign of Antichrist, p. 163
90   Culleton, The Prophets and Our Times, p. 24
91   Conte Jr., Ronald L. The Great Apostasy and the Abomination of Desolation. December 23, 2005. http://www.catholicplanet.com/future/great-apostasy.htm viewed 12/13/08
92   Pui-Hua, p. 109
93   Birch, pp. xlii-xliii, 555
94   Kramer, p. 228
95   Dupont, p. 90
96   Dupont, p. 31
97   Connor Edward. Prophecy for Today. Imprimatur + A.J. Willinger, Bishop of Monterey-Fresno; Reprint: Tan Books and Publishers, Rockford (IL), 1984, p. 25
98   Connor, p. 33
99   Connor, pp. 33-34. Note: Edward Connor reported, "There were no Protestants in the 14th century; the word perhaps should be "heretics" (p. 40).
100   Dupont, p. 13
101   Connor, pp. 35-36
102   Thigpen P. The Rapture Trap: A Catholic Response to "End Times" Fever. Ascension Press, 2001, p. 216
103   Connor, Edward. Prophecy for Today. Imprimatur + A.J. Willinger, Bishop of Monterey-Fresno; Reprint: Tan Books and Publishers, Rockford (IL), 1984, pp. 123-126
104   Dupont, p.19
105   Connor, pp. 7-9
106   Bander, Peter. Introductory commentary in The Prophecies of St. Malachy. TAN Books, Rockford (IL), 1973, p. 11
107   Devine, Arthur. "Prophecy." The Catholic Encyclopedia. Vol. 12. Nihil Obstat. June 1, 1911. Remy Lafort, S.T.D., Censor. Imprimatur. +John Cardinal Farley, Archbishop of New York. New York: Robert Appleton Company, 1911. 10 Mar. 2009 <http://www.newadvent.org/cathen/12473a.htm>
108   Bander, pp. 50-54
109   Bander, p. 96
110   Rossi, Gaudentius. The Christian Trumpet: Or, Previsions and Predictions about Impending General Calamities, the Universal Triumph of the Church, the Coming of the Anti-Christ, the Last Judgment, and the End of the World; Divided Into Three Parts, 4th edition. Patrick Donahoe, 1875. Original from Oxford Uni-

versity Digitized Sep 1, 2006, p. 203
111. Dupont, p. 93
112. Dupont, p.94
113. Dupont, p. 94
114. Chopra, R. editor in chief. Nostradamus Prophecies with Famous Examples. http://www.liveindia.com/nostradamus/famous.html viewed 11/29/08
115. Nostradamus. Les Propheties. 1840 Bareste edition. http://yowusa.com/nostradamus/c10/61.shtml visited 10/22/07 & 11/29/08
116. The Lost Book of Nostradamus. The History Channel. Original air date, January 2009
117. Kumar, Vijay. End of the World 2012. http://www.godrealized.com/2012.html viewed 01/18/09
118. Hindu Prophecies: The Kalki Purana. http://ww-iii.tripod.com/hindu.htm viewed 04/19/09
119. Horoscope of Shri Mataji Nirmala Devi – by Lalit Bhandari (given during Tour of Australia – 22 October 1991; http://www.adishakti.org/mayan_end_times_12-21-2012/shri_mataji's_horoscope_the_tribulation_and_satya_yuga.htm viewed 8/20/08
120. Raju Apr 22 2007, 01:06 AM. India Discussion Forum. http://www.india-forum.com/forums/index.php?act=Print&client=printer&f=10&t=1843 viewed 8/20/08
121. Kalki Avatar. Indian Mythology. http://www.webonautics.com/mythology/avataar_kalki2.html viewed 4/19/09
122. NEW AGE SPIRITUALITY a.k.a. Self-spirituality, New spirituality, Mind-body-spirit. Religious Tolerance.org http://www.religioustolerance.org/newage.htm viewed 03/14/09
123. Schneider L. A New Age of Peace. http://www.beliefnet.com/News/Peace/A-New-Age-Of-Peace.aspx viewed 03/14/09
124. Braden, pp. 74,78
125. Braden G. The Mystery of 2012: Predictions, Prophecies and Possibilities. Sounds True, Incorporated, 2009, p. 425
126. Weidner J, Bridges V. Harrington M. A Monument to the End of Time: Alchemy, Fulcanelli and the Great Cross. Aethyrea Books LLC, 2000, p. 173
127. Araujo, p. 75
128. Birch, p. 449
129. Culleton, The Prophets and Our Times, p. 193
130. Culleton. The Prophets and Our Times, pp. 179,180
131. Araujo, pp. 84-85

APPENDIX C: ENDNOTES

132 Epstein R. BUDDHIST IDEAS FOR ATTAINING WORLD PEACE. Lectures for the Global Peace Studies Program, San Francisco State University, November 7 & 9, 1988 http://online.sfsu.edu/~rone/Buddhism/BUDDHIST%20IDEAS%20FOR%20ATTAINING%20WORLD%20PEACE.htm viewed 03/14/09
133 Roerich N. Shambhala. 1930, Reprint, Vedams eBooks (P) Ltd, 2003, pp. 11-12
134 Cited in World Scripture, IRF, Paragon House Publishing, 1995, p. 786 per http://www.adishakti.org/prophecies/23_maitreya_the_three_mothers_has_incarnated_herself.htm 03/18/09
135 Ahlström, Gösta W. Prophecy in other religions » Prophetic movements and figures in the Eastern religions. Encyclopedia Brittanica Online. http://www.britannica.com/EBchecked/topic/479082/prophecy/34075/Prophecy-in-other-religions viewed 03/18/09
136 Here are two examples, Daniel 7:7-8. The Wycliffe Bible Commentary, Electronic Database. Copyright (c) 1962 by Moody Press) and The Prophecies of Daniel. The Original And True Douay Old Testament Of Anno Domini 1610, Volume 2. Prepared and Edited by Dr. William von Peters, Ph.D. Copyright © 2005, Dr. William G. von Peters. Ph.D. 2005 copyright assigned to VSC Corp., p. 732
137 Conway E, Monaghan A. Europe in deepest recession since War as Germany suffers. Telegraph - May 15, 2009. http://www.telegraph.co.uk/finance/economics/5331129/Europe-in-deepest-recession-since-War-as-Germany-suffers.html viewed 05/16/09
138 Culleton, The Prophets and Our Times, p. 182
139 Dupont, pp. 21-22
140 Connor p.84
141 Culleton, The Prophets and Our Times, p. 195
142 Birch, p. 553
143 Dupont, p.37
144 Birch, p. 553
145 Joannes Amadeus de Sylva, in Connor, p. 34
146 By Methodius of Patara, claimed 4th century as cited in Tzima Otto, p. 109
147 Matthew Henry's Commentary on the Whole Bible: New Modern Edition, Electronic Database. Copyright (c) 1991 by Hendrickson Publishers, Inc.
148 The Wycliffe Bible Commentary, Electronic Database. Copyright (c) 1962 by Moody Press

149 Walvoord JF. The Prophecy Knowledge Handbook. Victor Books/SP Publications, Wheaton (IL), 1990, p. 257
150 Primor A. A foreign army at the gate. Haaretz, Israel News, October 7, 2008. http://www.haaretz.com/hasen/spages/1027062.html viewed 03/11/09 and Mizroch A. Israel sees ties with EU as crucial Jerusalem Post - Feb 22, 2008; http://www.jpost.com/servlet/Satellite?cid=1203605149734&pagename=JPost%2FJPArticle%2FShowFull
151 As cited in Richardson J. Antichrist: Islam's Awaited Messiah. Pleasant Word, 2006, p. 48
152 Ibn Zubair Ali, Mohammed Ali. The minor signs of Last Days from: The Signs of Qiyamah. http://www.islamawareness.net/Prophecies/minor.html viewed 06/21/09
153 European Parliament Approves Military Use of Galileo Satellite. DPA news agency. Deutsche Welle - July 10, 2008. http://www.dw-world.de/dw/article/0,2144,3474226,00.html viewed 05/14/09
154 Lytle JM. US says GPS satellite coverage may fail soon. Maintenance delays mean EU's Galileo may step in. TechRadar UK - May 14, 2009. http://www.techradar.com/news/portable-devices/satnav/us-says-gps-satellite-coverage-may-fail-soon-599431 viewed 05/17/09
155 Pasztor A. GPS Satellite Glitches Fuel Concern on Next Generation. Wall Street Journal, June 17, 2009 http://online.wsj.com/article/SB124520702464422059.html viewed 06/17/09
156 Atkins W. Last magnet lowered into Large Hadron Collider. 02 May 2009. iTWire. http://www.itwire.com/content/view/24778/1066/1/1/ viewed 05/15/09
157 Israel sees ties with EU as crucial Jerusalem Post - Feb 22, 2008; http://www.jpost.com/servlet/Satellite?cid=1203605149734&pagename=JPost%2FJPArticle%2FShowFull
158 Culleton, The Prophets and Our Times, p. 136
159 Culleton, The Prophets and Our Times, p.137
160 Birch, p. 281
161 Connor, p. 31
162 Culleton, The Prophets and Our Times, p. 110
163 Tzima Otto, pp. 127-139
164 Kurz W. What Does the Bible Say About the End Times? A Catholic View. Servant Books, Cincinnati. Nihil Obstat: Kistner H., Schehr T.P. Imprimi Potest: Link F., Paul J.M. Imprimatur: Carl K. Moeddel, Vicar General and Auxillary Bishop, Archdiocese of Cincinnati, July 19, 2004. Servant Books, Cincinnati, 2004,

APPENDIX C: ENDNOTES

p. 68
165   Araujo, Fabio R. Selected Prophecies and Prophets. BookSurge LLC, Charlestown (SC), 2007, p. 132
166   Jerome. Commentary on Daniel, Preface and Chapter 11. Translated by Gleason L. Archer. (1958). p. 15 http://www.tertullian.org/fathers/jerome_daniel_02_text.htm viewed 12/20/08
167   Daniel 11:21-45 The reign of Antiochus Epiphanes. Matthew Henry's Commentary on the Whole Bible: New Modern Edition, Electronic Database. Copyright (c) 1991 by Hendrickson Publishers, Inc.
168   Snooks, Graeme Donald. The Ephemeral Civilization: Exploding the Myth of Social Evolution. Routledge, 1997, p. 173
169   Birch, pp. 317,326
170   Culleton, The Prophets and Our Times, p. 179
171   Dupont, pp.60,62,71
172   Emmerich, The Life and Revelations, Vol. II, pp. 77,279-281,290-291
173   Kirsch, Johann Peter. "Millennium and Millenarianism." The Catholic Encyclopedia. Vol. 10. Nihil Obstat. October 1, 1911. Remy Lafort, S.T.D., Censor. Imprimatur. +John Cardinal Farley, Archbishop of New York. New York: Robert Appleton Company, 1911. 18 Mar. 2009 <http://www.newadvent.org/cathen/10307a.htm>.
174   LeFrois, Bernard J. Eschatological Interpretation of the Apocalypse. The Catholic Biblical Quarterly, Vol. XIII, pp. 17-20; Cited in Culleton RG. The Reign of Antichrist, 1951. Reprint TAN Books, Rockford (IL), 1974, p. 9
175   Catechism of the Catholic Church, p. 194
176   As cited in Birch, pp. 515-516
177   Orthodox Christian Beliefs and Practices. © 2006-2007 Ukrainian Orthodox Church of Canada. http://www.uocc.ca/en-ca/faith/beliefs/ 08/18/07
178   Batiffel, Pierre. Transcribed by Elizabeth T. Knuth. Apocatastasis. The Catholic Encyclopedia, Volume I. Published 1907. New York: Robert Appleton Company. Nihil Obstat, March 1, 1907. Remy Lafort, S.T.D., Censor. Imprimatur. +John Cardinal Farley, Archbishop of New York
179   Thiel B. Universal Offer of Salvation: There Are Hundreds of Verses in the Bible Supporting the True Doctrine of Apocatastasis. www.cogwriter.com/apocatastasis.htm 2007/2008/2009
180   Ware T. The Orthodox Church. Penguin Books, London, 1997,

pp.255,262
181 BERNARD GUI: INQUISITOR'S MANUAL, Chapter 5. Translated by David Burr, History Department, Virginia Tech, Blacksburg, VA. http://phi.kenyon.edu/Projects/Margin/inquisit.htm 04/09/07
182 Thiel B. Universal Offer of Salvation: There Are Hundreds of Verses in the Bible Supporting the True Doctrine of Apocatastasis.
183 Bagatti. The Church from the Gentiles in Palestine, p. 58 and Bagatti. The Church from the Circumcision, p. 13
184 Pinay, Maurice. The Plot Against the Church, Part Four Chapter One. Translated from the German and Spanish editions of the same work. 1962
185 Cited in Tzima Otto, p. 135; Dr. Otto herself refers to those with Nazarene beliefs as "Christian traitors" on p. 240
186 Connor, p.26
187 Connor, p. 27
188 Culleton, The Prophets and Our Times, p. 154
189 Emmerich, The Life and Revelations, Volume II. p.292
190 Culligan, pp.127,128
191 Dupont, p.51
192 Dupont, p 114
193 Dupont, p. 114
194 Birch, pp. 364,553
195 Connor, pp.22-23
196 Tzima Otto, p. 113, 114
197 Tzima Otto, pp. 30, 31, 32, 50-51,52
198 Tzima Otto, p. 60
199 Connor, p. 37
200 Culleton, The Prophets and Our Times, p. 50
201 Flynn, p. 372
202 Connor, p. 31
203 Nine Major Approved Apparitions. Theotokos Catholic Books. http://www.theotokos.org.uk/pages/appdisce/nineapps.html 03/18/09
204 Culligan, p. 163
205 Culleton, Reign of Antichrist, pp. 217-218
206 Flynn, p. 326
207 Caldwell S. Pope orders bishops to root out false claims of visions. Telegraph, January 13, 2009. http://www.telegraph.co.uk/news/worldnews/europe/vaticancityandholysee/4223793/Pope-

APPENDIX C: ENDNOTES

orders-bishops-to-root-out-false-claims-of-visions.html viewed 03/20/09

208 Jackson P. ORTHODOX LIFE., No. I, 1997., Brotherhood of Saint Job of Pochaev at Holy Trinity Monastery, Jordanville, N.Y. pp. 18-22. http://fr-d-serfes.org/orthodox/theotokos.htm viewed 05/04/09

209 Dupont, p. 33

210 Dupont, p.76

211 Tzima Otto, p. 252

212 Raum T. U.S. national debt is a growing concern. AP. The Tribune, San Luis Obispo, July 4, 2009, p. B5

213 Tzima Otto, pp. 111, 113,114

214 Alleyne R. Food and energy shortages will create 'perfect storm', says Prof John Beddington. Telegraph, March 19, 2009. http://www.telegraph.co.uk/earth/earthnews/5015051/Food-and-energy-shortages-will-create-perfect-storm-says-Prof-John-Beddington.html viewed 03/19/08

215 Martin Dr. Gerald Celente: Food Riots, Tax Rebellions By 2012. Free Republic. Friday, November 14, 2008. http://www.freerepublic.com/focus/f-bloggers/2132164/posts viewed 05/03/09

216 Kramer H.B. L. The Book of Destiny. Nihil Obstat: J.S. Considine, O.P., Censor Deputatus. Imprimatur: +Joseph M. Mueller, Bishop of Sioux City, Iowa, January 26, 1956. Reprint TAN Books, Rockford (IL), pp. 81,181-182

217 Runningen R, Nichols H. Obama Says U.S. Long-Term Debt Load 'Unsustainable'. Bloomberg.com May 14, 2009 19:40 EDT. http://www.bloomberg.com/apps/news?pid=newsarchive&sid=aJsSb4qtILhg viewed 05/16/09

218 Taheri, A. Obama and Ahmadinejad. Forbes.com 10.26.08, 1:33 PM ET http://www.forbes.com/2008/10/26/obama-iran-ahmadinejad-oped-cx_at_1026taheri_print.html viewed 02/28/09

219 Markowitz N. "Just Wars" and "Winnable Wars": Obama and Afghanistan. Political Affairs, 3/20/09. http://www.politicalaffairs.net/article/articleview/8278/ viewed 3/23/09

220 Obama and Democracy. Wall Street Journal, June 6, 2009. http://online.wsj.com/article/SB124424627384290569.html viewed 07/02/09

221 Glasse C. New Encyclopedia of Islam: A Revised Edition of the Concise Encyclopedia of Islam, 3rd edition, 2008, pp. 143, 316

222 Reagen DR. Further Thoughts About a Muslim Antichrist. Bible Prophecy Today, March 16, 2009. http://bible-prophecy-today.

blogspot.com/2009/03/further-thoughts-about-muslim.html viewed 03/18/09

223 Nayouf, Hayyan. Translated from Arabic by Sonia Farid. Shiite scholar denies Obama link to Muslim savior. Dubai. November 4, 2008. http://www.alarabiya.net/articles/2008/11/04/59490.html viewed 05/19/09

224 The Qur'an. From chapter 43, known as AZ-ZUKHRUF (ORNAMENTS OF GOLD, LUXURY). http://www.usc.edu/schools/college/crcc/engagement/resources/texts/muslim/quran/043.qmt.html The Qur'an viewed 03/22/09

225 Fight the Smears. http://fightthesmears.com/articles/3/baracks-faith viewed 11/29/08

226 Martin J, Lee C. Obama skips church, heads to gym. Politico, 11/23/08

227 Olsen, Andrew. Nostradamus Obama Prophecies Revealed. Daily Squib, April 10th, 2008; http://www.dailysquib.co.uk/?c=117&a=1300

228 Reese, Ron. "FOUND IN BOOK OF REVELATION--OBAMA'S CONFIRMING OF COVENANT ON OCT. 29, 2008!!!", December 1, 2008. http://www.fivedoves.com/letters/dec2008/ronr121.htm viewed 2/28/09

229 Who is Barrack Obama? The Ghanaian Chronicle, Volume: 18, Edition No: 194, July 10, 2009 http://www.ghanaian-chronicle.com/thestory.asp?id=12800&title=%3Cb%3EWho%20is%20Barrack%20Obama?%3C/b%3E viewed 07/11/09

230 Luo. Junior Worldmark Encyclopedia of World Cultures, 1999, article pages 1 & 3. http://findarticles.com/p/articles/mi_gx5217/is_1999/ai_n19133319/pg_1?tag=artBody;col1 viewed 11/04/08

231 http://www.babynames.com/name/BARAK

232 http://www.babynames.com/name/HUSSEIN

233 http://www.babynames.com/name/OBAMA viewed 03/18/09

234 http://www.babyhold.com/list/Hebrew_Baby_Names/Bama/details/ viewed 11/16/08

235 "Visions of the Great Nyasaye, A Study of the Luo Religion in Kenya", Order of Sorcha Faal, Sister Mary McCrea © 1915; © February 13, 2008 EU and US all rights reserved. http://www.whatdoesitmean.com/index1070.htm viewed 4/17/08

236 National Public Radio. Obama Makes First Visit To Subsaharan Africa. http://www.npr.org/templates/story/story.php?storyId=106419765 viewed 07/10/09

237 Cardinal Stafford criticizes Obama as 'aggressive, disruptive and apocalyptic'. Catholic News Agency. Nov 17, 2008. http://catholicnewsagency.com/new.php?n=14355 viewed 03/01/09
238 Stafford, Cardinal James Francis. Cardinal's Address to Catholic University of America, November 13, 2008. Catholic News Agency. http://www.catholicnewsagency.com/document.php?n=780 viewed 03/01/09
239 Gardiner N. Barack Obama will back a federal Europe. Telegraph, March 18, 2009. http://www.telegraph.co.uk/comment/5005351/Barack-Obama-will-back-a-federal-Europe.html viewed 03/20/09
240 Bender B. Gates readies big cuts in weapons. Boston Globe, March 17, 2009 http://www.boston.com/news/nation/washington/articles/2009/03/17/gates_readies_big_cuts_in_weapons/ viewed 03/18/09
241 Obama discusses Daschle, the economy. CNN, AC 360, February 3, 2009. http://edition.cnn.com/2009/POLITICS/02/03/obama.qanda/?iref=hpmostpop viewed 03/01/09
242 Conway E. Britain showing signs of heading towards 1930s-style depression, says Bank. Telegraph, March 16, 2009. http://www.telegraph.co.uk/finance/financetopics/recession/4996994/Britain-showing-signs-of-heading-towards-1930s-style-depression-says-Bank.html viewed 03/31/09
243 Gibbon E. Decline and Fall of the Roman Empire, Volume I. ca. 1776-1788. The Modern Library, NY, p. 403
244 Babylonian Talmud: Tractate Sanhedrin Folio 97a
245 Gieseler, Johann Karl Ludwig. A Text-book of Church History. Translated by Samuel Davidson, John Winstanley Hull, Mary A. Robinson. Harper & brothers, 1857, Original from the University of Michigan, Digitized Feb 17, 2006, pp. 128, 166-167
246 Sungenis R. Good News and Bad News Regarding Scriptural Chronologies. Catholic Apologetics International. http://www.catholicintl.com/catholicissues/scriptural-chronologies2.htm viewed 05/12/09
247 Epistle of Barnabas, 15:1-5
248 By a certain Philip, disciple of Bardesan. Appendix after The Book of the Laws of Various Countries. Excerpted from Ante-Nicene Fathers, Volume 8. Edited by Alexander Roberts & James Donaldson. American Edition, 1886. Online Edition Copyright © 2004 by K. Knight
249 Irenaeus. Adversus haereses, Book V, Chapter 29, Verse 2. Ex-

250   cerpted from Ante-Nicene Fathers, Volume 1. Edited by Alexander Roberts & James Donaldson. American Edition, 1885. Online Edition Copyright © 2004 by K. Knight
250   St. Hippolytus of Rome, The Catholic Encyclopedia, 1910
251   Hippolytus. On the HexaËmeron, Or Six Days' Work. From Fragments from Commentaries on Various Books of Scripture. http://www.newadvent.org/fathers/0502.htm viewed 9/17/07
252   Culligan E. The Last World War and the End of Time. The book was blessed by Pope Paul VI, 1966. TAN Books, Rockford (IL), pp. 113-115
253   Rossi , Gaudentius. The Christian Trumpet: Or, Previsions and Predictions about Impending General Calamities, the Universal Triumph of the Church, the Coming of the Anti-Christ, the Last Judgment, and the End of the World; Divided Into Three Parts, 4th edition. Patrick Donahoe, 1875. Original from Oxford University. Digitized Sep 1, 2006, p. 233
254   Blair PH, Lapidge M. The world of Bede. Cambridge University Press, 1990, p. 266
255   Culligan, pp. 113-115
256   Catechism of the Catholic Church, p. 194
257   Bible Study Course. Lesson 2, Part 2, God 7,000-Year Plan. Living Church of God, Copyright © 2008 Living Church of God. http://online.twbiblecourse.org/bsc_lesson_content.php?lesson=2&page=5 viewed 04/19/08
258   There have been concerns about whether Terah was 70 or 130 when Abram was born. Here is one explanation from J. Sarfati, "Note that Abraham was not Terah's firstborn. Gen. 12:4 says Abraham was 75 when he left Haran, and this was soon after Terah died at 205 (Gen. 11:32), and the difference (205-75) means Terah was actually 130 years old when Abraham was born, not 70 (Ussher seems to have been the first modern chronologist to have noticed this point). The latter figure refers to Terah's age when the oldest of the three sons mentioned was born, probably Haran." Sarfati J. Journal of Creation 17(3):14–18 December 2003. http://creation.com/biblical-chronogenealogies viewed 05/23/09)
259   Thiele E. The Mysterious Numbers of the Hebrew Kings. Kregel Publications version, 1994, p. 80
260   Long, Jesse. 1 & 2 Kings: 1 and 2 Kings. College Press, 2002, p. 156
261   Thiele, p. 80

APPENDIX C: ENDNOTES

262 Canning, John. 100 Great Kings, Queens, and Rulers of the World. Taplinger Pub. Co., 1967, p. 52
263 Wood L, O'Brien D. A Survey of Israel's History. Zondervan, 1986, p. 253
264 Israel I, Silberman. N. David and Solomon: In Search of the Bible's Sacred Kings and the Roots of the Western Tradition. Simon and Schuster, 2007, p. 20
265 Emmerich AC. The Life of Lord Jesus Christ and Biblical Revelations. Schmöger edition, Vol. IV. Nihil Obstat: D. Jaegher, 14 Februari 1914. Imprimatur: A.C. De Schrevel, Brugis, 14 Februari 1914. Reprint TAN Books, Rockford (IL), 2004, pp.156,157
266 Birch, pp.267-270
267 Tzima Otto, p. 190
268 Connor, p. 37
269 Dupont, pp. 115,116
270 Culligan, p. 128
271 Dupont, pp. 34,60-61
272 Connor, p. 76
273 Dupont, p.45
274 Flynn, p, 255
275 Van Den Biesen C. Transcribed by Michael C. Tinkler. Apocalypse. The Catholic Encyclopedia, Volume I. Published 1907. New York: Robert Appleton Company. Nihil Obstat, March 1, 1907. Remy Lafort, S.T.D., Censor. Imprimatur. +John Cardinal Farley, Archbishop of New York
276 Culleton, The Prophets and Our Times, p. 132
277 Hildegard of Bingen. Scivias. Paulist Press, Mahwah (NJ), pp. 497,498
278 Newman, Barbara. Voice of the Living Light: Hildegard of Bingen and Her World. Published by University of California Press, 1998, p. 83
279 Connor, pp. 31-32
280 Connor, p. 73
281 Culleton, The Reign of Antichrist, p. 128
282 Culleton, R. Gerald. The Reign of Antichrist, p. 122
283 Catechism of the Catholic Church, #675, pp. 193-194
284 Culleton, R. Gerald. The Reign of Antichrist, p. 130
285 Rossi,.p. 203
286 The False Prophet. Living in the Final Generation. http://www.geocities.com/rebornempowered/ApparitionsofMary.htm 10/12/07

287 Kramer H., p. 318,320-323
288 Gerasimos, Bishop. At the End of Time: The Eschatological Expectations of the Church. Holy Cross Orthodox Press. October 5, 2004, pp. 28-29
289 José Hoíl, p. 77
290 The Catholic Almanac. By Franciscans: Province of the Most Holy Name of Jesus, Washington (D.C.). Holy Name College, St. Anthony's Guild, Paterson, N.J., 1952, p. 217
291 Kramer P. The Imminent Chastisement for Not Fulfilling Our Lady's Request. An edited transcript of a speech given at the Ambassadors of Jesus and Mary Seminar in Glendale, California, September 24, 2004.THE FATIMA CRUSADER Issue 80, Summer 2005, pp. 32-45 http://www.fatimacrusader.com/cr80/cr80pg32.asp viewed 4/15/08
292 Priest Kramer. As cited by Mario Derksen's article The Blind Leading the Blind Memo to Chris Ferrara, Father Nicholas Gruner and Father Paul Kramer: Please, please take off the blindfolds! in TRADITIONAL INSIGHTS October 7, 2005 Volume 16, no. 250; http://www.dailycatholic.org/issue/05Oct/oct-7mdi.htm 10/10/07
293 Tzima Otto, pp. xxv, 103, 122
294 REIGN OF THE FALSE PROPHET. Catholic Treasures. Audio ITEM #20104. http://www.catholictreasures.com/cartdescrip/20104.html 03/02/09
295 Berry E.S. The Apocalypse of St. John. First published 1921. http://journals.aol.com/langosh5/Father_E_Sylvester_Berry/ 10/12/07
296 Newman JH. The Patristical Idea of Antichrist, Lecture II. Newman Reader — Works of John Henry Newman. Copyright © 2004 by The National Institute for Newman Studies
297 Connor, p. 87
298 Dupont, p. 40
299 Spencer M. The coming evangelical collapse. The Christian Science Monitor, from the March 10, 2009 edition. http://www.csmonitor.com/2009/0310/p09s01-coop.html viewed 03/13/09
300 Ware, p. 255 and Aghiorgoussis, Maximos. The Dogmatic Tradition of the Orthodox Church. Copyright: © 1990-1996. http://www.goarch.org/en/ourfaith/articles/article8038.asp 08/18/07
301 Mastrantonis, G. The Ten Commandments. Copyright: © 1990-1996 Greek Orthodox Archdiocese of America. http://www.goarch.org/en/ourfaith/articles/article7115.asp 05/14/07

APPENDIX C: ENDNOTES

302   Clement of Alexandria. Stromata, Book VI

303   Ware, p. 278

304   Ware, p.296 and Harakis S. The Stand of the Orthodox Church on Controversial Issues. http://www.goarch.org/en/ourfaith/articles/article7101.asp 8/20/05

305   Clendenin D.B. ed. Eastern Orthodox Theology, 2nd ed. Baker Academic, 2003, p.67

306   Ott L. Fundamentals of Catholic Dogma. Translated into English by James Bastible. Nihil Obstat: Jeremiah J. O'Sullivan. Imprimatur + Cornelius, 7 October 1954. Reprint TAN Books, Rockford (IL), 1974, pp. 199-202

307   Damaskinos Papandreou, Orthodox Metropolitan of Switzerland. The Orthodox Churches and Priestly Celibacy. http://www.orthodoxresearchinstitute.org/articles/misc/damaskinos_celibacy.htm viewed 02/04/08

308   Fortesque A. Transcribed by Marie Jutras. Eastern Monasticism. The Catholic Encyclopedia, Volume X. Copyright © 1911 by Robert Appleton Company. Online Edition Copyright © 2003 by K. Knight. Nihil Obstat, October 1, 1911. Remy Lafort, S.T.D., Censor. Imprimatur. +John Cardinal Farley, Archbishop of New York

309   Ware, p.199

310   Thurston, Herbert. "Ash Wednesday." The Catholic Encyclopedia. Vol. 1. Nihil Obstat. March 1, 1907. Remy Lafort, S.T.D., Censor. Imprimatur. +John Cardinal Farley, Archbishop of New York. New York: Robert Appleton Company, 1907. 4 May 2009 <http://www.newadvent.org/cathen/01775b.htm>

311   O'Reilly, Thomas. "Apostolicity." The Catholic Encyclopedia. Vol. 1. New York: Robert Appleton Company, 1907

312   Duffy, Eamon. Saints & Sinners: A History of the Popes. Yale University Press, New Haven (CT), 2002, pp.2,6; Sullivan F.A. From Apostles to Bishops: the development of the episcopacy in the early church. Newman Press, Mahwah (NJ), 2001, pp. 13-15, 221-222; McBrien, Richard P. Lives of the Popes: The Pontiffs from St. Peter to Benedict XVI. Harper, San Francisco, 2005 updated ed., pp. 25, 396; Van Hove A. Transcribed by Matthew Dean. Bishop. The Catholic Encyclopedia, Volume II. Copyright © 1907 by Robert Appleton Company. Online Edition Copyright © 2003 by K. Knight. Imprimatur. +John M. Farley, Archbishop of New York; Kasper, Cardinal Walter. Keynote speech from the Conference of the Society for Ecumenical Studies, the St. Alban's

Christian Study Centre and the Hertfordshire Newman Association at St. Alban's Abbey, Hertfordshire, England, on May 17, 2003
313   McBrien, Richard P. Lives of the Popes: The Pontiffs from St. Peter to Benedict XVI. Harper, San Francisco, 2005 updated ed., pp. 20-22
314   Araujo, p. 68
315   Maas, Anthony. "Filioque." The Catholic Encyclopedia. Vol. 6. Nihil Obstat. September 1, 1909. Remy Lafort, Censor. Imprimatur. +John M. Farley, Archbishop of New York. New York: Robert Appleton Company, 1909. 15 Mar. 2009 <http://www.newadvent.org/cathen/06073a.htm>
316   Tzima Otto, pp. 5-6
317   The Voice of the Fathers is apparently a Greek Orthodox publication that opposes a Roman Catholic, as opposed to Greek Orthodox, Great Monarch, see Tzima Otto, pp, 34-38
318   Tzima Otto, p. 116
319   Tzima Otto, p. 111
320   Culleton, The Prophets and Our Times, p. 149
321   Weidner, p. 173
322   Weidner, p. 237
323   Andrew of Crete. Hom. in Dorm. Deipara, Homily 3 on Mary's Nativity, PG 97, 860 B-C. cited at http://www.bringyou.to/apologetics/a95.htm viewed 03/19/09
324   Flynn, p.349
325   Culleton, The Prophets and Our Times, p. 157-161
326   Schmöger, pp. 290-291
327   Huchedé, P. Translated by JBD. History of Antichrist. Imprimatur Edward Charles Fabre, Bishop of Montreal. English edition 1884, Reprint 1976. TAN Books, Rockford (IL), p. 24
328   Connor, pp. 36-37
329   Birch, pp. 276, 553,554
330   Culleton, The Prophets and Our Times, p. 170
331   Dupont, p. 79
332   Culleton, The Prophets and Our Times, p. 197
333   Irenaeus. Adversus haereses, Book V, Chapter 30, Verse 3. Excerpted from Ante-Nicene Fathers, Volume 1. Edited by Alexander Roberts & James Donaldson. American Edition, 1885. Online Edition Copyright © 2004 by K. Knight
334   Pui-Hua, p. 89
335   Kramer H.B. L. The Book of Destiny, pp. 318,319

APPENDIX C: ENDNOTES

336 Maas, Anthony. "Antichrist." The Catholic Encyclopedia. Vol. 1. New York: Robert Appleton Company, 1907. Nihil Obstat. March 1, 1907. Remy Lafort, S.T.D., Censor. Imprimatur. +John Cardinal Farley, Archbishop of New York. 10 Dec. 2008 <http://www.newadvent.org/cathen/01559a.htm>.)
337 Tzima Otto, p. 138
338 Annotations on The Second Epistle of Saint Paul to the Thessalonians. The Original and True RHEIMS NEW TESTAMENT of Anno Domini 1582 , p. 423
339 Victorinus. Commentary on the Apocalypse, From the 11th Chapter
340 Cyril of Jerusalem. Catechetical Lectures, Lecture 12, On the words Incarnate, and Made Man. Chapter 16
341 Kurz, p. 157
342 Kramer, pp. 256, 257, 323
343 Birch, p. 556
344 Dupont, pp. 29-30
345 Dupont, p.57
346 Tzima Otto, pp. 134,135,240. Note "public executioner of the Sabbatians" is how that portion of the phrase is shown as a translation on page 240 and seems to make the most historical sense of the Greek being translated.
347 Tzima Otto, p. 144
348 Schmöger, p.298
349 Schmöger, pp.279-280,283-284,292
350 Hildegard of Bingen. Scivias. Paulist Press, Mahwah (NJ), pp. 173-174,299
351 Hildegard, p. 457
352 Schmöger, p. 302
353 Schmöger, p.292
354 Schmöger, p.131
355 Schmöger, p.273
356 Matthew Henry's Commentary on the Whole Bible: New Modern Edition, Revelation 11:3-13. Electronic Database. Copyright (c) 1991 by Hendrickson Publishers, Inc.
357 Pui-Hua, p. 142
358 Hopi Civilization. http://2012wiki.com/index.php?title=Hopi_Civilization viewed 01/14/08
359 Visions of the Great Nyasaye, A Study of the Luo Religion in Kenya
360 Pinchbeck, p. 381

361 Connor, pp. 35-36
362 Ogwyn JH. Revelation: The Mystery Unveiled! LCG Booklet, 2006, pp. 17-18, 25, 26
363 Rossi, p. 165
364 Hippolytus. On Christ and Antichrist. http://www.newadvent.org/fathers/0516.htm viewed 12/17/08
365 Cyril of Jerusalem. Catechetical Lecture 15. http://www.newadvent.org/fathers/310115.htm viewed 12/27/08
366 Kurz, p. 96
367 Kramer H.B, pp. 81,181-182
368 Rheims New Testament, p. 556
369 LaHaye T, Jenkins J. Are We Living in the End Times? Tyndale House, Wheaton (IL), 1999, p. 159
370 LaHaye & Jenkins, p. 105, 147)
371 Walvoord, pp. 491-492
372 Walvoord, pp. 333,579
373 Ogwyn JH. Revelation: The Mystery Unveiled!, p. 27
374 Ogwyn JH. Revelation: The Mystery Unveiled!, pp. 22-23
375 Ogwyn JH. Revelation: The Mystery Unveiled!, pp. 38-39
376 Jaishankar A. Earth Hour. Deccan Herald. March 24, 2009. http://www.deccanherald.com/Content/Mar242009/environmet20090323125853.asp
377 Tzima Otto, pp. 82-83
378 Connor, pp. 31-32
379 Rossi, p. 44
380 Culleton, The Prophets and Our Times, p. 137
381 Culleton, The Prophets and Our Times, p. 126-127
382 Culleton, The Reign of Antichrist, pp. 128,129
383 Connor, p. 86
384 Connor, p. 84
385 Connor, pp.35-36
386 Culleton, p. 127
387 December 21, 2012 7 Prophecies Of Doom. Posted March 4, 2008. http://www.aprogrammingpro.com/2008/03/04/december-21-2012-7-prophecies-of-doom/ viewed 04/21/09 and Crowley, Original air date 03/01/07
388 G. Jeffrey MacDonald. Does Maya calendar predict 2012 apocalypse? USA Today. http://www.usatoday.com/tech/science/2007-03-27-maya-2012_n.htm viewed 01/14/08
389 http://www.upi.com/Odd_News/2008/06/23/Many_Dutch_prepare_for_2012_apocalypse/UPI-40461214263554/ and José Hoíl,

APPENDIX C: ENDNOTES

      p. 67
390 Braden, p. 330
391 Weidner, p. 173
392 NEW AGE SPIRITUALITY a.k.a. Self-spirituality, New spirituality, Mind-body-spirit. Religious Tolerance.org http://www.religioustolerance.org/newage.htm viewed 03/14/09
393 Culleton, The Reign of Antichrist, p. 163
394 Pui-Hua, p. 109
395 Ibn Zubair Ali
396 Alleyne R. Food and energy shortages will create 'perfect storm', says Prof John Beddington. Telegraph, March 19, 2009. http://www.telegraph.co.uk/earth/earthnews/5015051/Food-and-energy-shortages-will-create-perfect-storm-says-Prof-John-Beddington.html viewed 03/19/08
397 Pinchbeck, p. 381
398 Horoscope of Shri Mataji Nirmala Devi – by Lalit Bhandari (given during Tour of Australia – 22 October 1991; http://www.adishakti.org/mayan_end_times_12-21-2012/shri_mataji's_horoscope_the_tribulation_and_satya_yuga.htm viewed 8/20/08
399 Mayan Doomsday Prophecy, Decoding the Past. The History Channel. Original air date 08/03/06 and José Hoíl, p. 111
400 Tzima Otto, pp. 111, 113,114
401 Birch, pp. 268-270, 553-555; Connor, p. 37
402 Tzima Otto, pp. 30, 32, 50-51,52,190, 247-352
403 Taheri, A. Obama and Ahmadinejad and Nayouf H. Shiite scholar denies Obama link to Muslim savior
404 Emmerich, The Life and Revelations, Vol. II, pp. 77,279-281,290-291
405 Tzima Otto, pp. 127-139
406 Culleton, The Prophets and Our Times, p. 226
407 Dupont, p.18 and Connor p. 32
408 Tzima Otto, p. 316
409 Connor, pp.22-23; Pinay, part four; and Culleton, p. 157-161
410 Culleton, The Prophets and Our Times, p. 110
411 Tzima Otto, p. 240
412 Kumar, Vijay. End of the World 2012. http://www.godrealized.com/2012.html viewed 01/18/09
413 The False Prophet. Living in the Final Generation. http://www.geocities.com/rebornempowered/ApparitionsofMary.htm 10/12/07, Dupont, p. 34,60-61, and Connor, pp. 31-32
414 José Hoíl, p. 77

415 Tzima Otto, pp. 82-83, 138
416 The Sibylline Oracles, Book VIII, verses 188, pp. 184
417 Culleton, The Prophets and Our Times, pp. 50, Connor, pp. 31-32,36; Flynn, p. 326; ; Connor, p. 37; and Culligan, p. 163
418 Jackson , pp. 18-22
419 Dupont, p. 31
420 Kumar, Vijay. End of the World 2012. http://www.godrealized.com/2012.html viewed 01/18/09
421 Book of Mormon, 1 Nephi 13:4-5. Church of Jesus Christ of Latter Day Saints, Salt Lake City, 1991, p. 24
422 Dupont, p. 31and Hildegard, pp. 301-302; and Flynn, p. 372
423 José Hoíl, pp. 77,80
424 Tzima Otto, p. 252
425 Tzime Otto, p.274
426 Schmöger, p.298
427 Tzima Otto, pp. 132-136
428 Culleton, The Prophets and Our Times, pp. 131,132, 163; Culleton, The Reign of Antichrist, p. 135; Dupont, p.15; Connor, pp.30, 33; and Birch, pp. 308-309
429 Hopi Civilization. http://2012wiki.com/index.php?title=Hopi_Civilization viewed 01/14/08
430 "Visions of the Great Nyasaye, A Study of the Luo Religion in Kenya", Order of Sorcha Faal, Sister Mary McCrea © 1915; © February 13, 2008 EU and US all rights reserved. http://www.whatdoesitmean.com/index1070.htm viewed 4/17/08
431 As if Things Weren't Bad Enough, Russian Professor Predicts End of U.S. Wall Street Journal, Dec 29, 2008 http://online.wsj.com/article/SB123051100709638419.html
432 Culleton, The Prophets and Our Times, p. 163
433 The Sibylline Oracles, Book III, verses 188, 308-319, pp. 78,83
434 Culleton, The Prophets and Our Times, pp. 180, 193; Dupont, p. 76
435 Kumar, Vijay. End of the World 2012. http://www.godrealized.com/2012.html viewed 01/18/09 and Hindu Prophecies: The Kalki Purana. http://ww-iii.tripod.com/hindu.htm viewed 04/19/09
436 Markowitz N. "Just Wars" and "Winnable Wars": Obama and Afghanistan. Political Affairs, 3/20/09. http://www.politicalaffairs.net/article/articleview/8278/ viewed 3/23/09
437 Connor, p. 36
438 Araujo, p. 103

APPENDIX C: ENDNOTES

439 Tzima Otto, pp. 32, 76, 102
440 Culleton, The Prophets and Our Times, pp. 137, 179, 180; Connor, p. 27; and Birch, pp. xlii-xliii, 552-556
441 Cumming J. Sabbath evening readings on the New Testament. 1861. Original from Oxford University Digitized Aug 15, 2006, p. 234
442 Epstein R. BUDDHIST IDEAS FOR ATTAINING WORLD PEACE. Lectures for the Global Peace Studies Program, San Francisco State University, November 7 & 9, 1988 http://online.sfsu.edu/~rone/Buddhism/BUDDHIST%20IDEAS%20FOR%20ATTAINING%20WORLD%20PEACE.htm viewed 03/14/09
443 Dupont, p. 78; Culleton, The Prophets and Our Times, p. 168
444 DR. MENDELEYEFF'S STRIKING PROPHECY; Dead Chemist Foretold the Attack of Europe by a Regenerated China. WILL FIRST FIGHT INDIA Preponderance of Males the Cause -- Japan, Not an "Originator Power," Can Never Be Great. New York Times, August 11, 1907. http://query.nytimes.com/mem/archive-free/pdf?res=9B03E1DF103EE033A25752C1A96E9C946697D6CF viewed 04/21/09
445 Tzima Otto, p. 157
446 Babylonian Talmud: Tractate Sanhedrin Folio 97a
447 Gibbon, p. 403
448 Baldwin C. Holes in Earth's magnetic cloak let the sun in. Reuters, December 16, 2008. http://www.reuters.com/article/scienceNews/idUSTRE4BF79220081216 viewed 03/23/09; Brooks, Michael. Space storm alert: 90 seconds from catastrophe. New Scientist Monday, March 23, 2009. http://www.prisonplanet.com/space-storm-alert-90-seconds-from-catastrophe.html viewed 03/23/09; and Joseph, p. 16
449 Joseph, p. 16; Brooks, Michael. Space storm alert: 90 seconds from catastrophe. New Scientist Monday, March 23, 2009. http://www.newscientist.com/article/mg20127001.300-space-storm-alert-90-seconds-from-catastrophe.html?full=true viewed 03/23/09 and Jaishankar A. Earth Hour. Deccan Herald. March 24, 2009. http://www.deccanherald.com/Content/Mar242009/environmet20090323125853.asp
450 Schmöger, p.298 and Mother Shipton's Prophecies. http://www.crystalinks.com/shipton.html 08/26/08; Dupont, p. 32
451 Connor, pp. 84, 86
452 Gerasimos, pp. 28-29
453 Mayan Dresden Codex, last page

454 Cited in World Scripture, IRF, Paragon House Publishing, 1995, p. 786 per http://www.adishakti.org/prophecies/23_maitreya_the_three_mothers_has_incarnated_herself.htm 03/18/09
455 The Qur'an. From chapter 43, known as AZ-ZUKHRUF (ORNAMENTS OF GOLD, LUXURY). http://www.usc.edu/schools/college/crcc/engagement/resources/texts/muslim/quran/043.qmt.html The Qur'an viewed 03/22/09
456 Isaiah 9:7; 26:12
457 1 Thessalonians 4:16-17; Revelation 20:1-4
458 Kalki Avatar. Indian Mythology. http://www.webonautics.com/mythology/avataar_kalki2.html viewed 4/19/09
459 NEW AGE SPIRITUALITY a.k.a. Self-spirituality, New spirituality, Mind-body-spirit. Religious Tolerance.org http://www.religioustolerance.org/newage.htm viewed 03/14/09
460 Hopi Civilization. http://2012wiki.com/index.php?title=Hopi_Civilization viewed 01/14/08
461 LaHaye & Jenkins, pp. 98,100
462 LaHaye & Jenkins, p. 99
463 LaHaye & Jenkins, p. 100,194
464 LaHaye & Jenkins, p. 99
465 Lindsey H. The Hal Lindsey Report. Trinity Broadcasting Company, original air date February 27, 2009
466 LaHaye & Jenkins, p. 112
467 Walvoord, p. 544
468 Henry, Rev 12:12-17
469 Beza, Theodore. "Commentary on Revelation 12". "The 1599 Geneva Study Bible". <http://bible.crosswalk.com/Commentaries/GenevaStudyBible/gen.cgi?book=re&chapter=012>. 1600-1645. viewed 07/23/08
470 Jamieson R., Fausset A., Brown D.: Commentary Critical and Explanatory on the Whole Bible. Revelation Chapter 12. http://bible.crosswalk.com/Commentaries/JamiesonFaussetBrown/jfb.cgi?book=re&chapter=012 viewed 04/25/09
471 The Original And True Rheims New Testament Of Anno Domini 1582, pp. 556-557
472 Walvoord, p. 233
473 Thigpen P. The Rapture Trap Study Guide. Ascension Press; Stg edition, July 2003, pp. 39-40
474 Rose S. Orthodoxy and the Religion of the Future: "Jesus is Coming Soon". Copyright © 2003 - 2009 OrthodoxPhotos.com. http://www.orthodoxphotos.com/readings/sign/coming.shtml

viewed 06/07/09)
475 Culleton, The Prophets and Our Times, pp. 177-178
476 Culleton, The Prophets and Our Times, pp. 171,172
477 Birch, pp. 225,226
478 Jerome. Commentary on Daniel, Chapter 11. Translated by Gleason L. Archer. (1958). http://www.tertullian.org/fathers/jerome_daniel_02_text.htm viewed 12/20/08
479 Sarkozy Helps to Bring Syria Out of Isolation. New York Times, July 14, 2008. http://www.nytimes.com/2008/07/14/world/europe/14france.html?em&ex=1216094400&en=bfad08e20a1536e6&ei=5087%0A
480 Pay Attention to Daniel's Prophecy! Watchtower Bible and Tract Society of New York, Brooklyn, 1999; 2006 printing, p. 218
481 Pay Attention to Daniel's Prophecy!, p. 247
482 1 Nephi 13:4-5
483 Fausset, A. R., A.M. "Commentary on Daniel 11". "Commentary Critical and Explanatory on the Whole Bible". <http://bible.crosswalk.com/Commentaries/JamiesonFaussetBrown/jfb.cgi?book=da&chapter=011>. 1871. viewed 7/23/08
484 Holy Bible: Vine's Expository Reference Edition., p. 788
485 Gesenius HFW, Driver SR, Briggs CA, Brown F, Robinson E.
486 Jerome. Commentary on Daniel, Chapter 11.
487 Culleton, The Prophets and Our Times, p. 226
488 Jerome. Commentary on Daniel, Chapter 11
489 Jerome. Commentary on Daniel, Chapter 11
490 Culleton, The Prophets and Our Times, p. 151
491 Lytle JM.
492 Dupont, p.18
493 Tzima Otto, p. 316
494 Connor, p. 32
495 Gigot FE. Transcribed by Donald J. Boon. The Abomination of Desolation. The Catholic Encyclopedia, Volume I. Published 1907. New York: Robert Appleton Company. Nihil Obstat, March 1, 1907. Remy Lafort, S.T.D., Censor. Imprimatur. +John Cardinal Farley, Archbishop of New York 1907
496 The Original And True Douay Old Testament Of Anno Domini 1610, Volume 2. Prepared and Edited by Dr. William von Peters, Ph.D. Copyright © 2005, Dr. William G. von Peters. Ph.D., p. 2005 copyright assigned to VSC Corp., p. 741
497 Clarke A. The Adam Clarke Commentary, Daniel Chapter 11. http://www.studylight.org/com/acc/view.

cgi?book=da&chapter=011 viewed 04/25/09
498 In this Sign you will conquer with One Voice. Cyndi Cain's SYMPHONY OF SUFFERING column www.DailyCatholic.org September 3-5, 2001 volume 12, no. 148
499 Tzima Otto, p. 240
500 OT:6256 `eth. Biblesoft's New Exhaustive Strong's Numbers and Concordance with Expanded Greek-Hebrew Dictionary. Copyright (c) 1994, Biblesoft and International Bible Translators, Inc.
501 The Wycliffe Bible Commentary, Daniel 12:1
502 Dupont, p.31
503 Kramer H.B. L. The Book of Destiny. Nihil Obstat: J.S. Considine, O.P., Censor Deputatus. Imprimatur: +Joseph M. Mueller, Bishop of Sioux City, Iowa, January 26, 1956. Reprint TAN Books, Rockford (IL),pp. 296-297
504 Graff, Ron and Dolphin, Lambert. Thy Kingdom Come, Thy Will Be Done..., Chapter 11. Peninsula Bible Church, Palo Alto (CA), 1998
505 LaHaye T, Hindson E. The Popular Bible Prophecy Commentary. Harvest House, Eugene (OR), 2006, pp. 523-524
506 Hildegard of Bingen. Scivias. Paulist Press, Mahwah (NJ), pp. 301-302
507 Rheims New Testament, p. 556
508 Irenaeus. Adversus haereses, Book V, Chapter 34, Verse 3. Excerpted from Ante-Nicene Fathers, Volume 1. Edited by Alexander Roberts & James Donaldson. American Edition, 1885. Online Edition Copyright © 2004 by K. Knight
509 Hippolytus. On Christ and Antichrist, Chapter 61
510 Cyril of Jerusalem. Catechetical Lecture 15
511 Victorinus of Petau. Commentary on the Apocalpyse. Ante-Nicene Christian library: translations of the writings of the Fathers down to A.D. 325. Edited by Alexander Roberts, James Donaldson. T. and T. Clark, 1870. Original from Harvard University. Digitized Nov 16, 2006, p. 423
512 Tzima Otto, pp.190, 274
513 José Hoíl, p. 80
514 José Hoíl, p. 233
515 Ogwyn J. The United States and Great Britain in Prophecy. LCG Booklet, p. 42
516 Interlinear Transliterated Bible. Dan 11:36, 6213. Copyright (c) 1994 by Biblesoft
517 Gesenius HFW, Driver SR, Briggs CA, Brown F, Robinson E.

APPENDIX C: ENDNOTES

518 Culligan, pp. 118-119
519 Culleton, The Prophets and Our Times, pp. 131,132
520 Culleton, The Prophets and Our Times, p. 163
521 Culleton, The Prophets and Our Times, p. 137
522 Dupont, p.15
523 Connor, p.30
524 Culleton, The Reign of Antichrist, p. 163
525 Birch, pp. 308-309
526 Connor, p. 33
527 Tzima Otto, p, 116
528 Flynn, pp. 341,342
529 Flynn, p. A259
530 Lindsey H. The Hal Lindsey Report. Trinity Broadcasting Company, original air date May 1, 2009
531 Rossi, pp.16, 255
532 The Sibylline Oracles, Book III, verses 188, 308-319, pp. 78,83
533 Osborn A. As if Things Weren't Bad Enough, Russian Professor Predicts End of U.S. Wall Street Journal, Dec 29, 2008 http://online.wsj.com/article/SB123051100709638419.html
534 Culleton, The Reign of Antichrist, p. 163
535 Pui-Hua, p. 164. The ancient Chinese prophecy states, "Population mouth takes territories south of the Yangtze river. The capital is moved again. The two divide up the territories, of which each maintains and defends." This may be related to a deal that perhaps the Chinese will make in the future with Europe, as opposed to military conquest. It also may not be related to the taking of Australia or New Zealand, but perhaps might be.
536 Gardiner N. Barack Obama will back a federal Europe. Telegraph, March 18, 2009. http://www.telegraph.co.uk/comment/5005351/Barack-Obama-will-back-a-federal-Europe.html viewed 03/20/09
537 Dupont, p. 32
538 Culleton, The Prophets and Our Times, p. 172
539 Culleton, The Prophets and Our Times, p. 165
540 Seymour W.W. The cross in tradition, history, and art. G.P. Putnams sons, 1898. Original from Princeton University. Digitized Sep 19, 2008, pp. 910
541 Pui-Hua, p. 85
542 Cumming. p. 234
543 Connor, p. 36
544 Araujo, p. 103

545 Tzima Otto, p. 32
546 Culleton, The Prophets and Our Times, p. 157-161
547 Tzima Otto, p. 178
548 Jerome. Commentary on Daniel, Chapter 11
549 http://www.thenubian.net/nubtoday.php viewed 8/05/06
550 Tzima Otto, pp. 76, 102, 114
551 A Gold Mine Worth LE 23 Billion (and counting). Egypt Today, August, 2006
552 Dupont, p.45
553 Dupont, p. 78
554 Culleton, The Prophets and Our Times, p. 168
555 DR. MENDELEYEFF'S STRIKING PROPHECY, August 11, 1907
556 Tzima Otto, p. 83
557 Tzima Otto, p. 112
558 Tzima Otto, p. 157
559 Dupont, pp. 115-116; Connor pp. 76, 87; Flynn, p. 255; Rossi, p. 203

INDEX

Symbols

6,000 years 130·150·151·152·153·154·155·156·157·158·159·160·161·163·164·243
42 months 141·201·249
666 5·139·190·191·192·195·248·249·255·256
1260 years 41
2012 The Return of Quetzalcoatl 18·339
2012Wiki, Website 25

A

Abaye 151
Abomination of Desolation, The 74·87·121·216·218·248·299·301·302
Abraham 161·162·354
Adharma 63
Adso, Monk 88
Afghanistan 58·147·351·362
Africa 10·35·51·117·127·313·316·326·332·352
Agathaghelos, Hieronymus 89·206
Age of Aquarius 67
Age of peace 14·23·31·51·53·62·64·66·68·69·70·75·80·89·164·183·240·243·244·246·249·250·252·253·254·333
Albigensians 104
Alexander III, Pope 41

Ali, Hussein Ibn 132
Al Qaeda 133
Alten, Steve 17
Alumbrados 104
Amalek 290
Ammon 290·332
Anagata-vamsa 73
Andrew Fool-for-Christ, Saint 109·333·336
Anglicans 11
Anglo-American 130·226·248·249·292·299·316·318·321·323·325·330
Anonymou 112·167·182·318·331
  Paraphrasis 112·167·331
  Prophecy 182·318
Antichrist 3·5·44·45·47·50·51·52·60·71·80·90·91·100·101·106·107·115·116·134·135·139·140·141·142·143·145·168·170·171·172·174·175·186·193·194·195·196·197·198·203·205·206·214·219·221·232·234·235·236·237·238·248·250·261·283·288·290·298·301·303·304·311·318·331·344·345·348·349·350·351·355·356·358·359·360·361·362·366·367
Antiochus 90·91·92·288·304·349
Antiochus IV Epiphanes 90
antipope 5·47·55·56·57·60·165·168·169·172·173·174·175·

188·192·196·198·207·210·
230·236·241·285·302·303·
309
Apocalypse 2012 16·339
Apocatastasis 101·349
Apostolic Penitentiary of the Holy
See 146
Appointed time 131·132·146·148·
287·288·290·294·307·337
Appointed Time 151·294·295
Arabia 116·133·135·136·139·144·
243·296·303·325·329·330·
352
Arabic King 249
Arabized 332
Argüelles, José 68
Armageddon 59·142·222·227·
234·235·244·250
Aryana 141
Asdenti of Taggai, Sister Rose
189
Ash Wednesday 178·357
Asia Minor 10·33·34·35·36·191
Asian Currency Crisis 127
Asians 242·323·335
Asiatic Empire 334
Assyria 242·246·290·322·323
Assyrians 290·321·322·323·329
Atheists 117·176·185·194
Athens 10
Augustus, Caesar 52·286
Australia 316·323·346·361·367
Aystinger the German 88

B

Babylon 7·171·226·228·229·230·
232·233·242·294·313·322·
323·335·336·337
Bagatti, Bellarmino 40·103·341·
343·350
Bahar al-Anvar 132

Baktuns 17
Bama 144·352
Bandarra, Gonçalves Annes 71
Bander, P. 55
Bangladesh 336
Banil Asfaar 84
Barak 144
Bardesan 157·158·353
Bar Kokhba revolt 33
Battle of Armageddon 6·141·142·
222
Beast, The 45·50·65·66·77·81·85·
95·109·112·135·138·139·
140·141·147·192·195·196·
197·198·204·207·214·217·
224·227·236·249·250·256·
263·314·323·324·336
Beddington, Prof. 126·351·361
Bede, the venerable 160
Beginning of sorrows 121·122·
123·124·126·127·128·240·
299·300
Benedict XIII 56
Benedict XVI 7·56·60·160·181·
197·198·292·357·358
Berry, E. Sylvester 174
Bhagavatam, Srimad 65
Bhagwan Kalki 64
Bhutan 336
Bible Code 27
Bible in Basic English (BBE) 296
Biesen, C. Van Den 169
Binitarian 40
Birch, Desmond A. 51·80·88·166·
188·205·286·318
Blast, Robert 27
Blitzkrieg 302
Blond Nation, The 336
blood-vomit 23
Bouquillion, Bertina 44
Brahma 326
Bridges, V. 183·184

INDEX

Bridget of Sweden, Saint 71·105
Brigata, Saint 180
Buddha 7·64·73·74·327
Buddhism 70·72·73·255·326·347·363
Buddhist 3·5·12·13·62·70·72·73·243·244·252·327
Buddhist tenant 243
Byzantine 81·89·167·183·240·241·242·243·332·336

C

Caesar of Arles, St. 231
Cairo 133
Calvin, John 282
Cambodia 327·336
Canada 296·316·321·323·349
Canning, John 163
Canori-Mora, Elizabeth 108
Capuchin Friar 285
Cardinalate 56
Caribbean 296
Castañeda, Quetzil 21
Cataclysms 72·73
Catechism of the Catholic Church 100·170·349·354·355
Cathars 103·104
Catholic Almanac, The 172·356
Catholic Encyclopedia, The 37·180·304·341·342·343·344·345·349·354·355·357·358·359·365
Catholicism 51·71·92·171·319·326·331
Celente, Gerald 127·128·351
Celestine II 55
Charlemagne 285
Charles (Emperor) 88
Chastisement 51·80·108·188·344·356
Chilam Balam 19·21·22·23·30·172·312·339
Chile 282
Chiliasm 100
China 26·29·196·214·296·323·323·327·335·363
Chinese 18·27·51·196·214·240·323·329·335·339·367
Chopra, Deepak 68
Chopra, R. 59
Christ, Jesus 19·22·23·32·33·35·37·38·39·40·41·42·43·45·51·53·64·70·73·75·87·89·91·93·94·95·97·99·101·102·104·107·109·114·116·117·118·119·120·121·122·125·126·128·134·135·136·137·139·143·150·151·152·153·154·155·156·157·158·159·164·168·170·172·181·183·185·187·188·189·193·194·195·200·201·203·204·205·206·211·212·214·215·216·217·222·227·228·231·232·234·235·236·237·238·246·248·250·252·255·256·258·259·260·261·262·263·264·265·266·267·268·269·270·271·272·274·275·276·277·279·280·282·283·291·296·298·299·300·301·304·305·309·311·312·315·319·320·321·327·330·331·334·337·340·342·344·355·356·360·362·364·366
Church of God 42·107·186·230·354
Civil unrest 79·81
Clandestine 41
Clark, Adam 305·366
Clement of Alexandria 34·357
Clement VII 56
Climate change 126

Columbkille, St. 316
Commandments 356
Confucianist 25
Connor, E. 55
Constantine (Emperor) 35·36·38·39·112·187·220·286·315·341
Constantinians 37
Conte, Robert Jr. 50
Corinth 10
Crete 10·358
Crossbearers 185
Crusaders 42·133·184·242·327·328
Crusades, The 41
Culleton, Gerald 50·113·297·298
Culligan, E. 44·159
Cushites 332
Cyprus 295
Cyril of Jerusalem 203·218·359·360·366

D

Daily sacrifices 78·87·302·303
Dajjal 134
Dalmatia 330
Darby, John Nelson 282
Day of the Lord, The 6·73·118·222·223·224·225·226·228·231·246·249·250·269·270·333·337
Debt 7·123·351
December 22, 2012 15·16·27·61·240
Devil, The 20·22·310·312
Devine, A. 55
Dikpati, Mausumi 28
Diocletian (Emperor) 35
Dionysius of Luxemburg 79
Douay Old Testament 304·347·365

Douay OT 306
Dragon 22
Dresden Codex 7·9·18·19·20·22·23·61·244·254·364
Dupont, Yves 48·51·55·58·59·168·303
Dutch 21·339

E

Earth Day 68
Earthquakes 200·201·213·224·227·231·232·233·249·250·274
Eastern Orthodox, The 11·47·88·101·115·177·178·179·182·283·357
Economic blackmail 50·69·249
Ecstatic of Tours, The 50·80
Ecumenical religion 14·68·69·70·81·92·107·114·117·138·165·176·183·188·214·216·241·242·244·248·255·257·298·320·334
Edict Against the Heretics, The 36
Edom 290·332
Edward, Catholic Saint 318
Edward, Saint 317
Egypt 86·162·200·273·288·289·308·326·331·332·333·368
Ekadashi 65
Elias 203·204·212
Elijah (Prophet) 151·203·204
Elisha 203
England 48·60·282·297·316·317·318·319·324·325·334·358
Enoch 203·204·212
Ephesus 7·10·107·116
Ephraem, St. 286
Epiphanes, Antiochus 91·92·288·349

INDEX

Epistle of Barnabas 156·353
Eppinger, Mother Alphonse 52
Epstein, Ron 72
Ethiopia 332
Ethiopians 322·332
Ethnobotanist 27
Euro 333
Europe 29·42·50·52·71·77·78·79·
    80·84·89·112·117·126·127·
    135·140·147·177·227·240·
    285·289·291·297·298·300·
    307·313·320·323·330·334·
    335·347·353·363·367
  Europeans 84·85·147·288·298·
    302·323·329·332
  European Union 78·81·85·86·
    140·175·295·313·314
  European Union 348·352·362
  European Organization for
    Nuclear Research 85

F

Faber, Frederick William 175
Faithless age 80
False prophet 23·118·121·139·
    140·169·171·172·192·194·
    195·196·197·205·206·207·
    235·236·244·247
False religion 106·107·173·250
Famines 121·122·123·126·231·
    299
Fatwa 135
Ferrer, St. Vincent 174
Ferr, Vincent 205
Fifth cycle 17
Fifth Epoch 52
Finkelstein, Israel 163
Flemish 21
Flood 18·19·21·22·23·31·49·50·
    61·70·77·239·240·253·254·
    272·279·312

Flynn, Maureen & Ted 169
Forbes 13·132·136·351
Foreign god 165·175·315·325·
    327
France 81·88·230·331
Francesca de Billiante, Countess
    297
Francesca de Brillante, Countess
    334
Franciscan Friar 189·317
Francis de Paul, St. 185·331
Francis di Paula, Friar 217
Francis of Assisi, St. 170·174
Francis of Paula 166·167

G

Gabar 82
Galileo 85·348
Gameleo 188
Gautama 7·73·74
Gebal 290
Geneva Study Bible 277·364
Gerasimos of Abydos 172
Germany 18·80·81·114·169·207·
    289·325·347
Gibbon 37·340·342·353·363
Gibbon, Edward 150
Gieseler, Johann Karl Ludwig
    152
Global warming 228
Glorious Land 78·332
Godhead 40·194
Gods 95·313·315·326
Gog 134
Gold 165·201·202·243·249·269·
    314·332·333
Golden crown 286
GPS 85·348
Great exploits 304·305
Great Monarch, The 5·6·47·51·52·
    53·54·71·74·79·80·81·89·

108·109·112·113·114·124·
165·166·172·173·176·182·
185·192·207·216·229·230·
231·236·241·242·243·244·
245·285·286·292·303·307·
309·317·318·323·324·325·
331·332·337·344·358
Great Tribulation, The 6·22·53·
87·118·120·123·128·142·
146·149·163·199·215·216·
217·218·219·220·221·222·
223·226·249·254·255·263·
266·267·268·269·270·273·
275·276·277·279·281·299·
319·333
Greco-Roman 34·37·47·48·99
Greece 10
Gregory the Great, Pope 170
Guatemala 10·16

H

Habakkuk 123·131·146·148·248·
249·287·322
Hadith 132
Hadrat Haroon 84
Hadrian, Emperor 33
Hagrites 290
Hal Lindsey Report, The 272·364·
367
Haran 161·354
Hathaway, David 28
Haydes 229
Heavenly signs 120·223·224·246
Hebrew tradition 243
Hellenistic 90
Heresiologist 39
Herman of Lehnin, Abbot 302
Hexagram 27
Higbir 82
Hilarion, Monk 79·231
Hildegard of Bingen 7·232·310·
355·359·366
Hildegard, St. 47·169·170·237
Hindu 3·5·13·25·62·64·65·66·69·
70·138·240·241·242·244·
327·346·362
Hinduism 255·326
Hippolytus 158·218·311·354·360·
366
History Channel, The 17·339·346·
361
Hoìl, J. Josè 312
Holzhauser, Venerable Bar-
tholomew 52·176·236·286·
324
Hopi 3·12·13·18·25·62·215·240·
242·244·252·340·359·362·
364
Hopi traditions 3·12·242
Huchedè, Priest P. 187
humanitarian 321
Hurlbut, Jesse 38
Hussites 104

I

I Ching 3·7·12·15·25·26·27·62·
68·239
Iconoclasts 103
Icons 104·327
Idols 104
Imam 132·134·135
  12th 83
Imam Ali Ibn Abi-Talib 132
Immaculate conception 178
India 59·62·296·326·334·346
Indians 18·327·335
Indonesia 130·138·336
INRI 184
Interstellar energy cloud 30
Ireland 155·317·320
Irenaeus 34·99·158·190·191·311·
340·341·353·358·366

INDEX

Irenaeus of Lyon 34
Ishmaelites 290·331
Islam 83·84·111·132·134·135·137·138·139·243·255·327·329·348·351
Islamic 3·5·13·84·116·129·132·133·134·135·240·242·328·332
Israel 51·53·83·84·86·94·130·142·162·163·213·215·217·219·223·224·225·227·247·248·278·289·290·291·292·302·308·313·329·332·343·348·355
Istanbul 10·117·181·229
   Constantinople 7·10·40·52·101·105·117·124·181·182·336
   IstanbulConstantinople 343
Iximche 10

J

Jackson, Peter 115
Jainism 326
Japan 29·296·327·334·363
Jean de Roquetaillade 45
Jehoshaphat 19
Jenin 33
Jenkins, Dr. LaHaye, J. 222
Jenkins, Jerry 259·260·262·266·268·271·272·275
Jerome, St. 38·40·71·90·91·159·288·295·298·301·331·342·349·365·368
Jerusalem, Israel 19·33·34·36·70·77·78·82·88·103·117·154·156·171·225·227·241·248·250·256·272·290·294·296·302·303·340·341·342·343·348
Jesuit 282
Joachim, Abbott 168·170·229

John of the Cleft Rock, St. 45·52
John XXIII 230
Jordan 33·309
Josefa von Bourg 112
Joseph, Lawrence E. 16
Judaea 91
Judea 74·121·154·218·294·300·301
Judeo-Christian 34·37·43·62

K

Kalachakra 70
Kalki 64·65·66·346·362·364
Kattina, R. 151·152
katuns 17·23
Keil, C. F. 82
Kenyan 130·138·143·144·145·146·215·242
   Prophecy 242
Kingdom of God, The 69·151·214·255·267·268·337
Kingdom of the Romans 286
King of the North, The 5·6·45·76·81·87·88·91·92·118·124·132·135·140·147·165·167·175·192·218·224·245·247·248·249·250·255·285·287·291·292·294·295·296·297·298·299·300·301·302·303·304·307·309·311·313·314·315·323·325·326·327·328·329·330·332·333·335·336·337
King of the South, The 83·129·132·134·135·137·139·147·245·287·289·294·295·296·303·315·328·329·330·333
Kings of the east 59·335
kittim 295
Knights Templar, The 166
Koran 136·244

375

Korea 327·334·336
Kramer, Priest Herman B. 51·171·196·204·219
Kramer, Priest Paul 173·356
Kulkulcan 23
Kumar, Vijay 62·64
Kurz, Priest W. 204·219

L

LaHaye, Dr. Tim 259·260·262·266·267·268·271·272·275·278·309·360·364·366
Lama 72
Lampstands 199·201·205
Laodicea 10·43·281
Laos 336
Large Hadron Collider 85·348
LaSalette Prophecy 50
Latin America 296·307·313·316
Lavinsky, Priest 187
Leontios, Monk 229
Leo the Philosopher, Emperor 333
Leo XIII, Pope 46·344
Les Propheties 57·61·346
Liang, Zhuge 214
Libra 58·59
Libya 332
Libyans 332
Lindsey, Hal 272·273·319·364·367
Literal Translation of the Holy Bible 306
London 60·126·317·325·349
Long, Jesse 162
Lopez, Brother David 185
Luo 130·143·144·145·146·352·359·362
Luther, Martin 198·282
Luxembourg 79

M

Maas, Priest A. 196
Maccabees 90
Magog 134
Maha Avatara 66
Mahayana 73
Mahdi 83·116·132·133·134·135·139·147·240·242·245·328
Mahometan Empire 330
Maitreya 73
Majlisi, Mullah 132
Malachy Prophecies 54·55·56·58·59·60·61·171·172·254·317·345
Mandelbrot 27
Manhattan 29
Man of sin, The 111·246·266
Manuel II Palaeogous, Emperor 333
Maria díOria, Palma 105
Maria of Agreda, Blessed 117
Maria of Agreda, Venerable 235
Mary 7·113·114·115·116·117·136·184·185·211·241·319·329·352·353·356·358·362
  Apparition 114·115
Mas, Balthassar 324
Maurus, Rabanus 88
May 2013 30
Mayan calendar 3·13·16·17·21·25·68·141·184·239
McKenna brothers 27
Megiddo 7·227·234·235
Mendeleyeff 335
Mercury 65·158
Merkel, Chancellor Angela 289
Merlin 169
Message Version, The 292
Messias 89
Methodius, St. 52·89
Middle Ages, The 101·103·166·178·196·258
Middle East, The 41·51·226·246·

INDEX

247·255·302·332
Militaristic dictator 14·54·65·73·
  76·81·167·188·328
Milky Way Galaxy 15·16·65
Millenarianism 100·152
Millennialism 101
Milvian Bridge 35
Miriam 116
Moab 290·332
Modern King James Version 306
Mohammedans 117·170
Montanism 101
Montfort, Saint Louis de 113
Mormons 186·241
  Book of Mormon, The 293
  MormonsBook of Mormon, The 362
Moslemism 52
Mount of Olives, The 88·122·228·272
Mubarak, President Hosni 289
Muhammad 13·134·143
Muslim declarations 242
Myanmar 336
Mystic 47·96·109·166·180·186·
  232·309·310·319·334

N

Napuctun 30
NASA 7·28·30·340
Nasrdm 41
NATO 303
Naval forces 296·298·300
Naval power 295·296·297·299
Nazarene 32·33·34·35·36·37·38·
  39·40·41·42·43·48·86·87·
  89·93·96·98·99·101·102·
  103·104·107·124·152·153·
  195·198·205·206·211·212·
  213·220·226·247·249·252·
  254·255·288·299·300·309·
  315·340·341·342·344·350
Nazareth 32
Nelios the Myrrh-Gusher, Saint 183
Nepal 336
Nero 304
Netherlands 21·78
Neumann, Therese 319
New Age 3·5·13·23·62·66·67·68·
  69·70·165·240·244·252·
  256·339·346
New Age hopes 13·240·244
New Age Movement 66·67·69·
  70·165
New Age to come 3·62
New birth 23
Newman, Barbara 170
Newman, J. H. 174
New World Order 5·67·165
New York Times, The 335·363·365
New Zealand 316·323·367
Nicea 36
NOAA 30
Noah 124·158·160·272
Nostradamus 5·7·44·57·58·59·60·
  61·130·140·141·325·334·
  346·352
Notorious demagogue 243
Nuclear weapons 25
Nun Anne Catherine Emmerich 7·
  47·48·97·98·105·166·187·
  207·209·210·211·235·344·
  349·350·355·361
Nursing Nun of Bellay 107

O

Obama, Barack 3·5·7·13·57·59·
  60·61·129·130·131·132·
  133·136·137·138·139·140·
  141·142·143·144·145·146·

147·148·190·215·351·352·
353·361·362·367
Oba Prophecy 168
Ogwyn, John 160·162·191·216·
224·226·313
O'Brien, David 163
O'Connor, Priest 171·174
Olivet 272
Orge 265·266
Origen 34
Orthodox 81·89·101·102·104·109·
112·113·118·124·171·173·
176·177·178·179·180·181·
182·183·196·205·206·208·
229·230·240·241·242·244·
307·312·318·331·332·336·
344·349·356·357·358
Orthodox Interpretation 240·241·
242
Otrante, Werdin d' 52·318
Otto, Helen Tzima 173·196
Owalo, Johanwa 143·144

P

Pakistan 336
Papius 99
Paradisaical age 73
Paraea 33
Paraphrasis, Anonymou 112·167·
331
Passover 36·37·195
Patarines 103
Patmos 10
Patriarchate 7
Peace is the Way 68
Pella 33·34
Pentapolis 206
Pentecost 107
Pergamos 10
Persecution 34·35·36·37·41·42·
43·80·87·90·93·94·95·104·

106·110·118·124·173·196·
206·216·217·218·219·220·
231·247·249·252·278·279·
286·292·293·299·300·304·
306·307·309·311
Personal revelations 15·44
Pestilences 121·123·299
Petra 309·311
Pharisees, The 263
Philadelphia 7·10·43·86·93·94·98·
102·106·107·122·209·280·
281·291·298·300·305·307
Philadelphians 93·104·106·107·
108·118·209·271·280·293·
304·305·306·307·308·309·
310
Philistia 290
Philosophy 10·25
Pinay, Maurice 103·104·343·350·
361
Pius IV 57
Pius IX 114
Pius XII 58·174
Planetary alignment 18·126·141
Polarity 18
Polycarp of Smyrna 34·37·38·
107·158·190·191
Polycrates of Ephesus 107
Pompeii 10
Pontifex Maximus 196
Prefect of the Congregation for the
Doctrine of the Faith 160
Pregnancy 53·74·87·121
Pre-Tribulation 216·222·223·258·
259·261·262·263·264·265·
266·267·268·270·271·272·
273·275·276·278·281·282·
283·284
Pritz, Ray 39
Protestant 39·52·76·77·81·101·
102·115·143·152·176·177·
178·179·183·186·207·208·

INDEX

211·212·221·222·223·275·
277·278·281·282·287·294·
319·320·324·329·345
Protestant Reformation, The 211·
281
Pseudo-Methodius 331
Pui-Hua, Ruan 214
Pushya nakshatra 66

R

Randell, Eugene 141
Rasaullah 84
Rastifaris 71
Ratzinger, Joseph 100·160
Reagan, Ronald Wilson 190
Reb 60
Rehoboam 162·163
Religious Tolerance 67·346·361·
364
Repent 130·148·149·226·228·280·
324·325
repentance 80·148·149·225
Rhodes 10
Ricci, Priest Laurence 167
Richter, Jean Paul 79
Rocco, Brother Louis 80·117
Roman Empire, The 77·78·83·88·
140·171·172·174·175·190·
191·192·315·340·342·353
Romans 33·38·82·84·93·102·110·
182·191·199·213·246·247·
260·266·286·291·295·300
Rome 10·11·24·33·34·37·39·44·
55·91·97·105·115·160·168·
172·174·177·178·179·180·
181·182·189·191·196·207·
208·210·211·219·228·230·
231·250·285·297·336·354
Romulus 191
Roque, La 71
Rose, Priest Seraphim 283

Rossi, Priest Gaudentius 159·171·
320
Royer, Jane Le 71·106
Royer, Jeanne le 97·99·168·206
Ruler of the World 72·73
Russia 117·243·250·296·333·334·
335·336
Russian Orthodox prophecy 243
Russian prediction 242·243·335
Russians 323·329·335·336

S

Sabbath, The 74·121·151·152·
153·156·158·159·160·363
Sabbatian 206
Sackcloth 199·201·203·206·208·
213·274
Sacrifices 77·78·114·295·302·303
Sadhanas 67
Sahaja Yoga 65
Sardis 10·43·280·281·341
Sarkozy 289·365
Satan 22·46·100·106·111·153·
172·206·249·250·254·277·
280·293·312·328
Saturn 65·157
Satyayuga 66
Savonarola, Jerome 71
Scandinavia 29
Sceptre 88
Schaff, Philip 39·342
Second Coming, The 99·168·259·
260·261·262·263·264·265·
267·268·269·270·271·272·
282·283
Secret Sect, The 1·3·5·6·33·86·93·
96·98·102·104·118·252
Seer 11·57·90·131
Serpent 20·22·23·220·223·264·
276·279·310
Severus, Septimius (Emperor) 34

Shamballa 70·72
Sheen, Fulton 45
Shipton, Mother 48·50·317·344·
 363
Shri Mataji 65·346·361
Sibyl 323
Sibyl, Cumaean 24
Sibylline 24·239·241·242·322·
 323·339·362·367
Silberman, Neil 163
Simeon de Limena 166
Singapore 336
Snooks, Graeme 95
Sodom 200·273
Sola Scriptura 180
Solomon (King) 155·156·161·
 162·163·355
Son of perdition 111·169·266·310
Soufrand, Abbe 113
Sovereign Roman Pontiff, The
 180
Spaniards 19
Spencer, Michael 176
Sri Lanka 336
Sunni Muslims 133·134·135·136
Sunspots 28

T

Taheri, Amir 132
Taigi, Blessed Anna-Maria 105·
 169·334
Tai peoples 336
Talmud 3·151·243·353·363
Tang Dynasty 51
Tanna debe Eliyyahu, The 152
Taoist 25
Telesphorus of Cozensa 51
Terah 161·162·354
Terry, Milton Spenser 323·340
Tertullian 34·341
Thailand 336

The Ecstatic of Tours 50·80
The guided one 133
Theodosius 37·342
Theodosius (Emperor) 101
Theophilus of Antioch 34
Theravada 73
The Theology of History in St.
 Bonaventure 100
Thiele, Edwin 163
Thigpen, Paul 281
Third Lateran Council, The 41·
 343
Thyatira 10·43·280·281
Tibetan 25·70·184·240
Tibetan Kalachra 184
Tibeto-Burman peoples 336
Tikal 10·16
Time of the end 43·99·106·118·
 207·222·290·307·308·313·
 328·330
Torres, Ven. Sor Marianne de
 Jesus 47·96
Trappistine Nun of Notre Dame
 des Gardes 108
Trinitarian 40
Trinity, The 143
Tsunami 324
Turkey 10·116·117
Turks 80·117·170
Tuwaqachi 18
Two Witnesses 6·199·204·210·
 214·248·250
Tyre 290·313
Tzima, Helen Otto 303
Tzima, H. Otto 47·112·206·307·
 344·347·348·350·351·355·
 356·358·359·360·361·362·
 363·365·366·367·368

U

Union for the Mediterranean 288·

INDEX

289
United Kingdom 60·289·323
United Nations Environment Programme, The 127
United States of America 2·7·13·15·29·58·60·85·123·127·131·133·138·140·146·147·148·149·215·242·247·248·249·255·295·296·298·302·303·307·316·318·319·320·321·323·327·328·329·333·339·351·360·362·367
  Air Force 85
  Military 85
Universal Religion 67
USA Today 15·339·360
Ussher, James 155·156·354

V

Vatican City 10·44·99·100·114·115·173·179·181·182·197
Vatican II 182
Victorinus 203·311·359·366
Vietnam 336
Virata 65
Vishnu 64·66·326
Voclin, Abbe 108
Voragine, Jacob 90

W

Walvoord, Dr. 83·222·223·275·278·347·360·364
Walvoord, Dr. J. F. 83·222·223·275·278·347·360·364
Weather 18·29·126·240·253·313
Weidner, J. 183·184
Western lands 295
Wood, Leon 163
World War II 325
World War III 303·344
Wright, Jeremiah 139·140

Wycliffe Bible Commentary 82·308·347·366

Y

Yang 26·339
Yin 26·339

Z

Zenobius, Saint 170
Zion 223·224·229·246·294·308

2012 and the Rise of the Secret Sect is also available in other languages.

For German, 2012 und das Auftreten der geheimen Sekte, please go to www.diegeheimesekte.de

For Portuguese, 2012 e o Surgimento da Seita Secreta, please go to www.armazendanet.com

For Spanish, 2012 y el ascenso de la Secta Secreta, please go to www.lasectasecreta.com.com

International editions of the book, in all available languages (including English), can also be obtained from U.K. distributors such as Ingram International, Bertrams, and Gardners.

Electronic versions (including Kindle) are also available. Go to www.thesecretsect.com for details, future languages, and updates on distribution. The book has also been made available at websites such as barnesandnoble.com and amazon.com.

Those interested in world news and commentary of a prophetic nature, may wish to visit www.cogwriter.com

Those interested in 2012 and possible future updates related to this book, may wish to visit www.thesecretsect.com

Those who want more books on related topics, may wish to visit www.nazarenebooks.com